W9-DBG-037

ON TRYING TO
KEEP STILL

Also by Jenny Diski

ON TRYING TO KEEP STILL

JENNY DISKI

LITTLE, BROWN

LITTLE, BROWN

First published in Great Britain in April 2006 by Little, Brown

Copyright © Jenny Diski 2006

The moral right of the author has been asserted

All rights reserved.
No part of this publication may be reproduced,
stored in a retrieval system, or transmitted in any form
or by any means, without the prior permission in writing
of the publisher, nor be otherwise circulated in any form
of binding or cover other than that in which it is published
and without a similar condition including this condition
being imposed on the subsequent purchaser.

A CIP catalogue record for this book
is available from the British Library

ISBN 0 316 72525 0

Typeset in Horley by M Rules
Printed and bound in Great Britain
by Clays Ltd, St Ives plc

Little, Brown
An imprint of
Time Warner Book Group UK
Brettenham House
Lancaster Place
London WC2E 7EN

www.twbg.co.uk

To S. H.
now and then

Night-room

We're here because we like to keep things simple.
We like to think of nothing but ourselves.
This place is here for us.
This place is ours.
The nurses are all ours.
The drugs are ours.
All we have to do is do nothing.
All we have to do is ache with joy.

From 'Lou-Lou' by Selima Hill, 2004

Recently I retired to my estates, determined to devote myself as far as I could to spending what little life I have left quietly and privately; it seemed to me then that the greatest favour I could do for my mind was to leave it in total idleness, caring for itself, concerned only with itself, calmly thinking of itself. I hoped it could do that more easily from then on, since with the passage of time it had grown mature and put on weight.

But I find . . . that on the contrary it bolted off like a runaway horse, taking far more trouble over itself than it ever did over anyone else; it gives birth to so many chimeras and fantastic monstrosities, one after another, without order or fitness, that, so as to contemplate at my ease their oddness and their strangeness, I began to keep a record of them, hoping in time to make my mind ashamed of itself.

From 'On Idleness' (I:8)
The Essays by Michel de Montaigne, 1580

INTRODUCTION

Something about the idea of being a travel writer distresses me.
So this is not a travel book, though it contains some journeys. It
is a book on travelling and keeping still. Primarily, it is about the
wish to keep still. Something about the distinction between being
a fiction and a non-fiction writer distresses me, too. So I think of
myself as a writer. Period. I suppose that curiosity, the need to
know, is at the heart of it – at the heart of us. Writers (and others)
might qualify as that dreadful child frozen in time who repeatedly
asks 'why' in response to every answer to every previous question.
That's curiosity, but it's also the good sense a child has that she is
being lied to. Mostly the answers to her questions are wrong, or
at least insufficient, sometimes because of ignorance, sometimes
laziness, but often because the question was impossible to answer.
The problem about not knowing is that the question which is
supposed to elicit enlightenment is difficult to frame precisely,
because you don't know. Perhaps the point of asking questions is
not to receive an answer but to reiterate and refine the question
itself. I'm inclined to think that there is, essentially, only one

1

question. It is 'What is the point?' and in some form or another it is asked over and over again by those of us who have failed to mature enough to stop asking it.

Another question is: what is it like when something or nothing happens? Something or nothing happens all the time. The same question has been asked – more or less consciously, with more or less precision – by many others; let's say just about everyone, but notably for me by Michel de Montaigne in his *Essais*, along with Daniel Defoe in *Robinson Crusoe*, St. Augustine in *The Confessions*, Nietzsche in his *Notebooks*.

In 2000 I made a millennial move from London (where I was born, brought up and always lived) to Cambridge, for no other reason than that someone I loved – the Poet – lived there. Not quite travelling, not quite keeping still. But it can't be said that now I am alone most of the time. It troubles me no end – I worry about it while delighting in the company I chose, and choose. In the past year I have spent periods alone – in various ways, but usually deliberately – in New Zealand, in a farm cottage in Somerset, in Lapland. You are never alone with a mind, of course. *I am, therefore I think* – remember, wonder, obsess. You're never alone with a world. *No man is an island* – if only. The past and the present state of the world and of my regular life press in, no matter how I would wish my private space impenetrable. Levi-Strauss declared of totemic systems that animals are good to think with. Irritants and interruptions are also, much as I dislike them, good to think with. Anyway they are there, in and outside my head – memories, inconsequentialities, and the doings of the world.

Much worse, more alarming than anything else, there is also in solitude emptiness: a mind devoid of thoughts, or rushing away from them, which is more shocking than outside interruption. No peaceful blankness, but a mad, skittering nothingness. The perfect image of aloneness collapses into trivia and pointlessness. Boredom, perhaps, but I don't think so. It is more like a flat refusal to think. A compulsion to subvert the circumstances I have provided myself with. Not stillness, but a fretful pacing in my cage. This may be an altogether more authentic will to oblivion. A sorry truth that shines a light on my narcissistic notion of blankness and turns it inside out. Take travelling *and* keeping still, fiction and non-fiction with a pinch of salt.

PART ONE

ON DISTANCE

If I am not at home, I am always very near it.

Montaigne: Of Repentance

1

ON BEING VERY FAR AWAY

I may be the last person left alive who is still amazed each time I arrive in another country. In most other ways I have adjusted to modernity – I write on a computer, send and receive emails, even carry a mobile phone when I am out (if I remember it) – but I have never shaken off a sense of wonder each time I set foot in a foreign land. My sense of the extraordinariness of being in another country was strong when I travelled as a small child, by boat or plane with my parents to Belgium and Italy. We lived in London, mostly in our part of London. Knowing I lived on an island was central to my thinking about my geographical place in the world. Other parts of my island, south London or anywhere else in Britain, were simply places belonging to where I lived but which I didn't inhabit. But once I was crossing the defining boundary of the English Channel I felt like a space traveller setting off for a distant planet. A trip on a plane to Brussels or Alassio matched the folk-and-fairy-tale journeys I read of princesses, fishermen, woodcutters and youngest sons, travelling mysteriously in the dead of night to other lands, magical flights on carpets or winged horses, quests for their hearts' desire to impossible elsewherenesses.

It is my experience that the oddest of existences becomes normal, regular, ordinary, if that is what you are living, and yet the strangeness of getting to somewhere else, to another *country* (*pace* Scotland, Wales), has never gone away. I remember how I felt about those foreign journeys as a small child so clearly because I feel just the same now. I cannot get used to foreign travel. It has nothing immediately to do with difference in language or customs, but simply with arriving somewhere that is designated quite else. Somewhere talked of, seen on a map. Somewhere not *here*, where theoretically I always have been and am. A place that must be crossed over to. Over the border. It isn't that some places are more exotic than others. Amsterdam and the moon are equally other to me, and if I ever go to the moon, it will be quite as exciting as each time I arrive in Amsterdam.

Conversely, although it takes as long to fly to Manchester as it does to Paris, at Orly airport I am somewhere else, whereas when I set down on the runway in Manchester I am just in a place where I happen not to have lived. The distance in miles from one place to another has nothing to do with *distance*. It is more like that usefully untranslatable word Freud made so much of: *unheimlich*. Unhomelike, literally. Uncanny, as it is generally translated. For me, it is strangerness and a most particular vastly lost sensation that I can't help but define as homesickness.

I know for a fact that you don't have to have a home you want to be in to be homesick. I was at home during my four-month stay in the Lady Chichester Psychiatric Hospital in Hove at the age of fifteen; I was not at home in the children's home I was sent to four years earlier at eleven, when my mother and I were evicted from our flat. I was never at home when I lived alone with my mother (at times living with her was the very definition of *unheimlich*), but I was homesick when I was taken from living alone with her to the children's home somewhere on the coast, with its hospital-like dormitory of beds so tall I had to climb to get into mine. The first night, I tried to make my getaway after dark when everyone was asleep, but I was stopped by the matron who saw me sidle past her door. She sat me in front of the fire in her room, gave me cocoa and biscuits and asked me where I was going. 'Home' I said, which was nowhere just then, so I meant 'my mother', who was nothing like as warm and comforting as the kindly matron. I expect my mother loved me, but she *needed* me more, and vented her fears and grief on me. She terrified me sometimes and, worse, was always on the verge of terrifying me, but in the cosy chair of the matron's sitting room, where she gently asked me to explain my problem, all I wanted was to be back where I had been, where I *should* be, where I had always been, even though I was where I was now because the school truant officer had found me in an empty flat from which all the furniture, even the carpets, had been repossessed, my mother shrieking, me lying on the floorboards crying. When my father left, months before, he gave me the option, suitcase in hand, of going with him. I opted to stay with my mother, though he was the one I felt most comfortable with in all the world. The parent I loved. But I knew neither of them were trustworthy, and I must have believed that mere love would not prevent homesickness, so I chose my mother as the place where my home was. Simple inertia, perhaps. Homesickness is a longing for inertia – for never having moved in the first place. Which, unless I had a choice before conception, would make my mother the very emblem of home, however she and I got on. She was at least as close to the original inertia as I could get. And Freud, of course, places the source of the *unheimlich* in the maternal womb.

Forty-five years on, I am not at home at King's Cross Station at eleven p.m. taking the late train back to Cambridge. Even if I am with the Poet, with whom I am at home and almost live with, I am not at home waiting for (or on) the train. I am not at home when I am not at home but, strangely, I like to be in transit. To be in transit is a very particular condition: on the train to Cambridge is not in transit, it is just not yet home. On the train with no particular destination around America is fine; I'm not on my way, trying to get home from somewhere, not there yet. I cried once (not so very long ago when I was still living in London) outside Liverpool Street Station. It was eleven-thirty at night. I couldn't find a taxi to take me home to Kentish Town after I had been to Norwich to give a reading. Suddenly, looking up and down the empty road, the distance between Liverpool Street and Kentish Town was unbridgeable. It seemed quite possible that I would never get home. I was flooded with the certainty that this was the beginning of the rest of my life of homelessness. I suppose (even with a sore foot *) I could have walked home in an hour or so. But as well as the sense that *homeless for the rest of my life* didn't depend on the logic of effort but on some cosmic decision that had been pending and was now made, I had not the faintest idea in which direction to head. Liverpool Street is nowhere to me. It might have been a wind-blasted beach in Antarctica for all my sense of direction† was capable of detecting. I started to walk, but with every step wondered if I should turn around and go the other way. How is one to know which way to go if you *don't* know? That was when I began to cry – just a stifled sob or two. I have felt bereft on an Antarctic beach, but it was muted by the fact that I was there because I wanted to be there, and I knew that a dinghy was scheduled to take me back to the ship in three hours. I have never wanted to be at Liverpool Street Station. Yet I grew up roaming London: wandered around Soho and Charing Cross Road, took the bus alone from Tottenham Court Road to Camden Town every day to go to primary school, to Stepney when I started secondary school, ran away to Wembley when I was twelve, secretly met my father in Golders Green bus station. I was by both necessity and inclination an independent and resourceful child. But in my late forties I had to fight back tears because I was *stranded* at Liverpool Street – because I felt lost and alone in the world. After half an hour or so, a taxi approached with its light on. I felt at home in the taxi.

*Of which see later
†Of which see later

Homesickness has retained a powerful if ill-defined grip on me, but it seems to be at its most potent nearer to where ever home is conceived to be, rather than a world away. Distance is a difficult calculation. If it is defined by the time it takes to get from one place to another, then there's no difference going to London from Cambridge railway station, or Amsterdam by plane from Cambridge airport. Different speeds, of course, but the speed of the vehicle travelled on is irrelevant to the traveller's understanding of how far they have gone. Time is the thing. Not long ago it took me twelve hours to get from Inverness to London, in theory by plane. The airport was fogged over, so we were bussed to Aberdeen and then waited several hours for a plane, which left us at the wrong London airport thus taking much longer to get to King's Cross, from which the late train to Cambridge stopped at each station taking an age to get there. It would have been twice as quick to have caught a train home from Inverness. In the time it took me to get back from the north of Scotland, I could have returned to Cambridge from somewhere beyond Singapore. That journey was just modernity playing its regular cruel trick, but I had the same sense of panic as I had trying to get to Camden from Liverpool Street. I was too near where I was going to tolerate the difficulty. The only safe distance from home is the far distant.

Perhaps – after an initial refusal – I said yes to the New Zealand invitation because it was as far distant as it was possible to be. I was invited to the Wellington Readers and Writers Festival for eight days in the early spring, which was their autumn. I asked for the return flight date to be extended so that I could spend a couple of weeks travelling around on my own. Far, far away. In transit. A stranger, unwatched by anyone, no one's concern, wandering around or staying still at will, once I had finished my stint as a public writer. Wandering, not trying to get home. I daydreamed of driving a rented car through the most exotic of landscapes, and of being alone in forests and by the sea. I had a hankering for being completely on my own after the closeness of life with the Poet in Cambridge. I had a nagging worry that closeness was wrong for me. I missed being a stranger. I thought that strangerhood was where I really lived, and needed to get to it for a while. Quiet, no one else except for other strangers. The very warmth and pleasure of my relationship with the Poet seemed to me to deafen me. I wanted, I thought to myself, to *think* – meaning not be connected to anyone – so that I could hear the echoes inside my head. I felt I was avoiding something I ought to be listening to. I wanted to be alone as far from home as I could get: not that near-enough-to-home that causes homesickness, the unbearable *unheimlich*. I wanted *unheimlich* – it is essentially what I am always looking for – but of the right kind. Strangeness and strangerness without the blank despair. A matter, I decided, of no one nearby to care what I did, and the far, far distance. New Zealand fitted the bill almost perfectly: I have never particularly wanted to go to New Zealand, I knew no one in the country, and you couldn't get further away from almost anywhere.

After twenty-eight hours in transit, I got off the plane at Christchurch, New Zealand, to be informed by vast signs and paintings on the walls in the airport that I had arrived at Middle Earth. The journey had begun on the morning of 4 March in Drummer Street, Cambridge, when I got on the ten o'clock bus to New Zealand. To Heathrow, actually, but it felt as if this first step was the crucial one, and it entertained me that a journey of twelve thousand miles should begin on bus number JL717. (Of course, if the plane had crashed, it might have seemed to my surviving friends that the journey had begun in 1947 in the Tottenham Court Road, or back in 1912 and 1910 when my parents were born in the East End of London, or during the war when they met and she got pregnant while her then husband was overseas.) A young woman with her backpack beside her sat opposite me in the seat across the aisle. She held an old white rectangle of towelling, a nappy or a hand towel faded to grey with washing, and throughout the journey she lightly brushed its frayed edges back and forth across her lips, rhythmically, over and over, as she must have been doing for twenty or more years. The action rendered her completely private. Of course, I could see her doing it, but in some fashion, the hypnotic comfort of the remnant of cloth on her lips made me, and everything else, invisible to her – which, perhaps, is as private as a person can get.

We took off from Heathrow at dusk and flew into a night that lasted two days by the calendar or twenty-three hours by an unaltered watch. At some point along the flight path between London and Singapore, the world turned or I overflew its spin or whatever it is that happens, and a day disappeared. After a three-hour stopover, long enough for a shower, and another flight, I landed in Christchurch on the morning of 6 March. I don't sleep on planes. I tried for the oblivion of the girl on the bus, but lacked a towel or some other soothing fetish to take my mind off the world. I felt only that awful restlessness of waiting for a long time to pass. I fidgeted, ate the stream of meals that came to me, drank water, and fidgeted some more. I watched *Kill Bill 1* on the screen on the back of the seat in front of me, and tried not to watch *Love Actually*, which was on every screen in my peripheral vision throughout the journey. I listened to John Dowland's pavannes, to Rossini's *Petite Messe Solonelle*, to Tom Waits' 'Alice'. All of them, in retrospect, connected by a kind of mock or mocking melancholia. I read a book about reading. I took Temazapam and stayed wide awake. I got very close to watching *Love Actually*, but at the last moment began to watch Jack Nicholson and that *Annie Hall* woman in a film that tried to re-make *Love Actually* without its audience noticing. I switched it off and decided to watch the sublime *Kill Bill 1* again. I think I may have let a weary tear fall once or twice, sentimentalising over my book of lost stories and library closures. By the time we touched down I was barely sane, and certainly not sensible.

And when the signs insisted I had got to Middle Earth, I was groggy enough not to care where I was. New Zealand, Middle Earth, Tottenham Court Road, any place, so long as I was somewhere (although actually I still wasn't; only in transit to Wellington on the North Island. Another wait, another delay, another plane journey, another landing in another airport). So, being sick with lack of sleep, lagging a day ahead of myself, and overhearing one young man explaining earnestly to another, 'I was reading this Tibetan monk who said that we only use one per cent of our brains. Wow, huh?', Middle Earth seemed as likely a place to be as anywhere. Although it meant that time as well as space travel had to be involved because, for a few moments in my muddled brain, Middle Earth was the place I'd known in 1969, an underground club, literally and metaphorically, somewhere in a Notting Hill basement I think, where we ingested quantities of hallucinogens while dancing, or sitting cross-legged to watch the recombinatory adventures of hot coloured oils projected on to screens all around the dark, smoke and incense-thick room, and listened to the pixilated lutes, tambours and whining voices of The Incredible String Band:

> *And I've nothing to do,*
> *And I've nowhere to go;*
> *I'm not in the slightest way upset.*
> *. . . And I'm not even chasing the sunset . . .*

For a demented moment in Christchurch airport I wondered how anyone could possibly fault those tripping troubadours and their incredible string message. What other condition was there to aim for in my frazzled state, or in any state at all? No wonder I took the hippie route in the Sixties. It was my route home. I was a lizard and someone sweetly turned over a rock in front of me. Oh, God, yes, *that's* where I belong. *And I'm not even chasing the sunset . . .* Then I remembered all that was decades long gone, that I was in New Zealand and that the walls were simply reminding jet-lag bedevilled travellers about the dreary sourcebook of my drug-crazed somnambulistic hippie nights, *The Bloody Lord of the Bloody Rings,* which had been filmed there and recently won a regiment of Oscars. There are only about four million people in the country and it seemed as I travelled that almost everyone had either been in the movie (there were calls for extras apparently that required only those over six-foot seven-inches or under four foot to apply) or been inconvenienced by it, so it was a cause of great national pride. It's not for me to judge. As I say, I didn't, at that point, care where I was, though perhaps I would have preferred to be on the moon – the Sea of Tranquillity, say, which seemed just as probable as New Zealand – but I was still in that state of passive acceptance of life or death or finding oneself in surprising places, which is the only way to survive the stupefying effects of long-haul jet travel.

After I'd spent just a little time in the country, it seemed less surprising that the people of New Zealand should have embraced rather than resented their reassignment to Middle Earth, because there can't be a population in the world who so consciously feel themselves to be peripheral. My guess is that they would welcome being in Middle *Anywhere.* Everyone explained, almost by way of saying hello, how far away they are.

'We're so far away,' they kept telling me apologetically.

'Far away from what?' I'd ask, surprised, because they and I were both *here*, so far as it was ever possible to tell.

'Everything.'

In fact, of course, everything is far away from New Zealand when that is where you are. But perhaps that's easy to say if you are merely making a visit and you have a return ticket to the far away you came from. It doesn't help, I should think, that so many of the place names on the map are not Maori, but hankerings after some home that was home, if ever, generations ago: Christchurch, Wellington, Cheviot, Hastings, Richmond, Eltham, Oxford, Cambridge, Blenheim, Hamilton, Dunedin. Eltham, for God's sake.

As soon as they've met you and ascertained that you are from those parts, most New Zealanders tell you about their European trip; their year or five spent where far away isn't, as if on day-release from the penal colony. Or they say, with an unnecessary degree of passion and determination, that they are planning such a trip soon – or one day. Shop assistants and students, academics and artists, all earnestly assure you they have been or will go, like people conscious that they are illiterate in a world full of book-worms and promising to remedy it. I'd thought that the traffic was, these days, the other way, with backpackers and gap-yearers heading off for a trip of a lifetime to New Zealand. But either because the distance really is palpable, or because the New Zealanders' sense of wonder at where they already are in the world is so omnipresent and insistent, the feeling of separation grabbed me too, and I begin to think like a local. I've never felt the *distance* of distance so strongly. Not on that beach in the Antarctic, not sitting with my legs dangling over the edge of the jetty, gazing towards the end of the world through Drake's Passage at the tip of Tierra del Fuego, not even in the desolate, dusty nowhere of the station platform in Raton, New Mexico, staring off into the hazy featureless horizon looking for the pin-point that would be my train out of there. But this was not a remoteness like being in the grip of a depression or outside

Liverpool Street Station without a taxi. Not *unheimlich* in the sense of needing to get home and being barred from doing so. It was the 'world', whatever I and my New Zealand hosts meant by that, which was so remote. Not homesickness, but world-lostness. Not, so far as I was concerned, an unpleasant feeling at all.

During the first week, the 'international writers' at the book festival were a group. There were thirteen or so of us *internationals* all together in the *Hotel de Wheels* (which adopted its soubriquet when, a few years ago, after it was decided to put the *Te Papa* Maori museum in its place, it was hoisted up on to a hotel-sized trolley and wheeled from the harbour front across the road to the opposite pavement). Us thirteen international writers were locked together and on show because we were from far away. A group – bussed here and there, waiting side by side in the lobby for our various interviewers and photographers – because we all didn't come from there. We were from Israel, Germany, America, Australia, Canada, Singapore, UK. An arbitrary group (though pretty white and largely Anglophone) except that we all wrote – fiction, non-fiction or poetry – which gave us less in common than non-writers might imagine.

Our large bright rooms, with heavenly bathrooms and showers big enough for dancing in, opened out on to a continuous balcony where, together or separately, we could sit and watch the comings and goings on the harbour front, a place, like all harbour fronts these days, of play and sport rather than work and sea traffic. On the first afternoon we were driven in convoy to the Governor's residence to be welcomed in her immaculate gardens. Speeches in English and a bit of Maori. Shaking of hands, smiling smiles, as polite and grateful as we could manage; a very well-behaved collection of international writers. I miss the days I never knew of loud-mouthed, liquored, sexually rampant writers. How tame we were. Positively ambassadorial. How fearful that if we didn't behave – what? We'll never be published again? Never asked back? Sent to bed without our tea? During the week, morning and afternoon, we went off to the cinema (refurbished for the premier of *The Lord of the Rings,* and now in use for less glitzy delights) where the Festival readings and panels were held. A phalanx, a super-group of International Writers, some of us on stage, the rest in the two rows of seats reserved for us, opened the proceedings. Naturally, we formed our own subgroups or solitudes fast, according to our preconceptions of each other, how we supposed they thought about us, mutual regard or contempt for the work, and plain antipathy or attraction.

We collided in corridors, went off for lunch and gossiped about the others, and we met in the foyer in the queue (most often at three or four in the morning for those of us with European jet-lag) for the single computer with internet access. We waited edgily for our turn to get back in touch with the world and raised our eyebrows in recognition of our own absurdity to others who waited, while the person at the treasured machine made the most of their online time. Each one of us, once we had gained access to the computer, ignored the length of the waiting queue and huddled over the keyboard as if it were a security towel, tapping away at unheard-of speeds. One thing writers can do is type fast and look intense while they're doing it. I watched the hunched backs impatiently and with increasing despair, convinced (as, of course, it turned out was everyone else) that whoever was hogging the machine was keying in and sending the finest prose or most incisive poetry back to excited editors in their own countries, while I was just waiting to email frantic, barely literate messages home to the Poet complaining about being jet-lagged and overwrought.

There were parties and more parties, cocktails, dinner, lunches and launches, opening parties and closing parties. There were moments of escape, when I sat on the balcony and stared at the ever-present wind whistling round Wellington's corners and blowing old ladies against lamp posts. And there were the public performances where, separately and in various combinations, we took to the stage to read from our books and take questions from a reading public who here, as everywhere, wanted to know how we disciplined ourselves to work and where we got our ideas from. To which questions neither I nor anyone else seems to have a satisfactory answer (though my standard answers 1] by receiving gas bills and 2] desperation, seem as likely as any).

There were Maori greeting ceremonies almost daily. I have never been so greeted in my life. The first of these was a surprise, the second felt more like an assault, the third and later ones I skipped. The Maoris and the descendants of European settlers seem to have come to a very uneasy accommodation about who the place belongs to. Great battles were raging, while we were there, about who owned the offshore fishing rights. The left was accusing the right of racism. The right was accusing the left of racism. The Maoris were demanding their land under

21

the sea. The white New Zealanders were muttering about being discriminated against. The minority status of the original inhabitants was on everyone's minds, as conscience or victimhood, which resulted in extreme public displays of togetherness. All formal verbal greetings are said both in English and Maori by everyone, and both languages are taught compulsorily in schools. One of the organisers received a complaint that the International Writers were racist because none of us had learned any Maori in order to greet their audience bilingually. Heritage looms large in place of real cross-cultural ease. The Maori greeting ceremony was a version of what you see the All Blacks doing before a rugby match, but much more up close and personal. Its original intention was to warn off any visitor thinking of taking a liberty, with a show of the extreme warlike nature of their hosts. A twenty-minute choreographed assault by young men in loincloths making testosteronic gestures, offering violence against you (spears pointed, repeated fuck-off gestures with one arm inside the crook of the jerking other arm, eye-rolling, tongue lolling, bellowing, leaping within inches of you). Behind them, women do much the same thing, though you sense that their presence has more to do with equal rights within the ethnic group than authentic Maori warrior behaviour. And we white international authors, properly liberal, stood in our best or least creased party clothes, smiling gratefully at the assault. It became hard to say which party was most assaulted. Some of the young men drew blood as they beat themselves in their frenzied attempt to show us visitors who was boss. On the whole, it seemed to me that a handshake and a watchful eye is a wiser method of ensuring peace between strangers. Frankly, the amount of time and energy used up by the warriors displaying their terribleness would have allowed any real enemy to load their rifles in their own good time, take leisurely aim and fire. I had an image of a bloodbath, and astonished, dying young men gasping with their last breath, 'But we hadn't finished scaring you. Not fair.' Heritage, of course, but if a group of young men behaved like that to me anywhere else in the world, I'd have been inclined to tell them to fuck off and stamp on their bare feet. Or run a mile. But heritage, so we all responded (even the American author whose idea of fun was shooting holes in the books of those who criticised his) with the sensitive dead smiles of foreign dignitaries being entertained by the locals, as patronising as any imperial working party visiting the colonies.

After a week, the formalities were over, the readings were done, emails exchanged, and the international writers dispersed back to the wide world from which they had come. *Now* it was my time. I was simply far away, as far away as it was possible to get, on my own and purposeless. Almost free as a bird. A return date, a stop off in Auckland to see some people about a film they wanted to make of one of my novels, aside from that, nothing. I sat in the lobby of the hotel with a map, waving farewell from time to time to International Writers, and made a plan. To Auckland by plane. From Auckland to . . . I spotted a peninsula on the east labelled the Coromandel Coast. *Dum di dum di dum di dumdum* started to play in my head. *Dum di dum*

23

di dum di dumdum ... On the coast of Coromandel ... Edward Lear ... *The Yonghy-Bonghy-Bo.* The heart-wrenching story of a tragic love between the Yonghy-Bonghy-Bo and the Lady Jingly Jones.

> *On the Coast of Coromandel*
> *Where the early pumpkins blow,*
> *In the middle of the woods*
> *Lived the Yonghy-Bonghy-Bo.*
> *Two old chairs, and half a candle,*
> *One old jug without a handle,—*
> *These were all his worldly goods:*
> *In the middle of the woods,*
> *These were all the worldly goods*
> *Of the Yonghy-Bonghy-Bo,*
> *Of the Yonghy-Bonghy-Bo.*
>
> *'Lady Jingly! Lady Jingly!*
> *Sitting where the pumpkins blow,*
> *Will you come and be my wife?'*
> *Said the Yonghy-Bonghy-Bo,*
> *'I am tired of living singly,—*
> *On this coast so wild and shingly,—*
> *I'm a-weary of my life;*
> *If you'll come and be my wife,*
> *Quite serene would be my life!'*
> *Said the Yonghy-Bonghy-Bo,*
> *Said the Yonghy-Bonghy-Bo.*

'On this Coast of Coromandel
Shrimps and watercresses grow,
Prawns are plentiful and cheap,'
Said the Yonghy-Bonghy-Bo.
'You shall have my chairs and candle,
And my jug without a handle!
Gaze upon the rolling deep
(Fish is plentiful and cheap):
As the sea, my love is deep!'
Said the Yonghy-Bonghy-Bo,
Said the Yonghy-Bonghy-Bo.

But it was not to be. The Lady Jingly was married already to Mr Jones (*Handel Jones, Esquire and Co*) in England, who sends her Dorking Hens from time to time as a sign of his continued existence. She's sorry, she really is:

'Though you've such a tiny body,
And your head so large doth grow, —
Though your hat may blow away,
Mr Yonghy-Bonghy-Bo!
Though you're such a Hoddy Doddy,
Yet I wish that I could modi-
-fy the words I needs must say!
Will you please to go away?
That is all I have to say,
Mr. Yonghy-Bonghy-Bo!
Mr. Yonghy-Bonghy-Bo!'

Her desolated lover disappears off to beyond the sea on the back of a passing turtle and leaves the Lady Jingly Jones alone to wonder how, but for the fact of Handel Jones Esquire, things might have been so very different:

> *From the Coast of Coromandel*
> *Did that Lady never go,*
> *On that heap of stones she mourns*
> *For the Yonghy-Bonghy-Bo.*
> *On that Coast of Coromandel,*
> *In his jug without a handle*
> *Still she weeps, and daily moans;*
> *On that little heap of stones*
> *To her Dorking Hens she moans,*
> *For the Yonghy-Bonghy-Bo,*
> *For the Yonghy-Bonghy-Bo.*

And there was the coast of Coromandel on the eastern edge of North Island, just a bus drive away from Auckland (as well, of course, as on the south-eastern coast of India), just waiting for me to spend some solitary time in it.

I found something called a Farmstay in the guide book. It said:

As soon as your car heads down the long, fern flanked driveway you will know you are in another world. Settle in, then take a wander in the cool bush, paddle a kayak on a tranquil harbour or just walk and talk with the animals.

Or just sit and softly weep into a jug without a handle. I called and booked into one of the farmstay cottages – view of the hills and harbour, no other guests staying – for several days. There are geysers and volcanoes, rainforests and mountains – no end of places a person ought to see in New Zealand, and most visitors, knowing their chances of returning are fairly slim, see everything they can possibly fit in. But, although I only had about a week and a half after I finished talking to the animals on the Coromandel Peninsula, I had focussed now on the glorious sound of Doubtful Sound and I planned the rest of my time around my desire to get there. In a great flurry of deciding and telephoning, I booked everything from the sofa in the hotel lobby: overnight bed and breakfasts between destinations, the hotel in Te Anau in Fiordland which is the nearest town to the Sound, flights and buses, and the three-hour boat trip through Doubtful Sound itself. I finished just as the taxi arrived to take me to Wellington Airport for Auckland, and then the bus to the coast of Coromandel.

2

ON FALLING

There were a few hours between the end of my meeting in Auckland and the departure of my bus for the Coromandel Peninsula. The bus station was at the foot of Auckland's major tourist attraction: Skytower. I suppose most major cities in the world have somewhere tall from which to look at itself. London, Toronto, Paris, New York all have their panoramic towers, and I haven't been up any of them. Why not? Because they're there, I suppose. But here I was with time to kill and the bus station café, like all bus station cafés in the world, it seems, left everything to be desired. I purchased my ticket to the interior of the Skytower in the foyer and rode up the glass-fronted lift (11mph, 40 seconds to the main observation level – one thing about tourist attractions they give you the facts) to the Sky Lounge, 597 feet (you do the maths) above ground level for coffee with a view. I carefully avoided walking over the two-foot wide glass floor laid around the perimeter: the older I get the less I can tolerate chasms beneath my feet, but tall tourist-buildings flaunt their height as glamour models reveal silicone-enhanced breasts.

I found an empty table by the window and settled down to appreciate the city laid out below from a more gentle angle than perpendicular. Fifty-one miles of view on a clear day, the brochure announced. The only city where you can see a couple of oceans at the same time (the South Pacific to the right, the Tasman Sea to the left: it's a very thin country), a good many volcanoes, and on that clear day, looking east, as far as the Coromandel Peninsula. It was a moderately clear day. I saw enough. Nearby were rooftops and city blocks, grey concrete and hotel signs. Very nice. There were also, to be fair, oceans and harbours and a lot of pleasing sky and scudding clouds. I sipped coffee and thought about my three days and nights to come, alone, talking to the animals. First, a long lazy bus ride gazing out of the window at, everyone said, the most beautiful scenery to be had anywhere in the world. I was in a trance of anticipation. If there is a perfect moment in travelling, for me, then it is this sitting staring at the sky in a public space, knowing no one, waiting to remove myself to a space that moves through the landscape, taking me with it to another space where I can be alone and just sit and stare again. It's the essence of the pleasure of travelling alone, that anticipatory moment just before you head off to get to how you want to be.

Then a body dropped like a stone outside the window directly in front of me. There was a communal gasp, one or two people actually cried out. It happened very fast, so that it was hard to tell if you had seen what you thought you had seen. People looked

29

around and asked the question of each other. My eyes had barely picked up that something had fallen and that it was, fleetingly, the size and shape of a human being. It wasn't my imagination; the collective response made that clear. But although my mind preferred not to acknowledge that a body had fallen, I'd registered it viscerally. My pulse raced and my heart and guts knocked against one another. One or two people jumped out of their seats and rushed to the windows to look down, while the rest of us sat like stone for a second in that lost panic of watching a catastrophe and not wanting it to have happened (with the frozen hope that keeping still will do the trick of turning back time), and not knowing what else to do.

But the braver ones who went to the window to have a look established that it wasn't a catastrophe. It was fun. A young woman harnessed to a wire had landed lightly on the soles of both feet on the pavement 600 feet below. A hurried look at my Skytower brochure explained that she had jumped off a platform two floors above the café. *New Zealand's Highest Jump. Don't Dream It – Do It!* Mostly I dream it in order, I reckon, not to have to do it. Especially dreams of falling. Dreams mean different things to different folk, I guess. About fifteen minutes later, she jumped again, but this time she stopped and hovered in mid-air outside the café window, waving at us, swaying from side to side in the wind, with a broad, open-mouthed smile, miming the cavernous, toothy scream of happiness that is now an essential part of the public expression of pleasure. She beamed her joy in life and love of humanity and the pleasures of falling, with the kind of ecstatic, come-hither smile you see in toothpaste advertisements that mean: I'm having the best time I've ever had in my life, orgasm is nothing compared to this, and you too could feel like me, and by the way do you see how white and even my teeth are? Which they were – huge and perfectly aligned, young antipodean teeth. She was employed by the franchisees to perform this BASE jump (I learn it's an acronym for the starting points of Buildings, Antennae, Spans and Earth) every quarter of an hour from a jutting platform 630 feet above ground, in order to encourage the punters. Tickets to jump were on sale downstairs. For just a few New Zealand dollars anyone could hire a bright yellow padded, insulated suit, pull on the harness (the same as used in falling stunts in movies like *Batman Forever, Titanic* and *Entrapment*; a 'fan descender' for the technically minded or those who like the fact that things no one ever dreamed of as objects or that do things no one ever thought of doing acquire official-sounding names), and plummet to the ground at a rate of 47 miles per hour, or 68 feet per second, or .061 somethings-or-other of the speed of sound. The joy of tourist brochure statistics is contagious. Be warned, my next book may be made up entirely of large or interesting numbers.

Whichever way you measured it, there would be just sixteen seconds of empty air from the moment you stepped off the floor of the platform, until your feet touched solid pavement again. A sixteen-second thrill, a near-lifetime of living-death experience for anyone with vertigo. I once sat at the top of a slow descending Ferris wheel and failed completely to admire the view over Hampstead Heath. I experienced my moment of death for as long as it took for the swinging car to arrive at the bottom of the arc, which was an inordinate minute or two, and I understood that I was to be thereafter earthbound. Vertigo comes at you, like short-sightedness, with middle-age. I think it must be there to remind you that there are certain things that older people don't have to do any more, like experience all the fun of the fair. At any rate, I have to send someone to get books from the stacks of the London Library because I can't stand on the metal grating with plunging views which they call floors.

I watched the young woman fall twice more before I went up to the next stop in the lift to investigate the place where the Skyjump began. Two sporty-looking men in jeans, t-shirts and trainers lounged in a glass booth behind a high tech winch, one tipping far back on his seat, wearing headphones, the other flipping through a tabloid newspaper. They took no notice of me standing to one side of their booth. After a few moments the lift arrived and the young woman emerged in her skin-tight sunshine yellow jumpsuit, holding two Mars bars which she chucked to each of the men, while in the process of eating one herself. Apparently she suffered none of the stomach turmoil I had on the Ferris wheel, or even while watching her first fall. She was a tall, muscular looking beauty with a weight of long, straight, sun-blonde hair tied back out of her face. Her expression was of the blankest boredom as she tossed her empty Mars bar wrapper on to the table by the winch and stepped out onto the platform. The man with the headphones got up and routinely followed her out on to the platform to help her pull on the harness. I suppose there is nothing exciting about falling one eighth of a mile through the void if you do it every fifteen minutes for several hours a day. It's just another job. Probably child's play, but duller. They were a most unexcited threesome. The man behind the winch continued to read his tabloid until the other man called out that they were ready. Then he attended to his machine. The girl walked to the edge of the platform facing outwards into the void, followed unanimatedly by her assistant who, getting the nod from the back of her head, hooked her harness to the wire, and then gave her a casual but effective shove with the sole of his trainer on her bum off the platform and out into thin air where, for a split second before she dropped out of sight, I saw that blazing sunshine smile (of the same shade as her jumpsuit) instantaneously break across her bored face, lighting it up, animating her expression with joy so that the coffee drinkers at the windows below could see what fantastic fun she was having when she paused to astonish them in mid-air on her fall of 630 feet for sixteen seconds at about forty-seven miles per hour.

It was a slow day. No one else jumped besides the girl employed to do so. She continued to go about her business after I returned to the café, up and down, up and down, dropping off the building, riding the lift back up, four or five times before I became aware of a terrible knowledge that had crept up on me, fully formed as it seemed, but quite without my being conscious of it: *that I could give the people downstairs at the desk some money and do the jump myself.* Now that I noticed the thought, it was more urgent than *could.* I found that I was thinking I *should.* I could, therefore I should, therefore I *ought.* For the life of me I couldn't understand how this notion had snuck up on me. It wasn't anything I could possibly think. I don't think I ought to do even easy, quite pleasant things. Not even necessary things. But there the thought was, having appeared in my head as if someone had injected it into my bloodstream. Perhaps there was something in the air, an adrenalin residue perhaps (mine from long ago; obviously not hers – her adrenal glands were calmly dozing), that edged me towards taking the plunge. Jumping off the side of the Skytower seemed a reasonable thing to do. The correct thing to do. Perfectly right. In spite of the frantic signals from my body-memory of the Ferris wheel, the thought that I actually could do the jump myself had grown into a powerful conviction that I ought, really ought, to do it.

Only enormous inner resources prevented me from acting on the impulse.

On the bus to Coromandel, I puzzled about how close I had come to doing the jump. It wasn't bravado, not a response to the 'don't dream it, do it' challenge. It was much more mundane than that; more an *oh well, I better just get on with it then* sort of feeling. The pull of the possible. Even I, a mistress of stasis, was drawn by simple opportunity towards action. Can do, do do. I'm much more familiar with *can do, won't do* as a natural response. It was my first, and very late, conscious moment of *because I can*. And I didn't like it at all.

It was a four-hour road journey to Coromandel town where I would be picked up and taken to the farm, twenty minutes drive away. An hour and a half out of Auckland at Thames I had to change buses, after a bit of a wait. The driver of the first bus gave us a captain of the ship speech as we left Auckland. How to ride the bus. Generally it involved not running around or doing violence to him or our fellow passengers. There were also strict company rules, he told us, about food and drink on board. Neither were permitted. As an occasional train traveller trapped in carriages scented with people eating McDonald's or Burger Kings, I was delighted by this ruling, but the driver, though an employee of the company, was master of his own bus. It wasn't reasonable to expect people not to drink on a long journey, he said, so it was all right with him if we drank water – though it had to be *water* and from bottles. A benevolent dictator, unless you'd only brought orange juice in a tetra-pak with you. He had absorbed the current social rubric that water must be constantly drunk or dehydration would do its worst and shrivel the life out of you within hours. There weren't 50cl bottles of water to carry around when I was young, and I can't imagine how my genera-tion survived, having to wait until we were indoors somewhere to beg, rasping, for life-giving regular, minerally depleted tap water.

It was apparent as soon as we left inner-city Auckland that New Zealand is, as advertised, the most beautiful place in the world. We drove south-west towards the Firth of Thames across a mountain range and always in sight of a density of greenness that I've never witnessed before. For an hour and a half I gazed at a lush world passing me by to either side of the bus. Greener, darker, thicker and more abundant than anywhere I've ever been. It was as if we were passing through a narrow corridor created in a world made entirely of rampant foliage, which, I suppose, in a way we always are. Then we arrived at the town of Thames and its bus station. Not green or lush. A pragmatic town where dingy prefabricated stores provided the wherewithal of life; food, implements, clothing, for people who come to it from the dense countryside to purchase those things. A place to earn a living if you didn't have a farm or didn't want to stay on the one you grew up on. On its outskirts, opposite the squat warehouse of a no-nonsense supermarket, the bus station. A bus station is a bus station is a bus station. Bus stands of stained concrete, litter in gutters, over-full waste baskets; a shop that sold bus tickets to get away from Thames and tacky mementoes of moments in Thames (koalas by the dozen, on key rings, on pennants, on pencils, on postcards, though you'd have to go 1300 hundred miles south to an entirely different country to find their habitat) for bored and stranded tourists; two small, dank lavatories, his and hers, just one each for all the busloads of bladders arriving; and a café, grimy glass and plasterboard, plastic tables, self-service counter, a worn-to-nothing utility nylon carpet on the floor. At first glance that was all, as familiar and dreary as Oxford bus station where I'd waited for an hour or so some months before, but at the other end of the planet. As far as I know Norman Foster has never designed and built a bus station. Pigeons and people who will never have anywhere to go spend their days (and probably their nights) in them; travellers wait in them with Buddhist-like patience or fidgety desperation to get away; minimally-waged employees clean, serve, take money with dogged dullness and grim asides to their colleagues or no one in particular, waiting for the working day to end.

Somebody ought to make an effort to design a bus station that doesn't look and feel like Desolation Row. God, I hate bus stations.

But there I was at the bus station in Thames for an hour and more while I waited for my connecting bus to the solitary, pastoral bliss of Coromandel. With my wheeled suitcase – can hardly leave it outside with everyone transient – I negotiated the lavatory door which opened inwards into the minuscule space (why make it easy by having it open outwards?), hovered over the plastic seat, and then squirmed out, case first round the corner of the door, then me, and headed for the café to have a cup of tea and the blueberry muffin I knew would be there because muffins, from having been quaint unavailable remnants from the distant past in my youth known only from nursery rhymes, are now ubiquitous; no inhabited corner of the earth is without the blueberry muffin. Such is progress and the global spirit of humanity.

Just inside the café doorway I was stopped in my tracks. The interior was as bleak as any bus station café is supposed to be, no surprise there – but the far wall, opposite where I stood, was a little bit special. It was covered from floor to ceiling in a huge hand-painted mural so naïve in execution that it made Grandma Moses look like Dürer. It depicted the Four (considerably-larger-than-life) Horsemen of the Apocalypse, head on, galloping out of the wall (if only the painter had been able to master perspective) towards the tables of travel-weary customers sipping their English Breakfast tea and chewing on dismal blueberry muffins, waiting for their connections. The horsemen wore their credentials in bold black capital letters on white headbands, making them look rather like hippies (not I think, the painter's intention): CONQUEST, WAR, FAMINE and DEATH. They wore, or at any rate their bodies consisted of, white robes, and they bared their uncannily white teeth to prove they were up to no good. The horsemen were, of course, seated on horses, though you could only be sure they were equine if you knew who they were. Without their labels round their foreheads they might have been four people in nightwear sitting on large dogs, or deer, or any biggish and brownish animal with ears and four legs by no means in the right place.

There was a low shelf on the wall just below the horses' hooves on which were nine or ten piles of home-printed, stapled handouts offering scripture and advice. I looked through them before I got my tea. My favourite had a drawing, undoubtedly done by the same artist as had made the mural. A gigantic fore-finger surrounded by short pencilled lines of power radiating from it, pointed doomfully down at a tiny sinner cowering in terror on one knee, young by the look of it, jeans, t-shirt and tell-tale long unruly hair, surrounded by an arc of pairs of inverted commas to indicate that he was quivering with fear. A speech bubble came from the distraught little lad: '**But GOD I thought you didn't exist!**' The next page explained without regard to grammar and punctuation, '**We only need one ingredient, that is to be a sinner, have you ever lied? If we are TRUTHFUL the answer is YES.**' I spent longer trying to work out the sense of this than it deserved. Unless I didn't spend nearly enough time thinking through the wisdom it offered. I'm really not certain.

Sometimes I think that *anything*, even a sweet packet, is worth spending the rest of one's life meditating on. It wouldn't be more of a waste of time than the drivel I spend most of my thoughts thinking. I collected one of each pamphlet to peruse while I waited for my bus. The Borges essays I had planned to read stayed in my bag.

The woman behind the counter poured hot water on to the tea bag in the mug, put it on the tray with my muffin and took my money.

Another pamphlet had a drawing of the front of a book with **The Holy Bible** written on its cover and underneath in even blacker bolder type, varying capitalisation and dreadful grammar:

Passport for
LIFE
All who BELIEVES
IN ME
Will Have ETERNAL
LIFE

The next leaflet headed *Science and God* began:

AS ONE LOOKS through the modern telescope into the giant starry night sky and sees the vastness of space and all that there is to see, one will agree with the Bible, that Heaven declares the glory of God.

It continued:

SCIENTIFIC FACT

The earth is a huge sphere travelling through endless space, at 18.5 miles a second, without any visible support. In other words, the earth is travelling at this speed, and rotates, or turns, on its axis during its circuit around the sun to precise timing. For thousands of years all this perfection and speed, with no motor or anything to hold it in place or to control it known to man. Not just this, but the sun, moon, His whole universe all in perfect harmony.

'Feel free to take any of those with you,' the woman behind the counter said as she poured me a refill of hot water. She was in her early thirties, blonde and tired-looking, in a singlet and black see-through blouse. I assumed the bus station was run by true believers who found it the perfect place to catch travelling sinners. Where better to make conversions than a way station, where people linger in the middle of their journeys, waiting for the next stage to begin, often alone, in hiatus, in limbo, about to be taken home or to a better destination or a worse? It's pretty scriptural. Practically a conversion factory. But although people waiting for buses are probably in a highly vulnerable spiritual condition, I was the only person who looked at the leaflets. Maybe, in the only urban desolation for many miles around, travellers were content just to soak up the uncommon plainness of their surroundings. It's true that after all the hours I spent travelling around observing the visual glory of New Zealand, I found myself eventually beginning to long for a little inner-city blight.

Before I left to get the next bus, I asked the blonde woman behind the counter if the café was run by people belonging to any particular religious group. There was a vegan café near me in Cambridge run by a group of believers in something or other, and the best lemon meringue pie in Hampstead used to be served at a café run by Hare Krishnas, but I've never come across a religious cult running a bus station.

She shook her head. 'It's nothing to do with me. It's the boss. He's eighty-five years old. Says he's passing on what he's learned about life.' Her tone was neutral. She didn't care one way or another. Maybe when I'm eighty-five, I'll buy a bus station and know by then what it is that I want to pass on.

Werner, a Swiss German who had followed his Europe-touring girlfriend, Sylvie, back to New Zealand and married her, picked me up at the bus stop in his 4 x 4, and explained that I needed to buy some food for my stay on their farm. The cabins were self-catering. I hadn't realised, but I was delighted to hear it. He waited while I shopped. Coromandel Township is like a town out of the old American west, or at least old American Westerns. Painted wooden houses, a main street, a stream with ducks swimming in it. A car challenges the image every so often. A pretty place. A bit touristy with the odd knick-knack shop, but this was the end of the season, so it was empty except for local people. It had a small supermarket that sold bare and dull essentials like the tea and biscuits I purchased, and a delicatessen where I bought bread, ham and a wonderful smoked cheese crammed with chilli.

Werner took me and my shopping to the five hundred-acre deer farm and showed me to my cabin, one in a line of seven, all but mine empty. The raised cabin with plasterboard walls and a corrugated metal roof was as basic as the supermarket. It was an adequate DIY effort and had probably come flat-packed for Werner to assemble. A table, a sofa, a sink, kettle, toaster and microwave oven, a bedroom with basic shower room and lavatory off it. A practical lino floor throughout. There was a wooden veranda with a rail along the length of the sliding glass door that made up the front wall of the cabin. I put my things inside, made a cup of tea and some toast and sat out on the plastic chair with my legs up on the rail, waiting for the sun to set over the sweep of the empty harbour of blue and sparkling water a couple of hundred feet below. Here it was. The world well lost. Silence, peace almost, but for the continuing shriek of the cicadas, nothing and no one around. And a bright, silvery sunset in progress, the gentlest you could imagine. During the night it rained, pittering down on the metal roof of my cabin, to keep the greenness of this world intense. I woke to strange bird calls and blazing sunshine. And no one else at all. Of course, Werner and Sylvie, were long since up, having fed the domestic animals – goats, a cockatoo, two dogs (one blind), and a cat called Traitor, who lived up to her name by spending as much of her day as I would allow on my veranda, purring on my lap – and had taken their four children to school. In the high season, Sylvie cleaned the cabins, washed the sheets and towels and sometimes cooked for large parties, but now life would be a bit easier as the winter set in and visitors came just in ones and twos, occasionally.

For supper I ate bread and cheese, for breakfast ham and melted cheese on toast, for lunch ham sandwiches, in between biscuits, and drank tea. First thing in the morning I walked along the 'bush path' that Werner had cut through the untouched jungle that ran along the edge of the cultivated farmland and went down to the harbour. Above it, but hidden by the narrow strip of dense forest, were rolling velvet hills, looking, when you emerged from the bush walk, as soft as antler fuzz, where herds of deer and cows grazed. Undulating acres of incline and declivity disappeared into the far distance. When I got down to the beach, there was a kayak lying on the sand and I longed to take it out, but I also didn't want to move anything, to disrupt what was there. Then again, maybe, I wasn't too sure about kayaking in a strange, empty harbour. I am a rubbish swimmer. Instead, I stood on the beach and stared out over the bright water and let my eyes rest on the horizon. It's what my eyes like doing most. Then I wandered back above the bush walk across the hilly grazing land. Later, in the afternoon, I went to the pond. Werner had cut away a path in the tangled foliage around the edge to make another walk. It took fifteen minutes to circle the pond. Families of ducks moved from one side to the other as I approached where they were splashing and flapping their feathers, preening and cleaning, keeping themselves nice, if it were not for this interruption of human footsteps. The next day I spent in exactly the same way, except that I sat on the little wonky wooden jetty on the pond and let my legs dangle into the water. I sat for an hour or so and thought later that I probably hadn't had a single thought in this time alone, apart from: I wonder what that bird is called, and: listen, how quiet it is.

In between walking and sitting and staring, I read Borges'
collected non-fiction, sitting on the balcony, looking up from
time to time at the harbour tide come and go and make visible
and invisible the netting in the shallows where mussels were
farmed, or in the evening on the sofa with the curtains drawn, or
in bed. Reading someone else's thinking. Taking it in, but into
my thoughtless mind. More and more I am convinced that there
is nothing in my head, nothing arising out of anything, nothing
learned, and that the emptiness and quietness I want so much is
just that: empty and quiet for no reason and no use at all. I was
completely content, but completely pointless. At my most
depressed, I've been appalled by pointlessness, it has seemed an
entirely acceptable reason for suicide: the pointlessness of me
and of life; especially of life. But at my most contented, pointlessness *is* the point, and sometimes runs over with meaning.
During my time on the Coromandel Coast, I was somehow both
depressed and contented. At any rate, I seemed pointless, life
seemed pointless, I felt weighted with sadness – and I was contented as a cat. More contented than Traitor the cat, who
seemed to need even more than she was getting from her
devoted family, or needed to let them know there was more she
could get, so they had better not be complacent about her. I was
as contented as the huge blind dog that ambled slowly about the
place, stopping to sniff the world, pausing to be stroked if you
called out to him, taking what he could get, otherwise just passing through. At times depression and contentment come
together to create a joy that feels like what they mean by grace.
Not that thing they call clinical depression, which is implacable

and deadly, but a broader form of sadness, a generalised sorrow that seeps slowly towards something else – and joy, if you imagine it very quiet, balanced on an infinitely small pinpoint, is the word that seems best to describe it. When it comes, I take it with pleasure.

Sometimes, like on the balcony on the Coromandel Coast, I can arrange the conditions when joy might appear, but the right conditions don't guarantee its appearance. And of course, it passes, sooner or later, though always too soon, like a breath of wind on a sweltering day.

'Have you noticed that everyone wants to be loved?'

I had noticed.

'Well, there you are. You see?'

I didn't, though I knew from the tone of voice what was coming next.

Sylvie was driving me from the farm to catch my bus to Auckland. No one interrupted my silence while I was staying in my cabin, but now Sylvie had the twenty minutes it took to get to the Coromandel Township bus stop, to prove the existence of God to me. I hadn't gathered that they were evangelical Christians. I hadn't gathered anything much about them except that they worked hard and lived in the most beautiful place I could imagine.

'Everyone wants to be loved and that shows us God exists.'

'How?' This was a bit listless. Three days on my own had made me reluctant to engage in theological debate.

45

'Because the longing for love is every one of us wanting to let God into our lives, even if we don't want to know it and refuse to admit it. We all want God to love us and to love God, but the evil in us stops us from opening ourselves to him. Do you understand?' She glanced at me to see if the penny had dropped.

I might have mentioned Freud or Melanie Klein on the subject of what we want. Or Sartre on the terrible isolation of the self-aware individual and the horror of the certainty of absolute extinction. Or Marx on the subject of false consciousness. But in fact I said, 'Oh'. I said it as weakly as I could, trying not to imply either that her reasoning had cleared the mists in my mind to revelation, or that I was the Devil's messenger and intent on souring innocent faith with ugly doubt because, although the latter role was quite to my taste, I didn't have the inclination for argument and in any case knew, being as old as I am, that very little in the way of rational conversation can sour ugly faith with innocent doubt.

I just said 'Oh' in a mild, non-committal sort of way in the hope that it would do and we could get on to talk about deer farming.

'Do you see what it means? It means we all *know* the truth of God. That He exists. It's only being born evil that puts a barrier between us and Him.'

Sylvie had four children. I was suddenly engaged.

'When your kids were born, did you look at them and think they were evil?'

She was well up on this sort of undermining talk.

'You have to teach children to be good. You never have to

teach them to be bad. They already know how to do that,' she said triumphantly.

I desperately wanted to let nature and nurture pass, but could not quite let the natal moment go.

'But the first time you saw them, the moment they were born, did they strike you as evil in any way?'

Sylvie did not exactly answer this question. She just continued doggedly to insist that we were all born to sin. It is clear in the Bible if only I took the trouble to read it. Genesis. Original sin. Adam and Eve. Their disobedience, our curse. We were there-fore, every one of us, wicked from birth and had to learn how to be good. 'How to be *social*,' I muttered, getting a little sullen now. I had only recently emerged from writing two novels based on intensely close readings of Genesis. We were on my territory. I knew more about the interpretations of Genesis from midrash, and biblical commentators of all kinds of faith and lack of it, than she imagined. Her singular reading of Genesis was just one of a dozen I could have given her. It wouldn't have made any dif-ference. Sylvie, of course, did not distinguish human social relations from God-given regulation.

'God gave the rules. He called them the ten commandments. We follow them because God wants us to. We aren't complete until we let Him into our life.'

Sylvie knew all about this, and all about my faithless objec-tions, because she had once been sinful herself, she told me. As sinful as they come, I couldn't imagine how sinful. But when she came back from the tour of Europe she made at twenty, God had come into her life, in a flash of enlightenment, and now she thanked him every minute of every day for saving her. Werner, who she had met and had an affair with in Switzerland, had turned up in New Zealand, doubtless for more sinning, but when he saw the remarkable change that had been wrought in her by God, he had given up resisting the truth and adopted the Lord himself. They married, bought the farm and life was good. Paradise, really. They built their holiday cabins not just for the extra income but so that people who had no faith (as well as organized groups who had) could share some of the grace in the form of the glorious, peaceful surroundings that had directly resulted from their trusting and obedient faith in Jesus. They hoped heathen eyes would open, and already-Christian ones would be reinforced in their belief. They lived, I had to concede, in what seemed very like an Eden: Sylvie, Werner, their four blonde, blue-eyed children and the animals, on their beautiful farm, above the turquoise sea and in gentle silence, apart from their parrot which flew around free each evening and arrived on my veranda railing refusing to leave until I returned its repetitive 'Hello' with one of my own. On the other hand, there seemed to be no part of New Zealand (apart from bus stations and busy cities) that isn't breathtakingly beautiful, so perhaps what is necessary for a paradisiacal existence is not so much to let God into your life, as to want it enough to stay in New Zealand and hang the distance to, or as they see it from, everywhere else.

Sylvie left me, unconverted, by the bus stop, but I could tell that she had not given up hope that one day I might be saved. One of the things about being a believer, I suppose, is that you don't give up hope. One of the things about me is that I do. I

headed back past stunning views of mountains and sea to
Auckland in order to fly to Queenstown on the South Island. A
bus from Queenstown would take me to my final destination, Te
Anau, in Fiordland, because it was from there that I could take a
boat trip around Doubtful Sound. It seemed more and more to be
just the place for me, especially since my encounters with true
belief. *Make a doubtful sound unto the Lord*, kept running
through my head as I sat on the plane to Queenstown gazing
down at the mountain ranges and the lakes cupped in their vol-
canic cavities. There's a converse *Doubtless Bay* up in the north of
the North Island but it was too definite sounding for my taste, so
I had chosen to head down south where things apparently were
less certain. Perhaps that's it: not that I lose hope too easily, but
that I never have certainty. I'm always doubtful. Not good material for evangelicals.

In Queenstown I had a few hours to wait, again, this time for
the bus to Te Anau. Queenstown, it turned out, is to those who
like to play with gravity what Middle Earth is to lovers of hob-
bits. The desire to plummet is not confined to the Skytower in
Auckland but is everywhere evident in New Zealand. It seems
that people drop off any ledge, bridge, building or mountain they
come across. Indeed, many of the jumpers come from across the
world just for that purpose. Falling down is institutionalized in
New Zealand. But Queenstown is the capital of wilful descending. Getting off the bus from the airport I looked up and saw,
stark against the clear blue, half a dozen human beings, attached
to nothing very much, dropping from the sky. In Queenstown
you can fall to earth from planes, swing in mid-air attached to a

49

rope 130 feet high, tumble downhill inside a transparent plastic ball, fly the thermals under a pair of nylon wings, crash over rapids on jet boats or rafts, or drop off anything you fancy, attached to a rubber line, before being bounced back from bare inches off the ground.

I wandered into shops that sold these activities and collected brochures and information, before finding myself a handy noodle bar where I could sit, sip soup and learn. The first ever purpose built commercial bungee jump was created in New Zealand in 1988 by A.J. Hackett, a visionary who saw that people would pay money to fall from great heights if they could be guaranteed (more or less) to survive. With just the right kind of high-tech elastic rope, he mass-produced the adrenalin rush that previously only extreme adrenalin junkies prepared to die for their fix could achieve. For most of the history of the world, it has been the goal of humanity to attempt to get up into the air and stay there for as long as possible. *Up* was always the desired direction. The Babel builders wanted the heavens not the depths. Up. The big idea of Daedalus was to fly, not to fall. Up. Icarus may seem to be the patron saint of freefall, but at the time of his maiden flight he was a tragic failure. We looked at the birds with envy, longing to find a way to emulate them, not at the nasty mess under the tree that was all that remained of an incautious monkey that had been trying to make its way amongst the branches of the canopy. Apes were so pleased to get on to solid ground that they stood up on two feet and became hominids capable of clapping their hands and dancing a jig of happiness. Only the desperate jumped from great heights, and they expected to do it just the once. Mountains were climbed, apparently, because they were there, not in order to jump off them once you got to the top. Up, up, always up. Now mountains are jumped off because it's a thrill that you aren't likely to hurt yourself doing, and the serious danger-monkeys climb them without ropes or crampons.

All the rhetoric of the falling industry is about overcoming fear. *Embrace the fear*, challenges a pamphlet for *Nzone*, the ultimate jump in Queenstown, a skydive operation that allows you to leave a plane at 15,000 feet and not pull the parachute cord for as long as you dare. *Our goal. Terminal velocity. 200km/hr (124 mph). Achievement doesn't come sweeter.* The brochure goes on to ask, *Why climb a great mountain that does not know you exist?* Which makes the climber sound like an unrequited lover trying to impress himself on his beloved. The answer, apparently, is that:

Deep in the human consciousness is a pervasive need for a logical universe that makes sense. But the real universe is always one step beyond logic. We do these things. It is something deep within us, the need to feed our voracious appetite for danger and glory. It is the spirit of man.

Quite how this makes the universe make more sense is not quite clear to me, but you do get a certificate after you land. *Take the plunge. Be brave*, the pamphlet whispers to those of us to whom the call of glory is not quite enough, *even if you're not, pretend to be. No one can tell the difference.* But the choice, they make it clear either to make the challenge more inviting or to cover themselves in case of accident, is yours: *To go through life able to say 'yes, I did it', or to go through life knowing that you had the opportunity, but you turned it down and walked away from becoming the complete person you could have been.* That's all you have to do to become a complete person: leap. Well, Kierkegaard wouldn't disagree. Actually he would. The risk between a leap of faith and a leap out of a plane is not commensurate. As to which has the higher value depends on you. I suspect that the complete person you become after taking a flying leap is the same sort of complete person you would become if you were, like Sylvie, to take Jesus into your heart and follow biblical instruction word for word. Go for it, but remember the harness. It takes a certain kind of person, according to *Nzone*:

> . . . *to step out of an aircraft at 15,000ft into thin air. It takes courage. The fact that you are harnessed by space age materials to an experienced qualified Jumpmaster makes little difference.* **You step out that aircraft door and for some 60 seconds you plummet towards the ground at 200km/h.**

In fact, the harness makes quite a big difference.

Though I was quite unmoved by the exhortations to take my cowardice in hand and develop my full person, there was just a nanosecond when there I was again, my heart thumping and wondering if I ought not to, just for the experience, just because I could, because other people had . . . But I thought very hard about those long seconds while I would be falling, about seeing all that space between me and the ground contracting, and I decided against it. Once, when I was about seven, I was staying in the country and the local boys had rigged a rope with a large knot on the end from a branch of a tree. The branch wasn't 15,000 feet above the ground but it was high enough to be a deadly fall. I was perfectly happy to climb trees but terrified of launching myself off one to swing helplessly backwards and forwards until gravity brought me to the ground. I've never been one to choose to be out of control. However, there was not the slightest doubt in my mind that I was obliged to climb up to the branch, sit on the knot, hang on tight to the rope and throw myself into the air, to fall and swing, or fall off and die. It was necessary not just so that I could be accepted by the local boys (though that was of the greatest importance), but so that I wouldn't have to go through the rest of my life knowing I had walked away from becoming the complete person I could have been.

I didn't die. I swung about like a vervet monkey on a liana. It was fun – or such a relief that it felt like fun. But decades on, it turns out that I've discovered an even greater thrill and more pervasive satisfaction than ever higher falls or even the certainty of God: I simply walk away from the complete person I could have been and live thrillingly with the vertiginous knowledge of all the opportunities I have turned down to make me the curtailed person I am today. So I climbed on to the bus for Te Anau and the prospect of a cruise through Doubtful Sound without so much as a final upward glance at the sky full of plummeting bodies.

3

ON GETTING WHERE YOU
WERE GOING

Another beautiful bus journey. From Queenstown to Te Anau
took two and a quarter hours. Lakes, mountains, a wilderness
covered with rare and protected red tussock grass, up more
mountains, down to more lakes, and everywhere green, green,
green. A passing sheepdog in the back of an open truck barked
at us. Traffic was an occasional truck or car as we wound on
through the valleys, mountain ranges with snow on their peaks,
and alongside the lakes that looked untouched, deep blue, still
and bottomless. It might have been that no one else existed
except our busload and the dog and his master driving the truck.
My fifteen fellow passengers were all under thirty, young travellers with mountainous burdens on their backs which needed
the help of the driver or each other to slough off and heave into
the luggage space before they climbed into the bus, light and
free; all the girls' midriffs were bare, otherwise they were
unidressed with distressed jeans, hems torn and trailing along

the ground, and ruined trainers that might have been new when their parents dropped them at journey's beginning in Australia, France, Germany, Holland, England and America. They all had MP3 players wired to their ears. One or two of the young women read books while we drove. Most of the men sprawled with their legs jutting into the gangway, dozing while their music met in the middle of their brains. I sat at the back of the bus and watched them when I wasn't watching the mountains and lakes. The bus driver didn't mention anything about eating and drinking. His busload was a snacking and drinking generation. They fished around in their bags, like cavernous sacks, and brought out chocolate bars or biscuits, and everyone had the essential water bottle with a nipple to drink from, in their bags or clipped to their belt, which they sucked on at regular intervals like babies on a demand feeding regime. Things down south were less rule-bound apparently than up in Auckland, or the clientele were so young that there was no point invoking the company rules on refreshments.

Along with my travelling companions I sucked on my bottle of water and listened to John Dowland through my headphones. It was an easy-going ride. People from far away, moving from one place to another, for no particular purpose. To see this sight, or meet that person, or just because the bus was going that way and they had been where they were long enough. What an oddly fortunate and pointless way to live. And how dream-like. How exactly the way I wanted it to be. A limbo of movement to get to another place to be still in. From keeping still by the pond or on the veranda at Coromandel to Doubtful Sound to sit on a boat

55

and look at the mountains, the water, and the stillness of the fiord as they passed by me.

The only thing wrong was that intermittently I had cramping pains in my stomach which didn't seem to ease up. By the time we arrived in Te Anau they were seizing at my guts with a steely grip every few minutes. My fellow passengers were distributed in ones and twos around the town of Te Anau to an apparently infinite number of backpacker hostels that proclaimed their friendliness and astonishing cheapness on large placards on front lawns. Then the driver dropped me off at my hotel. A proper, internationally bland, four star job, beside Lake Te Anau, all mod-cons I hoped, after the basic cabin of Coromandel – one of the entitlements I reckoned of being much older than twenty-five. I'd made two bookings while I waited in Queenstown for the bus: one to visit the glow-worm caves the following evening (because, well, you would, wouldn't you?) and the other to take the boat that sailed around Doubtful Sound, the culmination of my travels south, the day after.

I checked into the hotel and went to my bathroom and large bed – in that order. I had an awful night, with the pains in my stomach waking me whenever I dropped off. Unaccountably, for me, I had run out of painkillers. I always have some for headaches, but I must have taken them all and forgotten to replace them. I spent the night racked with cramps and a thundering headache. Also I wanted to throw up, but spent enormous amounts of energy controlling it. There is nothing I like less than vomiting. It feels like dying. It feels catastrophic. I will do anything to avoid it, making myself feel twice as ill as necessary, but at least not being sick. Perhaps it's a kind of phobia, like my horror of spiders. Then again, perhaps it's something to do with the memory of my mother vomiting into the toilet bowl: huge heavings, terrible noises. She had been having a fight with my father and he hit her, or hit her back. Too hard – she fell back against the wall (bumpy Anaglypta, cream, I think), I heard her head crack against it and then she slid down slowly to the ground. Like a mime pretending to be a rag doll. She seemed to be unconscious, her eyes were closed. Or, for all I knew, dead. I was eight or nine. My father suddenly shouted, 'Don't just stand there, get a bowl of water!' He sounded angry, but was probably panicked. I ran to the kitchen and he fetched a flannel from the bathroom, soaked it in the bowl of water I brought, and held it wet to her head. Soon her eyes opened. She got up slowly without a word and then staggered for the bathroom where the vomiting started. I went to the bathroom door and watched her, on the floor, throwing up for what seemed like hours. I thought she was going to die. I think my father also thought she was going to die. And ... the memory finishes. No resolution. Did we call a doctor? Take her to Casualty? Certainly, we should have: she had lost consciousness and was vomiting. I didn't know that then, but surely my father did. I can't remember anything beyond watching her embrace the white ceramic bowl and groan in between retching, now a dry, rasping sound, with nothing to come up. Since she didn't die, I suppose I ought not to feel that vomiting is so lethal. But I do. Maybe it doesn't have anything to do with my mother.

By the morning I was wretched. I went down to reception to

ask where the nearest pharmacy was. The young woman behind the desk gratifyingly said I looked awful. I longed for sympathy. I told her about my stomach cramps, awake all night, sick . . .

'Oh, it's a bug going round,' she said decisively. 'I had it last week. You have really bad stomach pains, a terrible headache and you keep vomiting.'

She sounded satisfactorily compassionate in spite of the sharp edge of her attenuated New Zealand vowels and her air of being practised at this particular discomfort: someone who'd been there first, got through it, gone beyond it. I asked humbly how long it was likely to last. She was the authority on my future wellbeing. I now feared it going on for a week, taking up all my time in Te Anau as well as the journey to, and night in, Christchurch and the twenty and more hours flying back to Heathrow and then getting to Cambridge, dirty washing, clothes creased, washing things somewhere at the bottom of my suitcase. I decided I would just stay where I was for as long as it took, rather than travel feeling like this. Never mind airline tickets, I'd stay in my satisfactorily anonymous hotel room in the enormous bed, right next to the bathroom in case I finally lost control of my vomit reflex. Until I felt better. The hell with going home. The hell with anything.

'Three days. Then I was fine. The doctor gave me paracetamol. There's nothing else you can do. Just stay in bed and drink a lot of water, he said.'

That made two days to go. Today's trip to the cold, dark, damp glow-worm caves was out of the question, but tomorrow, my last full day in Te Anau, before I returned to Christchurch, and the plane back to the UK the next morning, I ought to be feeling better – enough to make an effort at least. I am not a great one for making an effort, but being so far away, and longing to be rocked gently on the fathomless waters of Doubtful Sound . . . The receptionist took pity on me and gave me some paracetamol (which I signed for, absolving her and the hotel of any consequences) and I went back upstairs to my bed to wait it out. I called and cancelled the glow-worms, had no alternative but to let them go for ever (when would I be in Te Anau again?), but left the scheduled Doubtful Sound trip as it was. Some things you can't bear to cancel. If I wasn't feeling better I wouldn't go, but I couldn't bring myself to ring up and rule it out there and then. Doubtful Sound, for God's sake.

Back in bed, my body devoted to my racking pain and vomit control, I read about what I was going to miss that evening. In spite of, or because of, my fuzzy state of mind, it seemed easy enough to replace the actual experience I wasn't going to have with a close, imaginative reading of the brochure:

Have you ever seen limestone passages sculpted by water up close? Or a cascading waterfall underground? Have you drifted in silent darkness beneath the luminous blue-green shimmer of thousands of glow-worms?

No, I hadn't, and now I never would. But I had the brochure. It wasn't hard to imagine an underground waterfall, or silent darkness and a blue-green shimmer. And drifting, in between my bowel seizures, was like falling off a log. What's more there were colour photographs of it all and a map of the caves, so I needn't even worry that my imaginings were inaccurate. One of the photographs was of the boat. It had ten people in it, all smiling, their eyes shining with wonder, gleaming in the glow-worm light. It was crowded with a properly constituted family – mother, father, two small children – a young couple, an older couple, and two young women. *My* boat, on the other hand, just had me in it as I drifted in the underground dankness, dampness dripping down the granite walls, past the thundering waterfall, to the whirlpool cave, through the narrows to emerge finally '*beyond the roar of the stream to a cavern of silence, the magical glow-worm grotto*' where I continued to drift '*under the starry shimmer . . . an unforgettable experience for all ages*'. I still haven't forgotten it. And I didn't have to listen to anyone talking me through it, or the oohs of appreciation of my fellow tourists, or the click and whirr of cameras. I didn't even miss out on the science – so much a part of any sightseeing activity. It was, I learned, the larvae of fungus gnats which produce '*a brilliant internal glow through the oxidation of the chemical luciferin in its digestive system. The light can be turned on and off at will when disturbed by unusual noises, light, humidity and temperature. It also varies in intensity depending on the desire for food. Flying insects are attracted to the collective display of lights in the dark cave that mimic the night sky and are caught up in the sticky silk threads that hang from the glow-worm nests. The 'fishing lines' are then hauled in and the captured insects devoured.*'

Devoured, so much worse than being eaten, I think. And *luciferin* pleased me no end. A chemical called light, like the disobedient angel. And the glow-worms that lit up at will – have will, will light up. I watched these sublime, wilful, intensely desiring creatures with their fishing lines a-dangling, winking and blinking above me as I lay in the mattress-soft, pillowed bottom of my boat, my blankets pulled up around my chin. Every now and then my gut went into spasm, but the twinkling lights and the rising and falling of gossamer fishing lines held most of my attention. I had to agree with Lawson Burrows who discovered the caves in 1948, after a three-year search of the three hundred miles of lakeshore: 'It was a fantastic sight . . . it looked like a page out of a space fiction picture book, a weird place but not at all frightening.' Outside in the real world beyond the hotel window, the weather had taken a stormy turn. A wind howled through the air conditioning ducts, and the trees along the lakeshore whipped from side to side. To have taken the actual boat across Lake Te Anau to the caves and be inside them in this weather might well have been a bit frightening – miserable at any rate. Even, possibly, cancelled. Some time in the late afternoon, there was a cracking explosion outside. I opened my eyes and looked out of the window. The entire canopy of the tree directly opposite my window by the lake side had snapped and crashed to the ground. A seriously large amount of trunk, branches and foliage lay defeated on the promenade, pelted by huge raindrops falling from a steely sky. I sent up a prayer of smug thanks to the evolutionary process for the gift of imagination.

The next morning my insides were still cramping, my head still hurt, but both with less intensity, and the desire to throw up had faded. I was feeling feeble but, enchanted and dry though I had been by my private tour of the glow-worm caves, I decided with an unfamiliar resolve to ignore my discomfort and take the actual rather than the virtual boat trip through Doubtful Sound. Paracetamol at four-hour intervals would keep me going. Of course I had the brochure and could have lain in bed imagining myself sailing on still waters between sheer towering cliffs, passing through mists, hearing the birdsong and waterfalls in the wilderness to either side, seeing dolphins breech the glassy surface and fur seals lolling on islets, maybe even blue penguins playing around the bows of the boat. But for some reason, in spite of my wish (one I invariably grant myself) to stay in bed and where I was, I was really determined to do the actual deed and be there. Something to do with being far away, perhaps. The weather had only very slightly improved. No trees would keel over in the wind, but it was dull and showery, with just the occasional hint of a bold blue sky somewhere up beyond the clouds. I got up, bathed, and steeled myself for reality.

Although Te Anau is as near as you can find a bed to Doubtful Sound, the actual getting there turned out to be much more of a journey than I had supposed. Imagine a trip to glow-worm caves and there you are, already in them as soon as you decide to make the mental effort. I have always much preferred making mental efforts to physical ones. To take an actual cruise through Doubtful Sound, however, required catching a bus outside the hotel at eight-thirty a.m. to take me to Lake Manapouri, an hour or more away. We journeyed through the rain-soaked day, and a mist strong enough to see the droplets in the air, cold, wet and stony, in spite of which the driver stopped to allow people to get out in scenic spots and take photos. I stayed in the bus with my stomach ache. We stopped for a double rainbow, a torrent cascading down to a chasm where a swollen river roared under the bridge we were crossing, and anything else that was picturesque and would make a talking point back home. Everyone except me climbed out to grab the memories and store them in their little silver memory containers or, a modern touch, this, their phones. I didn't have either, as usual, but I kept dry. Eventually, we got to Lake Manapouri and boarded a boat for the forty-five-minute cruise across it to reach the next bus which would drive us over Wilmot Pass, through dense rainforest to, at long last, Doubtful Sound itself.

I already regretted having got up, but before we reached Wilmot Pass there was a supplementary tour of the Manapouri Underground Power Station. I don't have enough skill to describe how uninterested I am in power stations, nor how particularly uninterested in this power station, at this time, I was. Doubtful Sound seemed forever in the distance; unreachable. In fact it was only reachable by driving down into the bowels of the earth through a tunnel cut in a mountain and staring down from the viewing deck at the Machine Hall, empty apart from four, I don't know, *turbines* let's say, at each corner of the huge underground room. I don't doubt for a moment that there are people who are fascinated by power stations, perhaps some of my fellow travellers were, but I stood and looked down on a cavernous space with four yellow structures in it that did something involving a low but insistent hum which provided a lot of power, and felt my life drain away. The building of the power station and how it worked was explained in photographs, pictures and diagrams on the viewing deck for those who tired of looking at the four yellow

63

structures. I tried to persuade myself that any form of education is a good thing, and that, at least, it would be something to do until the enthusiasts had had enough. But somehow, only by staring fixedly at the yellow structures did it seem possible for me to survive the half-hour allocated to our visit, so to this day I know nothing about power stations and I have only myself and my increasing wish that I had stayed in bed to blame. But it was only because of the building of the power station that the pass through the mountains existed, indeed this 'fascinating 22 kilometres road', the brochure explains, is the most expensive piece of road in New Zealand. Without the power station, Doubtful Sound would have been inaccessible, so I really should have been grateful and impressed with this monumental human effort. But I am not a grateful person.

At last we were allowed to leave and climbed back into the bus, drove through the granite tunnel and came out into the granite daylight. Still raining. But that's what happens in rainforest country. Apparently, rain is more or less constant in Fiordland. I wouldn't have minded if I had been in my hotel room, looking out through the window and imagining the majesty of sea cliffs and silent water as I cruised Doubtful Sound from the comfort of my bed. I would have had no trouble imagining 'the many moods' of the Sound. *One minute clear, blue and sun-drenched, the next mysterious and mist-shrouded.* The brochures gave me just what I needed to pass a contented day in my bed. *You will be struck by the quality of silence – a silence broken only by birdsong, or maybe the rushing of a distant waterfall.* I had been waiting to be struck by this for days.

At last we got to the Sound and boarded the catamaran for our three-hour cruise. And so did several other busloads of seekers after silence who had arrived from other starting points. By the time we were all decanted onto the catamaran it was standing room only. The seats inside were taken, and the decks were full. I sat inside sharing a table by the window with a rugged-looking American couple who travelled the world doing wilderness walks, each of whom jumped up every few moments to photograph some unforgettable rock formation or fall of water, and an older New Zealand couple whose daughter lived in England. They explained their concern to the Americans at the number of Asian immigrants who had settled in New Zealand. 'They keep to themselves . . . They don't want to integrate . . .' I went outside to stand on the deck, but the wind whipped the rain into my eyes and my stomach cramps got worse. Still, it *was* beautiful. Misty and majestic, even if the mystery was fatally undermined by the squash of humanity appreciating it and making sure they could take it home with them. Video cameras whirred, commentaries were added, people held digital cameras out at arm's length in the new manner of taking photographs – even more distant than the old method which at least demanded a physical connection between lens, viewfinder and eye. I was wet and cold. I hate wet and cold. The life seeps from me. Bereft, again. I stood and watched what my eyes told me was the grey, rainy, windy beauty of Doubtful Sound and wanted to cry. It wasn't that everyone else was having such a great time, indeed quite a few looked miserable, standing in the soaking, almost freezing air, but I didn't see anyone fighting back tears.

The high point of the trip came when, in the middle of the captain's broadcast commentary, he told us the high point had come. Now we were going to hear the 'sound of silence', the sound of Doubtful Sound. He asked for all camera clicking and conversation to stop. He turned off the engine. For a full two minutes there was – silence. Of course, the sound of water lapping against the boat, the drippings of rain, the rush of wind, though no birds – they were sheltering from the wet rather than singing – but it was silence in that no humans or their machines made any sound for a hundred and twenty seconds.

Unfortunately, there was the sound of listening – a kind of buzz of people *not* doing anything in order to hear what people not doing anything was like, and the sound of expectation, of folk appreciating nature. The silent scream of appreciation gradually transmuted into a silent anticipation of the breaking of the silence. Then the captain turned the engine on again, cameras resumed their capture of the natural world, people exclaimed on the magical quality of the silence they had heard, and we chugged off towards the widening of the Sound at it reached the open sea. The boat began to bounce, then to rock and reel. The captain explained that he'd seen much higher waves at this point, as the sea made the Sound turbulent here, but that this was pretty rough and he didn't think it was wise to go any further. Several people had begun to look sick, and although I don't get sick as a rule in rough seas, my stomach was in no fit state to meet any kind of challenge. I returned to my vigil of the day before and devoted myself to suppressing my vomit centres. Even so I enjoyed the liveliness of the ride, the boat lurching upwards as if it was starting to climb a hill and then falling down before slapping up against the next wave, rather more than what had gone before.

And that was Doubtful Sound. A disappointment? Well, all anticipations are some kind of disappointment. I enjoyed my ersatz glow-worm visit more. What would have been the difference if I had actually gone to the caves? Only the fact that I had physically been there. But nothing will persuade me that the mere fact of being in a place is enough in itself to justify the effort of getting out of bed to become a tourist, or even a traveller. I don't have the slightest wish to be intrepid. I don't want to prove myself to myself or to anyone else. I don't care if no one thinks me brave or hardy. I have no concern at all that I did not have whatever it is that I should have had to take a dive out of a plane or off a building. None of that matters to me in the least. I don't even mind that I missed hundreds of wonderful things to see in parts of New Zealand I didn't get to as a result of my wish to be quiet and solitary and sit on a veranda on the Coromandel Coast, and my failed fantasy of silence and stillness drifting through Doubtful Sound. So, aside from doing my bit as a professional writer, was there any need for me to go to New Zealand, or anywhere else? None, I think. All the places I imagine myself in are solitary, silent and visually appealing. That is as good a description of my workroom as it is of anywhere in the world. So what about staying home? Not strange enough, perhaps, and not solitary enough. Then somewhere else, but without the need to be a traveller. Keep still, quiet, read, think, listen to what's going on in my head. Make a doubtful sound. Isn't that what I do for a living, really?

PART TWO

ON STILLNESS

Well, they are gone, and here must I remain,
This lime-tree bower my prison! I have lost
Beauties and feelings, such as would have been
Most sweet to my remembrance even when age
Had dimm'd mine eyes to blindness! . . .

From 'This Lime-Tree Bower My Prison'
by Samuel Taylor Coleridge

4

ON BEING HOLED-UP

The following autumn I rented the converted granary on a farm in the Quantock Hills for two months. The idea was to be isolated and alone, like a proper writer should be, and, writer or not, like I should be. To think, to read, to listen. This is an account of that period.

Week 1

I don't think there has ever been less disappointment in an arrival. Stillcombe – which it was not, of course, really called – is a sheep farm nestled in the West Country hills of Somerset. The small cottage I rented was a converted granary, which was built on to, but faced away from, the back of the large stone farmhouse. It was perched low down on the side of a tiny but precipitous valley. The windows of the cottage looked out on to steep, encircling, grass-covered hills, on which some of the three hundred or so sheep, a small herd of cattle, and a couple of ponies grazed. It was like being held in a cupped palm. The world was circumscribed by the line of trees at the top of the hill, blazing rich reds and golds in the autumn sun, the bronzed bracken above the fields, and a blue and cloud-patched sky. The cottage was advertised on a website as a holiday let. I booked it for two months, from October to the week before Christmas to sit still in, alone, be silent, write, read. A bit of a risk, having seen only a few online photographs. It looked right but who could tell?

No place is ever what it seems to be from pictures or description – not because of dishonesty of the photographer or describer (though there is always that possibility) but because of the images the mind makes from just a fragment of this or that, and the clutter of memories that come drifting into limited information to form themselves into a desired imagined space. Inside my urban head, country cottages all look like the gingerbread house deep in a forest clearing (though with the sea incongruously in view). Minus the gingerbread, the reality of Stillcombe was not greatly different from my idealized imaginings. Most remarkable. It was perfect. Small, remote, comfortable, simple. A green desert island, with all amenities (I have never wanted a rugged solitude) where, once I delivered the Poet to the train station, expelled after a weekend in his idea of heaven back to the wilderness of Cambridge, I would be left behind. Stable doors, wonky floors, window seats, old wood creaking, mist, sheep over there, a couple of horses in the field opposite the kitchen window, hills all around, secluding the cottage completely. The farmhouse, behind its old granary which was now my cottage, was invisible until you were outside the cottage gate (yes, there was a picket fence around it). The Farmer lived

there, no one else. I was as near as possible to being alone. Except
that the Poet was with me at the beginning. He drove me down and
was spending a couple of days here. A two-day holiday for him. He
was delighted by the place. It was a walker's dream. As soon as we
settled in he tramped about the hills and wished he could stay.

The Poet left mid-morning. I took him to the station, seven miles
away, and then drove back through the lanes, heading contentedly
towards being alone for the best part of two months. The
Somerset country lanes were single track roads lined with tall
hedgerows and overhung in places with the branches of trees
which have grown across the tops of the hedges and formed a
canopy over the tarmac. The leaves were turning, their colour
warm and rich. Light and shadow strobed as the overhanging
trees blocked the blazing autumn sunshine and then thinned out
to allow the brightness to burst back. Sometimes on the return
journey from the station I was plunged into a dark tunnel of
leaves, as if I had dived underwater or underground, until I
emerged gradually through dappled shade and then broke
through into a sudden blast of sunlight and the extraordinary
lush, brilliantly-coloured foliage, red, orange, gold, bronze – the
colours of metals, warm or fiery. Not sharing this was wonderful.
No need to describe verbally or point out; just drive through it, be
in it. I laughed out loud from time to time, more like a gasp at the
fact that it was possible for me to be here, doing this, being this.
How could this have happened? How could I have made this
happen? I am always astonished to find myself in beautiful

places. Odd really, when all it takes is the effort to be in them. I thought during those moments, though I almost never use the word even to myself silently in my head, that I was uncomplicatedly happy. I remember that thought with trepidation, as if even to have thought it once, let alone mention it now, is a dropping of my guard. Guarding against what? Misleading myself. Letting myself sink into a stupor of easy sentiment. *Happy* strikes me as fuzzy description; I have a genuine uncertainty about the meaning of the word. *Delight* is a better word. Much more precise, to my mind. I was delighted as I drove back from the railway station to my cottage in its sequestered hollow.

I returned slowly along the narrow lanes, stopping and backing up to let cars coming in the opposite direction pass me, the other drivers and I smiling at each other when our windows levelled, separated only by inches, as if we were parties to some private joke (nature, combustion engines, an abstract delight in incongruity). I was in no hurry. I pulled in to passing places so that cars coming up behind me could overtake and leave me far behind. Radio 3 was playing, something idiotically appropriate – though perhaps almost anything would have been. And I noticed I was smiling: a private smile, for no one, a smile that blossomed of its own accord deep inside me, from my solar plexus, and spread beyond my internal boundaries to become the outward, physical expression of the contentment that seemed simultaneously to float down and enclose me like a gossamer caul. Contentment: also a much better word for what I felt than happiness. (But perhaps happiness is after all the only word to use since it is the word that everyone equates with the kind of condition I was in. Possibly I shouldn't be so picky.) Going back, returning. On my own for a great uninterrupted swathe of time. This was the first hour of two entire months. Day, night, day, night: running together to become an indistinguishable block of timeless time. Up the stony lane to park close to the cottage, out of view of the kitchen window at the back of the farmhouse. No sound or sign of the dogs. No one around.

The cottage was empty and waiting for me. I closed the car door quietly and crept in, wanting to do nothing to interfere with its silence. The occasional sound of a creaking floorboard, or the hum of a radiator filling up only emphasised the choice I had not to break into the quiet with any human noise. Unless I wanted to. I could speak aloud to myself, or play music into the empty air. I could do those things if and when I wanted to relish the sudden addition of sound to silence, and then its subtraction. There were other noises. Birds outside, of course, and sheep bleating occasionally. The previous day, and this morning before the Poet left, the Farmer's quad bike roared out of the garage, into the cobbled yard beside my cottage, and she set off accompanied by barking dogs to feed and check on the animals. Mid-morning, the post-office van arrived in low gear up the stony track and thrummed gently, idling while the postman delivered letters to the farm-house lobby. Curiously, they were not intrusions or irritations, as cars and motorbikes were in the street outside the house in Cambridge, but chiaroscuro, a shading of sound and silence that didn't interfere at all with my sense of peace and quiet.

I set about taking possession of my newly solitary living quarters. It involved walking about – I'd already decided in which chintz-covered armchair I would read and write: it faced the hill opposite, the line of trees, bright with autumn, silhouetted on the skyline, the horses coming in and out of view as they wandered around their field grazing. To the left of my chair a window, with my books arranged on its ledge, looked out on to the back of the cottage garden and the rising hill behind, and let in the sound of the spring water running through a stone gargoyle and splashing into a small pond. Because the house was built on a hill, my living room was upstairs and beside the window to the left of my chair a great old wooden door led out to the garden overlooked by the farmhouse. I never went out that way.

The bedroom was across the landing from the living room, on the other side of the stairs, and looked out further to the right of the horse field and hills. Bathroom next to that. Downstairs, on the right of the front lobby was a small spare bedroom, and at the back another bathroom with a shower. The kitchen at the front of the cottage had a range as well as a stove, and a scrubbed pine dining table. A door at the back of the kitchen opened on to a lobby that linked the cottage and the farmhouse, where the post was left, and the Farmer and her visitors came and went.

This wandering around, taking possession, was virtually tip-toeing. I was always conscious of the farmhouse at my back, of not being completely alone (though I couldn't tell if the Farmer was in or out). I didn't want to make any kind of noise that could be heard in the farmhouse. Not because I worried about disturb-ing the Farmer, but because I wanted to be invisible, not noticed. I didn't want to give any cause for being thought about. I wasn't sure how sound worked between the two houses. To be quite certain, I was extremely careful. In order to be properly alone it is necessary to be convinced (rightly or otherwise) that no one is aware of you. I was not really at ease, but cautious and creeping around like a thief. I walked about, trying to make the place my own, but conscious that someone else might be behind the wall and might be aware of me. I could only steal solitude.

I went to bed and slept for two hours in the afternoon. That was an important part of taking possession. To sleep and wake at my own choosing. Schedules were mine alone.

When I woke, I sat in my chair and read Donald Frame's biography of Montaigne, which I was half way through. Montaigne was central to my project of being alone usefully. My bookshelf was carefully chosen: highly organised reading with a purpose.

My Window Seat Bookshelf From Left to Right

Charles Taylor	*The Sources of the Self*
Bernard Williams	*Problems of the Self*
Camus	*The Myth of Sisyphus*
Michael Shermer	*Why People Believe Weird Things*
William James	*The Varieties of Religious Experience*
Pascal Boyer	*Religion Explained*
Edward Engelberg	*Solitude and Its Ambiguities in Modernist Fiction*
Anthony Storr	*Solitude: A Return to the Self*
May Sarton	*Journal of a Solitude*
Sue Halpern	*Migrations to Solitude*
	The Viking Portable Nietzsche
Nietzsche	*Writings from the Late Notebooks*

James Reeves	*Selected Poems of Emily Dickinson*
Emerson	*Selected Essays*
Unamuno	*Tragic Sense of Life*
Rudiger Safraniski	*Nietzsche*
Thoreau	*Walden and Civil Disobedience*
	The Cloud of Unknowing
Kierkegaard	*Sickness Unto Death*
Julian of Norwich	*Revelations of Divine Love*
St. Augustine	*Confessions*
Patrick Leigh Fermor	*A Time to Keep Silence*
Thomas Merton	*The Seven Story Mountain*
Zeman	*Consciousness: A User's Guide*
Stephen Jay Gould	*Dinosaur in a Haystack*
Freud	*Vol. 13 On the Origin of Religion*
Diana Souhami	*Selkirk's Island*
Swift	*Gulliver's Travels*
Daniel Defoe	*Robinson Crusoe*
Henry James	*The Wings of a Dove*
Rousseau	*Confessions*
Xavier de Maistre	*A Nocturnal Expedition Round My Room*
Bencivenga	*The Discipline of Subjectivity*
Van den Abbeele	*Travel as Metaphor*
Frederick Rider	*The Dialectics of Selfhood in Montaigne*
M. A. Screech	*Montaigne and Melancholy*
	Montaigne – The Complete Essays
Donald Frame	*Montaigne – A Biography*
	Michel de Montaigne –
	The Complete Works

A row of books about what I thought I wanted to think about. Though I'd long since given up imagining that I actually think about anything. I read and I write: thought, if I can give it the name, is something that happens invisibly in between – or not at all. I drift. I daydream. I run over old events and conversations. I wonder in a vague way about things I don't know the answer to. But thinking? Never. Not in any way I understand the word.

That's how it was the first afternoon alone. I stopped reading and stared out of the window to watch the dusk gathering inside the little valley. Not thinking, not reading, not anything. Time passed and night fell, deepening the empty silence of the absolute country darkness outside.

Got up. Silence. Performed the usual morning ritual, automatic, but in a new place – shower, brush teeth, dress. Make tea. Silence. Settled in my chair with my tea. Silence. Read Montaigne. Stared out of the living room window. Silence. Hills, trees, sky. Sleep. Stared out of the bedroom window from the bed. Hills, trees, sky, further to the right. Watched afternoon TV (keeping the sound low in case it was overheard and my presence suspected). Two American detective series on the trot that I haven't seen before. *Monk,* a hyper-observant private eye who suffers (and benefits) charmingly from obsessive/compulsive disorder, bringing hope to mildly obsessive/compulsive viewers like myself or despair to the more seriously afflicted, I imagine. Also a filmed version of Rex Stout's snobbish, fat, orchid-loving detective, Nero Wolfe. Nicely tart. Perfect Saturday afternoon.

Read Montaigne. Listened to Beethoven late quartets as it grew completely dark. Watched the news and wondered if I should. Slept. Closed the living room curtains for darkness, opened them for daylight. Showered. Read. Looked out of windows. Slept. Saturdaysunday. Whenever I was hungry, I made toast, and ate it with salami, cheese, peanut butter, or marmalade. No more cooked meals now that the Poet had gone. Made four or five or six cups of tea (Assam, Harmutty Gold) each day. Microwaved my hot wheat bag innumerable times and hugged it to me happily. Not that I was cold. The cottage was centrally heated and the sun shone all weekend. But comfort was the thing (no contentment without a direct source of warmth). Looked out of kitchen window – though carefully, to ensure that no one was passing by to see me looking. A perfect weekend alone. Every moment was a pleasure, doing what I was born to do. Still not thinking, but reading other people's thoughts. Uninterrupted. Read *Robinson Crusoe*, finish it, read Diana Souhami's story of Alexander Selkirk, finish it, read Montaigne. No interruptions. And most important, none expected. A car drove to or from the farmhouse occasionally. Voices sometimes in the yard. The sheep bleated in the distance, not much, they were too busy gestating. So am I, I told myself – hopefully. I was very watchful, of course, as I went about the place – the arachnophobia* never lets me entirely relax and even less so in the country. But this was as peaceful and calm and doing exactly as I want, as I could ever hope for. Not thinking, it's true. Not being a writer. Not being

*Of which see later

anything at all. Just a transparent and pointless ghost flitting around an empty house without a purpose or intention. Timeless, without substance, invisible.

'Are you all right? I've been worried about you.'

It was the Farmer. She knocked on my door at ten the next morning. I leapt out of my chair as if a lynch mob had come for me. A knock on the door! I opened the top half of the stable door and peered anxiously out into the daylight. She looked relieved to see me. I managed a smile and a greeting – sometimes spending time alone makes you uncertain about the first moment of contact with the outside world – will my face look right, will my voice sound normal?

'Are you all right? I've been worried about you.'

'Worried? Why?'

'I haven't seen or heard you since your friend left. I didn't want to interrupt you, but then I wondered if you were all right. I suddenly thought you might have had an accident . . . I'm really sorry to bother you.'

All that weekend alone, I hadn't been. My lack of coming and going had been noticed. The Farmer couldn't believe that anyone could stay indoors for two entire days and not be febrile, paralysed or dead. First the noticing, then the worrying. I was mortified on both counts. I really didn't want her to be bothered about me for both our sakes.

'*Please* don't worry about me. I'm all right. I always am. I just like to stay in.'

I meant this with every cell in my body. I was horrified that those past three days the Farmer worried about me, thought about me, wondered where I was and what I was doing. Stupid, of course, because I was in a cottage attached to her house. How could my presence be ignored? People who rent her cottage go out. They go for rambling walks, to explore the local villages and towns. They fish, or bicycle. They ride or drive. They are on holiday, or even if they are more in retreat, they get out and tramp about moodily. Who could disappear in a tiny cottage for three days and be all right?

I could see that although she was relieved that I was all right, she wasn't convinced that I would continue to be. How would she know I was all right if she didn't see me out and about? How would she know I was not dead if I didn't show my face for days on end? I didn't know the answer to this. To tell her not to worry about whether I was dead or alive was unreasonable. I could hardly reassure her that it was impossible that I could be dead. I wasn't this time, but how would she know in the future? I might be dead. It wouldn't concern me, I would be dead, but it would be a tremendous nuisance to her, as well as upsetting. She worried about her sheep and lambs, and not just because they were her livelihood. Naturally, she'd worry about me if I didn't appear from time to time. I would worry, but she especially would worry because she could not comprehend a person not wanting to get out of the house at least once a day. The whole point of being there, for her, was that she was daily part of the astonishingly beautiful landscape, the dense green, the birds, butterflies, the glory of these hills and what lives in them. Why be here if you don't want to be in it? How could you be anything other than incapacitated or dead if you did not go out into this glorious world you'd paid money to be in the middle of? She knew well enough about the pleasure of sitting quietly, reading, but how could anyone stay indoors *all day*, for *three days*? The fact of having been out, working hard, making the animals comfortable, feeling the odd mix of autumnal chill and belated summer warmth on your face and then getting home and settling down for the evening was what made sitting quietly in front of the fire such a pleasure. I saw her point of view perfectly, and also that, in a million years, she would not see mine. I couldn't make very good sense of it myself. She thought I might be dead. I could see that.

It was true that one day I might not be all right, alone in a house, unable to reach the phone, no one expecting a call or a visit from me. I think of the splendidly named Mrs Hope of old newspaper advertisements; a nice, well-coiffed elderly lady, clearly a little frail, delicate boned, an uncomplaining sort of woman quite unlike me, who in the photograph has fallen to the floor and in all probability broken her hip. Anyway, she can't get up and she can't call out loud enough for the neighbours to hear. What hope is there for Mrs Hope, looking hopeless. She has managed to rise a little on her forearm, but dreadfully – terminally, I shouldn't wonder – out of reach of the phone. That'll teach her not to get out and make contact with people regularly. I wonder if her phone bill is as small as mine. But the whole point of the doom-laden scenario is that Mrs Hope has hope after all. Her loving, though absent, family have bought her a device on a chain that she hangs round her neck at all times, an electronic thingy, a button that she can push (assuming that she *can* push), so whenever the inevitable happens and Mrs Hope falls, as old people do, or scalds herself making a cup of tea, or hears the dull thud of trainers jumping late at night through her kitchen window, or feels a searing pain in her head that is nothing like a normal headache, she can simply press the button and help will be summoned. Somewhere, perhaps in India or Taiwan, a twenty-four hour watch is kept on the light that illuminates when Mrs Hope presses her button and, instantly, a member of her family can be alerted that their old mother is in trouble. A phone call to emergency services, and rescue will be only minutes away if the ambulance the caring children have called is immediately available and doesn't get stuck in traffic. Of course, if Mrs Hope suffers a stroke that paralyses her arms, or falls unconscious for some reason, then even her button will not help her. But there are risks in life. It is not possible to take all eventualities into account. Sometimes things happen that can't be prevented or resolved. Mrs Hope must hope that she doesn't suffer any misfortune that prevents her from pressing her button, but then so must we all. And in the end, in spite of all electronic precautions, we will each of us be beyond help.

The Farmer was correct as well as kind. I might have not been all right. How can I expect people not to worry, if they are decent people and strangers, if I don't show myself to be all right every now and then. I was ashamed at my thoughtlessness. I apologised. She apologised for disturbing me. I apologised again. I had just finished reading her extraordinary autobiography, published some years ago but now out of print. She was in her seventies and had been a shepherd since she was a teenager. She determined at eleven that looking after sheep was what she wanted to do with her life, and then had to prove herself (a very young woman from an academic family) to farmers who were not very inclined to employ her. She seemed not to notice discomfort or physical deprivation and had lived every kind of Spartan existence caring for sheep, including living alone with a flock on an uninhabited island in New Zealand for a year, before she met her husband, bought this difficult hill farm, and had several children. She and he worked alone to make the farm a perfect habitat for wildlife as well as sheep, though he worked in London and was only there to help out at weekends. Now the children were all grown up. Her husband died suddenly just a few years ago. Since then she had lived alone in the farmhouse. She had a wood burning stove in the living room, but no heating upstairs. One of her sons and his family lived in a house down the lane and shared the farm work. She writes, not just her autobiography, but novels too. An extraordinary woman. Dauntingly committed to the natural world. Daunting to me, at any rate. We are precise opposites in how we want to live our lives. I felt faintly ashamed of being me in her presence, though there was not the slightest doubt in my mind that me is who I am, and she is who she is. One of her two working dogs had cancer. He hawked and coughed in the morning, but, unless he was feeling particularly bad, he went off with his mistress every day to herd the sheep, running in front of the quad bike on which she toured the farm. The vet says when he stops going with her it will be time to put him down.

I felt terrible about making the Farmer worry about me and I apologised again. And terrible that I had made her think about me. I explained that I like to stay in. She looked baffled.

'Ah,' she said.

She wondered if I would like to take a trip round the farm? Perhaps tomorrow? When she'd finished feeding the sheep and the back of the quad bike was empty, she could take me for a ride. I was quite excited at the idea of riding on the back of a quad bike, of being shown around the farm by the Farmer and finding out how all those fields related to one another. But tomorrow was too soon for me, psychologically. I said that I was planning to go to the sea tomorrow, and then I had to work, but what about the day after tomorrow? I love that long phrase, it sounds so far off. A whole day and night away. One word doesn't do it. Two weeks is only a *fortnight*, but a day and a night takes three words to get to. Not that I don't know the truth about time passing: that it does. But I am beguiled by the words. And it's near enough too to look forward to something I want to do. Wednesday morning, then, she says.

I am, it turns out, not alone. Of course, I should have known this. Perhaps I even did know it. I was living in the cottage alone, but I couldn't cut myself off entirely from the human race. I can't just say, imagine I'm not here, or rather don't imagine me at all. I had a moment when I wanted to pack up and go back home. It was no one's fault. If I wanted to be really alone, I'd have to be more isolated and renounce the comforts (central heating, Tesco deliveries, a microwave oven to heat my hot wheat bag) which I require for my sybaritic non-farmer's life. Maybe I even want an eye on me, so that should I fall on the floor and not be able to reach for the phone someone will worry enough to come and find me. I feel both disappointed and fraudulent after my perfect, phoney-solitary weekend.

But even before the Farmer knocked on my door, I'd woken that morning in a kind of moral panic. I had been perfectly content with being indoors for two and a half days. But . . . but . . . but . . . I ought to go for a walk. Because? I ought. Need to explore my surroundings. Don't want to. But need to. Why? If I don't go out I won't get lost, so there was no need to know my way around. But I ought to see trees and grass and nature, and where the lane at the bottom of the valley goes. I'd enjoy it. And even if I would-n't, I should. Think and walk. Walk and think. Like you're supposed to if you're a writer. But when I used to picture myself (or anyone else) being a writer, I was – and they were – sitting in a study reading and writing and making notes. Never mind Wordsworth and Coleridge. What about Emily Dickinson, Proust, Raymond Roussel? And Montaigne . . .

What I chiefly portray is my cogitations, a shapeless subject that does not lend itself to expression in actions. It is all I can do to couch my thoughts in this airy medium of words. Some of the wisest and most devout men have lived avoiding all noticeable actions. My actions would tell me more about [chance]than about me.

Whenever I am feeling guilty about staying still, it is to Michel de Montaigne that I apply for justification. And as a rule it works

87

fine, but I was now ground down with the necessity of going for a walk. I put on outdoor jeans, a vest, a jumper, socks, trainers and anorak (not the cotton pull-ons and sloppy t-shirt and cashmere bedsocks I wore to be in all day) and set off.

5

ON EMPTINESS

I find it very difficult to believe that there is anything under my skin. I think of my body as the outer envelope: what I can see and clothe. I can't convince myself that the envelope contains anything. Bones, muscles, nerves, organs, cells, DNA, nucleotides, amino acids, peptides, hormones – they are, so far as I am concerned, mythological, though, of course, I don't doubt their reality as far as others are concerned. Other people and animals are full to bursting with that stuff, I am sure. It's how they function, it's what makes them what they are – their biosystem. Obviously. How else can they be living, breathing, functioning beings? I may have spent more time reading about the insides of sentient beings than anything else, because I'm everlastingly fascinated by the neatness and the unholy mess of the biology of living things. It's just that I don't believe that I have anything inside *me*. Of course, intellectually, I realise there must be, but I simply can't credit it in the place where knowing is more than intellectual, even when confronted with irrefutable evidence. A stomach ache, a broken bone, stiff neck, a bladder infection, what else are these things but proof that my interior is crammed full, just like everyone else's? It's not that I am disgusted by viscera – on the contrary. I'm delighted by inner organs – to look at, to eat, to think about – pulsing and squirting and contracting in ignorant harmony.

Those improbably organic parts that make the whole add up to a something that appears to be coherent and self-aware. A pretty good trick. Still. Even so. The idea of all that stuff inside *my* body strikes me as impossible. How can I disbelieve in what is demonstrably true? An irrefutable fact? I haven't got an answer. I can't explain my obtuseness. I just don't believe in it, any more than I believe in God. God is, at best, an optional extra in the explanation for creation and the continuing existence of life, but biology is certainly not. Easy enough not to believe in God, much harder to disbelieve in biology.

Nonetheless, the claim that I must have insides is as unlikely to me as the assumption that I possess an 'unconscious' or an 'imagination'. I've never been able to credit myself with those either. Actually, in the case of the unconscious and the imagination, although I have seen evidence of both in the activities of other people, I don't really believe in their existence at all, for anyone, except as metaphors for human inconsistency. That's another story . . . well, the same story, but a different part of the forest. It's the body that concerns me at the moment. Yes, I know they are supposed to be related. Psyche and soma, a subtle relationship. And, of course, I've seen evidence of that as well. But psychosomatic harmony or dysfunction too is a narrative we charm ourselves with, if you ask me. Another modern myth that our surreptitiously superstitious minds have sneaked into the contemporary credo. Minds. Now, minds – yours, mine, everyone's – minds, I believe in. If ever there was evidence lacking, it's for the existence of the human mind. If we are going to believe in the fact, the there-it-is-you-can-see-it fact of physicality, then minds must be the stuff of wishful thinking. *I am, therefore I think*. But still, illogically, mindlessly, I believe in minds.

My doctor once thought he heard my heart murmur.

'Nonsense,' I said. 'I don't have a heart.'

'Yes, you do,' he insisted, not as surprised as he ought to have been at my assertion, but waving the end of his stethoscope at me. 'I can hear it, and I think there is a murmur.'

Of course, I was flattered by the inclusive notion that I actually had a heart, just like everyone else, and very taken with the idea that it might be murmuring.

Doesn't believe in me, eh? Yeah well, I don't believe in her! I imagined it murmuring, or would that be more of a mumble?

Day and night, night and day, beat, beat, beat, and what thanks do I get for it? Or would that be more of a mutter?

All I want is a little fibrillation. Is that too much to ask? More of a moan, perhaps.

Murmuring is more dreamlike, a private conversation with oneself, going about one's own business with no thought that there might be any other business in the world. 'Oh, my paws and whiskers. I'm late, I'm late.' A rabbit disappearing down a hole watched by a curious child; a heart missing a beat and causing the doctor to send your envelope to the hospital for an ECG.

My purported heart murmur allowed me to toy with the idea of this busy little factory within me, to visualise the organs and endocrines pumping and purifying and catalysing. A drop of this chemical making me want to get up in the morning, a splash of that suffusing me with desire or disgust, a shortage of another causing a blackness darker and bleaker than a homeless winter's night. I work at the idea of my arm-shoulder-neck muscles contracting and expanding as I pick up a cup and put it down. I picture a scaffolding of bones preventing my collapse into a sagging, wet and bloody mess on the floor. So many labourers in my fields, ununionised, whose only purpose is the furtherance of me. Or conversely, and perhaps even better, a colony of blindly egotistical bits and bobs, each devoted exclusively and passionately to its own continuation. Heart pumping so that heart will keep pumping. Heart forever murmuring to itself: *I am that I am.* Kidneys purifying away to ensure that they can keep on purifying away. No glimmer of the big picture; no comprehension that they are merely parts servicing a whole, and that their entire existence depends on some inexplicable being beyond themselves. Mind. Whatever.

Anthropomorphic, or what? I try and get the bald facts of evolutionary theory into my head, the random but increasingly, accidentally optimal accumulation of sub-systems that allow an organism to function and survive and reproduce itself. So random, so unanthropomorphic, that they don't even stop doing what they do when what they do is no longer needed. Long after the organism's reproductive life is over the pumps go on pumping, the components go on doing what they do (which makes the mayfly, for example, a truly advanced entity, since, job done, everything stops, though that thing they call imagination lets us believe that a single day feels an entire life to a mayfly – what does an entire life *feel* like to a mayfly?). Redundancy is a proof that there is nothing intentional whatever in the bloody, spongy, sinewy bits that make up a functioning life form. It may not be true that hair continues to grow after death, but it's a fine metaphor for the pointlessness, the disinterestedness of the biology which, in a small number of cases, amounts to us. Language, however, and the human mind (one and much the same thing, I suppose) make it impossible to consider a system of working parts without intention. We can't escape using the word 'want' some way or another. Being, doing, acting, all carry connotations of desire. The gene reproduces itself. And instantly there is an image of a busy little gene working away at survival. A veritable Abraham of a gene, ensuring the existence of its offspring. Only the language of maths gets us out of our anthropomorphic hole, or possibly, as Wittgenstein suggested, the language of lions; but to my great sadness I don't understand either tongue.

You might suppose that my disbelief in my own internal organs is some kind of innate Manichaeism, an unanalysed Cartesianism. A body/spirit split in my self-consciousness. If not innate, it does go back a long way. At primary school I looked at the kids with physical problems – asthma, alopecia, eczema, a hole in the heart – with envy. They had 'conditions', they said with a tinge of pride. They were excused swimming, the teachers announced, because of their 'condition'. I yearned for a condition. They 'suffered' from named things. To suffer from something was a mark of distinction. I longed to be able to say in that almost otherworldly voice that 'I suffered' from something. It wasn't only because it seemed to me so special, so glamorous to be unincluded, to be set apart, let off bits of the otherwise ineluctable routine of daily life. They sat fully dressed by the side of the swimming pool, unable to join in because of their condition, while I struggled across its width, cold and miserable in the water in a horrible woolly swimsuit. They had days off in order to see specialists about their condition. They stood alone in the playground, particular and apart, like royalty, because their condition meant they couldn't join in the screaming, rushing games that I too couldn't join because the other kids didn't want me, and anyway I couldn't catch the ball or skip the rope. It was so useful to have a condition. So wonderful to be excused from activity and groups. And to have a mark of distinction. Even the ones with braces on their teeth were to be envied. Sometimes, in return for sweets, they took their braces out and let me try them on. And as for the polio kids with callipers, they glowed for me like stars of stage, screen and radio. They were so heroic, so superior to the able-bodied rank and file. But aside from their glamour, their conditions proved, too, that they were proper human beings, because only components that exist can fail to work.

I never had anything wrong with me, apart from threadworms

from time to time which caused me to become hysterical at the horror of living, squirming things inside me, and my parents to shout at me for 'making a fuss about nothing'. Where a weak heart after a bout of scarlet fever conferred glitz and a solidity of being, threadworms were merely shameful and vile. No one said that I couldn't do things because I 'suffered' from threadworms. You didn't suffer from threadworms, you 'had' them, and you certainly didn't announce them to the world. Your mother spoke in an undertone to the doctor and whispered at the chemist. Threadworms – just a letter away from *threat*worms I notice – lived inside you and crept out of your bottom in the dead of night. They cavorted around your anus as you slept, laid their eggs and tempted you to scratch ('Don't scratch!'), then you sucked your thumb to keep yourself quiet and comforted and transferred the eggs into your gut where they grew into more threadworms. What was I but their mere plaything; their life-cycle assistant? Terrible to be host to something that wriggles. Thousands of them. Millions, maybe.

Let's move away from the psychoanalytical opinion you are edging towards and try for a more pragmatic child's-eye view. Perhaps it was indeed those pale, writhing visitors from outside of me (uncooked pork? Lavatory seats? Sitting on radiators? What?) which convinced me that there was nothing of my own inside me: whereas a cardiac arrhythmia or asthma proved that the sufferer had a heart or lungs, an infestation of threadworms only demon-strated that there was empty space inside me for them to get in and multiply. I imagined their seething millions taking up all my internal space.

Nonetheless, I admit (and I'm loath to, doubting as I do the existence of a devious metaphor-making unconscious) that the sensation of emptiness was after all more likely a response to the emotional carry-on of life at home. It sounds good. Good enough to base novels on. The kid vacated her building, there's no one in, she cannot be touched by the terrors of living with her madly miserable mother and father. But, looking back, I see the emptiness I constructed inside me as more a creation than a nega-tion. I didn't make myself disappear, I made a place of retreat for myself. To be empty then was not to be non-existent. I *did* have an interior: it was hollow and cavernous, a vaulted cathedral of vacant space. I must have chucked out all the wet and soggy stuff inside in order to fashion a place of safety where I could go when I needed to. My memory of contentment and pleasure in my childhood is largely made up of my visits to that place, a vast empty dark-red chamber inside the deceptively compact envelope of my skin, where I would spend hours of my day sitting cross-legged. Dr Who's Tardis was no news to me when it came, I was only surprised at how cluttered and peopled it was. Not my kind of enclosure at all.

This place I had excavated for myself was where I would go when my parents were screaming at each other, or at me, or to pass the time when my mother was asleep in a darkened room clutching her big white box of Codis. It became the place I liked to be in best. I went there to read, to play imaginary games – dramas with princes and princesses and rescue in which I would play only the heroic or innocent parts (who played the villains I cannot say) – and, crucially, to find out if my mother was right when she said I was 'no good, just like your father' and 'incapable of love' or 'a bad lot'. Looking back, it was spatially extraordinary. No question that it was inside me, not outside: like a modern-day free diver I actually had to descend into myself to get there, from behind my eyes, down my spine to the very centre of me, to reach my solar plexus and lower abdomen, and lose contact with my actual surroundings. It was where *I* was. A great uninhabited room, a ballroom perhaps, in which there was something the size of a pebble lying on the floor, a small kernel which looked very like a walnut, or retrospectively, a tiny brain, a gnarled and compact sphere. That nugget was how I checked myself against the complaints made against me, and where I confirmed that my mother, or teachers or other children were wrong – I was not bad, I was good. Somehow, by what mechanism, I don't know, I bounced my questions off it and it radiated answers or certainties back at me, assuring me that I was essentially good and well-meaning. Very, very, useful. (I had another useful imaginary stone: it was at the front of my forehead. Looking back, it was a file system. When I was asked a question at school or at home, the small stone, dark red, like a cornelian, began to move slowly but smoothly, beginning at my right temple and heading in a semicircle towards my left temple. All the time before it reached the mid-point at the front of my head, it was possible to retrieve the information I was asked for, but once it had passed the mid-point, I knew that I did not have the information, or did not have access to it. No point in trying. No, don't know the answer. It was a handy sort of thing, my memory stone. It avoided wasting time looking for what could not be found.)

I remember vividly the feeling, when I dived down to the nugget place, of discovering again that I was good. That was the word that it reflected back at me. There was relief, nothing self-righteous; it was just a reality check. No, I was good. OK. The grown-ups, the others, weren't right. Not born bad. Not bad through and through. I learned to distinguish between what I was and what I did. It became clear to me that behaving badly, being naughty, or what I was told was naughty, was different from being essentially bad. My mother did not make that distinction. I was horrified by the idea that I might have been, as she said, born bad. It meant there was nothing to be done about it. That was the implication in her accusations. Incorrigible. A bad lot, wrongly made. If I were a vegetable, I'd be twisted and rotten ('through and through'), wormy probably, and be thrown away. As it was, being a human child, I couldn't be. It was her misfortune. Bad is what I was and ever would be. Sometimes when she said that, I felt quite despairing at the ineluctability of my wrongness; that I would never be able to get good. But the small, hard nugget inside me was what I trusted to tell myself the truth. My mirror, mirror on the wall. It was always risky: I might have discovered that they were right, I was bad. But I didn't. (There's a surprise.) And then, that sorted, I could relax and get on with living in that extraordinary inner space where I was what I was, and not born bad; making stories, reading, daydreaming. But I could only be alone there. In order to rejoin the world – 'It's dinner time.' 'Get on with your homework.' 'Don't just sit there, go and find some-one to play with.' 'Tell your mother to pass the salt.' 'Tell your father I hope he rots in hell, I'm not his skivvy.' 'I said, what is seven and five?' – I had to surface. It didn't matter, I knew my place – it had no name – was always available. My reality was down, or in there. The geography of the place was down and in, but the space there was infinite, and what were nowhere to be seen, were internal organs. There was just my mind, situated behind my forehead (was it that cornelian-coloured stone?), diving down to meet my tiny, separate, implacable, impenetrable nut-hard self, and then hang out in the great empty playground, ballroom or living room. Inside there were no insides.

And that is how it feels to me today. My room without a view, however, is long gone, nothing more than a memory. That place, and the small kernel of me curled tight into an impenetrable ball that lived there (as well as my memory stone), has disappeared. I have no idea when. By the time I was twelve it had gone. I can't remember any moment when I tried to get there and failed, only lots of moments of diving down and being unable to gain entry (like Peter Pan, it strikes me now, looking in through the locked window of his home). My self had shut up shop. The world, perhaps, had got too great a hold. By twelve something, some otherness is lost, I think. A capacity for being elsewhere. Oh my paws and whispers, I'm late, I'm late. Anyway, there it wasn't, and soon I gave up trying to get there. I no longer had any way of checking the state of my goodness or badness. No means of verifying my sense of myself. I must have felt bereft. I don't remember. Perhaps I felt grown up.

When I was fourteen, I came to the conclusion – I recall the moment vividly, on a train, taking me back to school for a new term – that bad was by far the most desirable thing to be. I longed for badness, for argument, for transgression, with a passion. I set myself in the way of badness. Goodness had no attractions. Look at the good ones and the bad ones. Which do you want to be? No contest. Badness was bold and special. Badness was a *condition*, one, unlike a hole in the heart, I could achieve for myself. Later that term – smoking, going to all-night parties and drinking cider in the woods, finding myself an inappropriate boyfriend from the town, stealing ether from the chemistry lab and inhaling it – I was expelled. I was just old enough not to have to go back to school.

My father decreed I would not take my O levels, A levels, go to university. I would go to work in a local grocery shop. I began a new future the next day. I was frightened by how effective my newly discovered capacity for badness was, but I was gleeful, too, astonished by its power and purity, filled with admiration at myself that I could achieve such a dark reputation, such a break-away from everything to be expected so quickly and easily. Proud that I could effect such a cataclysmic change in my life. The world became the place that used to be inside me, where I checked out what and who I was, and it reflected badness back at me, just as the other place had confirmed goodness. I discovered that it made not the slightest difference to my sense of myself which quality I recognised myself by. Good and bad were neither here nor there, so long as I was doing the choosing. Good was unavailable, but bad would do. I couldn't remember why it had bothered me so much when I was little that I might be bad. It was invigorating, exciting, something I could suffer from.

*

As it turned out, the scan proved that I still didn't have a condition. I didn't suffer from a heart murmur after all, but it did bring me eyeball to organ with the incontrovertible fact of my heart throbbing lumpishly, doggedly away inside what I had to accept was me. So the technician assured me. Electrode on my chest connected to wires that plugged into the machine. The little device that rolled over my skin sent back messages to the console that were transformed into a visual image. It might have been a set-up, a con, like the moon landing taking place in a film studio, or Princess Diana's death being mocked up with trick photography so that she and her former in-laws could live happily and less inconveniently ever after. But I managed to persuade myself (for then at least) that it was unlikely such a performance would have been organised and enacted just so that I might believe I had an organ inside me. In any case, the last time I looked at an image on a screen of something inside me, it came out, as real as real could be, and became my daughter. Sometimes, you have to stop arguing. Sometimes you have to trust that the world is not entirely arranged so that you might be deceived. This is not easy for me. I do suffer from megalomania, in a quiet, harmless sort of way.

There is a small, mad (oh, I do so hope it is mad) part of myself that has believed for a long time (since I was twelve and lost my inner apartment?) that I am the subject of an on-going world-wide experiment. It was set up – by God? The UN? Princeton Social Science department? – to test the results of affirming the qualities of someone entirely without them. Beginning as a child, tested by The Authorities, I was proclaimed massively intelligent, to possess an IQ the size of the Empire

State. They told me so when I was eleven, repeatedly. Later in my life, several people said that I was attractive and even, once or twice, quite interesting to talk to. Later still, it was arranged that while I was in some sort of waking trance, I would write books and that they would be published (not best-sellers, of course, that would clash with the intelligence affirmation). 'You are a remarkable person,' people in authority (doctors, headmistresses, social workers) would tell me when I was plainly a stupid, formless, adolescent mess. And the more I replied I wasn't, that I was blank, ordinary, thoughtless and without the smallest item of interest about me, the more it seemed to prove that I was remarkable indeed.

I felt trapped. The truth, when I spoke it, was received as an affirmation of its opposite. There was nothing I could do to let people know how wrong they were about me. I longed to find a way to make them believe I was a fraud. And here the psyche and soma did in fact meet. I was empty. I knew I wasn't clever – all I knew was how much I didn't understand, and I was certain I was crashingly boring. I had not a single thought worth thinking in my head and therefore nothing of interest to say. It could only be explained, this perverse affirmation of what I knew not to be true, by a deliberate and concerted action, which only made sense if it were an experiment. The child psychologists who had tested me when I was eleven had found the perfect specimen – the child without qualities – on which to prove or disprove the effects of positive reinforcement on a negative reality.

I realise, of course, that this theory made me the most important person in the world, the focus of international attention. My sense of absence and incapacity lived perfectly contentedly side by side with an ego the size of the universe. I was the most important and the least important creature in existence. Well, obviously. Aren't we all? Instead of the *what if it's all a dream world*, I inhabited the *what if it's all an experiment planet*. Of the two propositions, I'm inclined to think the latter most likely to be true.

How am I doing, guys?

6

ON TAKING WALKS

Yet still the solitary humble-bee
Sings in the bean-flower! Henceforth, I shall know
That Nature ne'er deserts the wise and pure;
No plot so narrow, be but Nature there,
No waste so vacant, but may well employ
Each faculty of sense, and keep the heart
Awake to Love and Beauty! and sometimes
'Tis well to be bereft of promis'd good,
That we may lift the soul, and contemplate
With lively joy the joys we cannot share.

From 'This Lime-Tree Bower My Prison'
by Samuel Taylor Coleridge

I've never been a great one for taking walks. I am sloth-like in my nature; resistant to movement. A bit Newtonian. Inertia is my thing. The status quo, the still point of the present moment are what I aspire to. I am obdurate in this, not merely passive. The cry of 'Go and do something' rings through my childhood and adolescence. I was sitting daydreaming or reading. I *was* doing something. Always. Every cell in my body wants to keep still, and wants it all the more passionately at the suggestion that it should change its state. Imagine the fervour of the millions – or is it billions? – of those cells that amount to me each not wanting with all their tiny but cumulative might. You would think you could move mountains with such desire. I have achieved not climbing any.

There are two distinct aspects of not going for walks. One, which happens when I'm alone, is the simple joy of continuing not to move, in spite of internalised voices telling me to *do* something. The other, which can only occur when I'm in company, is the profound pleasure of being left behind. The exhortation of others works wonders of indolence on me. Fresh air, nature in its season or the adrenalin rush of the inner city, when pressed on me, though I don't doubt their charms and excitements, make me shrink in my chair, wishing the room smaller, the windows shaded, the chair deeper, the door locked. *Leave me alone*, was, I think, born with me, my invisible twin, before language, when company was nothing but an incoherent threat of alteration. *Leave me alone* must have been my embryonic remonstration with whom-or-what-ever it may concern about the whole damn bother and dislocation of being born, and it stuck. I was not born idle, I was foetally idle. I can imagine with a clarity far more piercing than memory the dreadful initial interruption that signalled the end of my perfect, timeless, still existence. I like small rooms; I love to float and hate to swim – I am temperamentally suited to uterine life. Others I have spoken to about this say that they are sure they longed to get out of the maternal confines, to get on with being in the world; kicking and wriggling in the battle for space and the powerful need to join in the fun. Not me. I can only picture my embryonic self managing a lazy stretching of a limb now and then, or the necessary upheaval of turning over in order to experience inactivity from the other side. I'm sure I would not have kicked – I wouldn't have wanted to give my presence away if I had the slightest inkling that anything was out there. There was nothing I wanted, what was there to kick against? Even now, nearer the end than the beginning, I can feel the aftershock of the horror: the calamity and outrage of being given notice to quit my perfect existence. The awful pressure of those rippling, muscular walls labouring to squeeze me out of my infinite space into a world full of air into which I would never fit so perfectly. I continue to mourn the contraction of my unbothered existence into a born being. The studies that suggest the foetus can hear the world beyond the womb mortify me. I choose to believe that I managed to ignore the disruptive sounds of the world (*my father groaned, my mother wept*) and lived only with a background rhythm of two beating syncopated hearts, one fast, one slow, like the tocking of old clocks in an empty house, and the gentle babbling and gurgling of digestive juices. Then *leave me alone* tore into my life as my expulsion got under way. Until that moment, like any ego persisting in its private eternity, like God before the creation, everything was just fine. Imagine not even knowing that interruption was possible. Blissful oblivion. Hypnagogic drifting ad infinitum. And then, disruption and the absolute end of eternity. Of *that* eternity. Of course there will be the next, and let us hope final, one, but to look forward to it excessively is only another way of fearing it excessively.

It's surely that memory of my reluctant beginning which causes my love of being left behind alone. No, you go ahead. I'll stay where I am. It is a particular, quite physical satisfaction to hear the door shut, and the fading footfalls of the walking party who have or has gone off without me. Being left behind is one of my great luxuries. Just the fact of being left on the island, of turning my back on the retreating boat even when it is still within waving distance: that would be my luxury on *Desert Island Discs*. The relief and contentment at the diminishing sound and sight of others as they leave, the growing noise of the silence that takes their place, the holes in the air which were once filled with people. All to be savoured as an extra treat on top of staying still. There is nothing quite like a place that has had people in it and now has only you. A weight lifts, the spirit expands. Let's be clear, I am not a party person.

Even so, visceral as the pleasure is in finding myself alone at last, there is an even greater satisfaction in not having to state my preference for being left alone in the first place. I want the certainty that no one is going to suggest a walk, because no one being there to do so is the perfect circumstance. At least in principle. I yearn towards the condition, but find, when I am really alone for any length of time, that I have my own nagging company to contend with. To suppose that being alone truly means that no one is present is an elementary but inescapable error. The auto-social consequences of having been born are no less indelible than the trauma of the birth itself. There is a good deal more to consider about solitude than the mere avoidance of walking, but my sense of an obligation to go for a walk became a serious and unexpected issue daily during my two-month stay at Stillcombe.

For a while, you can sit and just listen, stare, immerse yourself in the new reality, adjusting to where you are. But one day you wake up feeling guilty, or the Farmer wonders if you are all right – and then . . . and then . . . staying still becomes the subject of a decision that has to be made. I think it must be the business of getting up, the routine preparation for the day ahead, that enables the regular resurgence of the superego. Like a switch. Go! Dreamtime is over. The teeth are fresh, face spritzed, body needled awake with falling water. Even if the rest of the day isn't routine (travel to office, open letters, write letters, lunch . . .) you are set into starting mode. There is some need to make a decision about the rest of the day, perhaps because the nature of *decision* requires activity to show it has been made. And so on that third morning, into my washed-brushed-and-all-dressed-up-with-nowhere-I-needed-to-go mind came a thought in the words of someone who could not have been me, but must have been because the words were inside my head and no one else was around: *I ought to go out, get some fresh air, and explore my surroundings.* I don't even know how to write that sentence so that it sounds like me.

But the impulse to knowledge seemed reasonable. How could I live in this encircling valley and not know what was beyond the immediate view? The cottage and farmhouse were near the base of the hillside. The land rose on three sides of my lines of vision, stitched with fences and gates to keep the livestock in or out of particular fields. To the right of my downstairs kitchen window were some old brick pig pens used now for housing sick sheep, and directly facing me was a complicated sheepfold, a maze of gates and small enclosures for isolating groups or single animals from the flock. Beyond that, further down the slope, at the valley bottom, I could see from the upstairs windows that there was a gate leading to a shadowed lane with a stream running beside it. It disappeared intriguingly from my angled view. And beside the pig pens to the immediate right of the cottage was the stony path that led out on to the public road which took me to Taunton where I had dropped the Poet three days ago, and, in another direction, with the aid of a map I now got out and spread on the kitchen table, to the sea, just seven miles away.

The simple choice of moving or staying still was no longer clear cut. My aim, my imaginings previous to getting to Stillcombe, was to sit. I did also picture myself wandering (wandering, not *walking*) around the farm, but not that I would have to make my mind up to do so at a particular moment, and choose a direction to go in. In my anticipatory country-living thoughts before I left Cambridge, I simply *was* wandering about the fields, or sitting in an armchair reading or writing. Always already. There was no initial condition when I had actually to make the decision to stay in or go out, and then an intermediate state when I dressed according to the weather: put on suitable boots, gloves or not, a hat in case of rain, tried to remember my stick, left the house, entered the world, and chose a direction. None of these tiny quotidian decisions had been taken into account by my notion of *wandering*. Most of all I had not allowed for the power of social conditioning – something it is essential not to allow for when imagining the perfect existence. The great Ought swooped down and landed. I could pinpoint the position in my brain (low down, in the outer portion of my left parietal lobe) where this *ought* resided. I could see it as on a brain scan, a tiny neon pink pulsing point in a mass of laid-back blue and yellow, glowing hotly to signal its right to be heard. I despised it, but I got up to start the day properly, scrubbed the night away, got fresh, got dressed. But why? (Jung, of whom I am not a great fan, asked a blocked writer to describe his day in detail. 'I wake at seven and get up . . .' 'There! That's your problem,' interrupted Jung, 'Getting up.') And then, readied for the day, it seemed that something ought to be done with it beyond choosing a book and settling into the armchair. Ought to begin the day with exercise, then I could justify sitting down and reading. These thoughts nagged me as if they were mine. A terrible morality which I utterly disown came over me. A literary morality at that. The shades of Coleridge and Wordsworth, just down the road, striding about these very coombes, arguing and composing for all their worth, sucking up nature like poetic bumble bees, wagged their fingers at me. That's what writers do. Walk and think. Think and walk. Think by walking. That's how it's done. The names of writers who spent day after day sunk deep into an armchair and lived in the country only behind glass completely evaded me. (Proust spent a lot of time in bed, of course, but he was a party animal when he wasn't reclining.) Was I a writer? Then I must go for a walk. But who was there watching me, alone in my country retreat, to notice or care? Guilt. Who should I feel guilty towards? Just hot pink omniscient, omnipresent lord or lady Superego. You are never alone with a superego.

So, washed and dressed, ready to start the day (though it had already started, long since, without me and was managing perfectly well), I thought, *I* thought, that I would go for a walk. I pulled on my specially bought, pristine Prada walking boots (no, really), and an old, in case I ever find myself in the country, jacket. I opened the front door, stepped outside, and stopped dead. I discovered that I had a functional problem with the act of going for a walk. The question was: *where* should I walk? In the field up behind the house to my left; down the hill to the dappled lane; across to the gate at the end of the field opposite; or down the stony track towards the road? I was going to be there for two months. I could take each direction in turn, several times over. But the problem of where to begin, of the first walk, was exquisite. I was convinced as I stood outside the front gate of my cottage that there was a correct direction in which to go. The important walk to take. The main route. The right path. I stood quite paralysed at the thought of taking a merely peripheral mistaken walk. *You went which way? Oh. Why would you do that?* Like that sense I had when I was young that any party I was invited to was the wrong one.

I just don't know how to go for a walk. I've never figured it out. In London, I lived for fifteen years just two hundred yards from Parliament Hill Fields. At first, I did what I knew I was supposed to do. I went for a walk quite regularly – cold, wind and rain, of course, excepted. That is, I walked the two hundred yards to the end of the road in order to go for a walk on Parliament Hill. This struck me as silly. It made more sense to drive around the one way system to get to Parliament Hill, so that I could start to walk where the walk started. I tried to consider the two hundred yards as part of the walk, but it clearly wasn't. I couldn't shake off the sense as I went along the pavement that I was on my way to somewhere, and when I got there, to the neat grass fields and tarmacadamed paths filled with dogs, runners, cyclists, real walkers, I stood, as I stood outside my cottage, wondering what on earth to do next. The problem was destination. I needed one. I have an inner certainty that walking, a forward propulsion of the body through space and time, must by definition take you somewhere. I fail to see how to just walk without intending to go any place in particular. I worried at every step about when it would become necessary to turn around and go back the way I had come. Unless I didn't. Why stop walking once I'd started? Obviously, I would have to return home or all the rest of my life would be a walk. So, shall I turn around here? Or here? Go back now . . . or now? When my feet start to ache? No, before they do, so that I can get back comfortably. But how shall I know how long I've got before it becomes a pain? Shall I give myself a time scale? Take a watch with me. Should I set the alarm, or keep looking at it to see if it's time to turn round? So much to worry about, so much to decide. Not a moment left to think about what I see or mull over important things, or daydream a new chapter or whatever it is that people do when they go for a walk on the Heath.

The answer was to take a circular route to avoid the anxiety of decision. This was easy enough on landscaped, managed Parliament Hill: up to the top where the kites are flying, turn right and go straight along, right again down the slope opposite, then right again, along the bottom path, past the café and the children's playground (where when I was twenty and living on a parallel road I used to go and swing at three in the insomniac miserable mornings all alone and in the dark), to arrive back at the top of my road and walk along the pavement the two hundred yards home. All right once or twice, but a repetitive sort of stroll. Hardly wandering. Might as well walk round and round the athletics track next to the playground. Parliament Hill has trees and grass but it is not so wild or natural that it affords much in the way of visual splendours. Better, if you're interested in nature, to squat down on the grass and watch the insects going about their business. I can always find a reason for staying still. But then what is going for a walk for? Is it about looking? Is it about thinking? Can you look and think? I look at things and wonder what they are called, and I hardly ever know. Wondering about the names of things is hardly thinking. Mmm, there's a pretty flower, I wonder what it's called. A lesser celandine, perhaps, or a mare's tail. Search me. I'm quite proud even to know that there are such things as lesser celandines – though I immediately begin to worry about how it can be distinguished from the greater or the regular sized celandine. I become fixated on names and classification, a veritable Linnaeus I'd be if I had any knowledge of what was what. I could think up new names for things, but I really want to know the 'real' names. I want to know that I'm looking at a lesser celandine, and then ... Well, and then I would know. Then I begin to worry about this, about why I want to know what everything is called. My walk becomes an effort of trying not to wonder what the name of everything is. Eventually, all I can think about is what I should think about when going for a walk. Wordsworth wandered lonely as a cloud and wrote his poems as he did it. Ah, but didn't Coleridge also stay home and wander lonely on opiates? This was much more my way. If walking was so good for thinking, how come Coleridge added the laudanum?

It is so unpleasant, so constipated. However, if instead of doing the circuit, I turned left just fifty yards from my entrance to the Heath, I came to an exit that led along to South End Green and the Italian deli. After a few days of unsatisfactory walking I took the left turn, having spent about two and a half minutes on Parliament Hill, bought some fresh pasta and pesto from the deli and walked back home through the streets. Instead of going for a walk, I went shopping, an activity I understand – and shopping is just a yawn away from deciding that I'd rather stay at home. I hardly ever went on to Parliament Hill Fields again.

As I stood outside the gate of my cottage, the problem of a right direction in which to take my walk was resolved by Belle, who came racing up to me from her place by the back door of the farmhouse as soon as she heard my gate open. Pat, the other sheepdog, weighted down with his tumour, was older and wiser. He just watched dubiously as Belle paused beside me for a second, panting and wagging, then raced off to the left of my cottage and flattened herself under the gate of the field that rose behind it. She stopped, turned and looked at me, and squeezing under the gate again, raced back, bouncing her readiness to go, go, go and take me with her. I stood bemused, not familiar with dog-talk, but finally got it when she belted back to the gate, under it, and waited as if on tiptoe, barely able to contain herself, looking back at me, puzzled at my immobility, alert for the slightest signal that she could charge on to her goal. There was a dog-sized hollow in the earth under the gate from Belle's and Pat's many wrigglings beneath it, too excited to wait for it to be opened. Belle knew there was indeed a right path, and she was deliriously willing to take me for a walk in the proper direction.

I was to learn that Belle was the most enthusiastic and most nearly useless of sheepdogs. Her heart was in it, totally, her whole purpose and only desire in life was to herd sheep, but too much so. She could not help herself. She herded sheep whether they needed herding or not. She made all the moves, running, stalking, crouching, driving, but she didn't wait to find out if these things were wanted. She herded sheep with all the goodwill but none of the self-disciplined obedience that is, apparently, the main requirement of a working dog. Thick, but well-meaning, the Farmer called her, shaking an affectionate but aggravated head over her as Belle sat looking up, tail wagging proudly, wet-doggy-eyed, for the pats and praise she believed she deserved for frightening the sheep witless when what was needed right then was calm uneventfulness in their lives as they gestated next year's lambs. But I knew nothing about Belle's deficiencies that morning. Here, I thought, is an expert in how to go for a walk. It

115

wants to take me; I will be led. If Belle was prepared to go for a walk with me as if I were a proper country-walking person, then I would accept the offer gratefully. This sort of misunderstanding occurs between travellers and indigenes in all times and all places.

I turned left and walked towards the metal gate, where Belle waited and wagged. I saw something that might have been doubt in her eyes as I struggled to open the gate, taking several minutes (really, minutes) to discover that lifting it allowed me to release the metal loop that kept it closed. Once I was through, Belle dashed across the field to another gate at the top and I followed. This is a very perpendicular part of the world and I am not fit. I was heaving to catch my breath and drenched with sweat by the time I was halfway to the top gate. Once again I wondered what exactly the benefits of giving up smoking were. Belle reached the gate and stood for a moment, looking back, giving me one last chance before deciding finally that I was not, in fact, a substitute Farmer, that I was a hopeless impossibly slow know-nothing holding up the urgent sheep work she had to do. If she hesitated for another moment, it was only because she was a polite, well-mannered dog. But when I stopped, ripped off my jacket and gasped for breath, Belle gave up and ran off out of sight across the upper field. I had lost my companion. Still I continued, slowly, to follow her direction. There were two other gates I might have walked towards, but Belle remained my guide, even if she had lost patience with me. I struggled on up the field and wondered how it was possible to walk and think when, aside from the difficulty of breathing, there was the business of trying not to fall over. Walking on steeply sloping grazing land requires a good deal of concentration. Avoid the cow shit, step over or around the boggy spots that clog the boots (Prada walking boots are very comfy, but they scream if brought in contact with cow shit.) Careful of molehills and dips that might make you turn your ankle. Look down, watch where you place the feet. Not quite the careless wandering I'd imagined.

Trust your feet, they said at Esalen, the New Age holiday and enlightenment camp I visited in California in 1973. It was on Big Sur and not just hilly, but perched on the side of a rocky cliff over the Pacific ocean. At night, when we returned from our encounter groups we had to find our way back to our cabins. Pitch black, no lights, no torches. Trust your feet, they said. It seemed to work. Feet put themselves one before another and no one ever fell over or tripped or tumbled into the Pacific ocean thrashing below. That was in 1973. In 2003 in Somerset, I tried to trust my feet, but the effect was not the same. As soon as I stopped looking or worrying where I was going, I tripped on some hump, or tipped down a hollow. Too old perhaps to trust my feet; either I had lost the knack of trusting, or my feet had become less trustworthy. New Age long gone, Old Age approaching.

At the top of the field I tried to open the gate, failed, and climbed over it. Belle heard me and, giving me yet another chance, returned to my side. There were sheep, thirty or so, dotted around the upper field, beyond the next gate. Belle raced off towards it once again. Now, it finally crossed my mind that Belle was not just taking me for a walk, but thought we were off to herd sheep. I explained to her that I was not a shepherd, that I was ignorant of sheep and that, as a mere visitor, I was not to interfere with the livestock.

'I'm just going for a walk,' I explained.

I really do have a sense, that if you speak simply and clearly to animals and very small children, they will understand. It's not that I'm under the impression that all creatures speak English (James I believed that if you took an infant at birth and left it alone on a desert island, it would naturally turn out to speak English) so much as a conviction that if you avoid patronising the world around you, reasoned communication is possible with all things. It has hardly ever proved to be the case, not even very often with grown up human beings, but I continue to try, with animals and small children at least. In spite of my explanation, however, Belle showed no lessening of her desire to get to the sheep and work them.

'No, no, no,' I said, simplifying my point.

'Woof,' she replied and squirmed under the gate into the field of blameless sheep while I stood calling her name, feeling foolish and inadequate, and hoping no one could see me trying and failing to get her to heel like a good dog should.

'Belle. Belle, come back. Here, Belle . . . Lunch . . . Please . . .'

Urbane cats I can deal with and retain some authority, but dogs and horses, bucolic creatures with dopey eyes though they may be, instantly sense my deficiency with all things natural.

The sheep, comfortably spread around, room for everyone, heads down, munching grass with not the slightest interest in the world, not bored, nor concerned with time, or the fact that they were carrying around what would one day be platesful of roast lamb and sweaters, existing in a perfect present, looked up and realised how wrong, yet again, they had been. If only they could remember that this happened to them every day. Belle ran towards them. They shivered alertness and started to gather, forming a nervous, fidgety crowd along the boundaries of which Belle ran to and fro, frightening the stragglers back into the group. Belle was satisfied with the assembly she had created. She crouched low, a few feet from the sheep, now wired with anxiety and pushing urgently into a tighter formation as though they might, if they pressed together hard enough, become one great saviour sheep who would turn massively on their small persecutor and run her out of town. Belle wagged and waited in her crouch for the boss to give her the next instruction. Who, to my astonishment, was me watching from behind the closed gate. Belle gazed at me and waited. All nature waited – at least the sheep and dog – for me to do the right thing, and knew what the right thing was.

At last, Belle lost faith in the omniscience of all humans and got on with it on her own. She began running from side to side, keeping a low crouch, maintaining the sheep in their compact group, but pushing them fearfully away from her and towards me behind the gate. The sheep at the back, nearest Belle, scurried away from her, jostling the sheep ahead of them until the sheep at the front of the group were pressured enough to break into a nervous trot and the whole bunch were on the move in the right direction, which from their point of view was away from Belle, and from Belle's was towards me and the gate. A herd of sheep with a dog behind them is a perfect forward-motion machine. This must be the basis of their reputation for stupidity – like British Prime Ministers they have no reverse gear. Apparently it was Belle's plan to move the sheep into the field I was in. I had gathered a little about keeping livestock: animals need to be shifted from field to field as they use up the grass. When I arrived the Farmer told me that the sheep were pregnant. They were being kept as quiet as possible and should not be alarmed. A hill farm runs on a tiny profit margin. An aborted lamb is a deficit.

'Make sure the gates that are open are left open, close the gates behind you that are closed, and don't get so near to the sheep that you disturb them,' was the simple instruction I was given about not causing trouble on the farm. I waved my arms and raised my voice to make Belle stop, which Belle, of course, took as affirmation.

The sheep pressed hard against the gate, trying to escape Belle by melting through the metal bars and going wherever she wanted them to go so that they could be left alone again to do what they did best, graze quietly, harmlessly, helplessly, the live-long day. But the gate was closed. If I opened it the sheep would be herded into the next field where they weren't supposed to be. The sheep were throwing themselves at the ones in front of them, and the unfortunates by the gate were being crushed against the metal bars. It was horrible. My first walk was a disaster. I began to panic, visualising little caul-wrapped packets of dead lamb foetus lying scattered around the field after the sheep had finally freaked and run crazy, their uteruses contracting frantically in terror. All my fault, a typical urban trouble-maker, who thought a dog was for taking for a walk, not for serious livelihood-making-or-breaking work. The sheep would all abort, the Farmer would lose her tiny profit which my rent would barely cover. I would be obliged to confess and apologise and then I would be expelled from the farm, and even if I weren't, I would no longer be alone and invisible: the Farmer would *think* about me, annoyed at me, wondering what I was up to now. I was actually wringing my hands with distress at all this. I wished the last half hour away, as you do when things go stupidly wrong, trying to backtrack on time. I had never thought about going for a walk, never left the cottage, never imagined I could go for a walk with a dog, like some *countrywoman* going for a walk with a dog. Roll back. Make this never have happened. Imagine Coleridge causing sheep chaos. This was not at all the calm, peace-absorbing soul I had foreseen wandering aimlessly but with underlying meaningfulness in my rural imaginings. And out there in the middle of nowhere, I felt myself to be observed from the farmhouse, whose windows gleamed in the morning sunlight, or from behind trees, or looked down on from the top of the coombe. No calm of mind, not alone on my desert island, but watched by critical eyes. Belle at any rate was observing me and wondering when I would break the mysterious deadlock and open the gate to release the sheep into the lower field. Desperate to end the fiasco, to save myself from further humiliation at the paws of a dog, and the foetal lambs from an even more untimely end than they would otherwise have, I turned and walked purposefully back to the previous gate, calling for Belle to follow in a voice that I tried to make severe. I sneaked a look behind and saw Belle waiting for me to return, and the sheep shoving and shuddering. I was down near the cottage before I dared look back again. No dog. I went in and stood at the window, consumed with fright, and considered how to explain all this to the Farmer.

Ten minutes later, to my relief, Belle appeared back in the yard, passed my cottage without a glance, and settled comfortably down beside Pat (who did not bother to open his poor, tired eyes) for a well earned rest, her job done to the best of her abilities and it certainly wasn't her fault that the dumb human wouldn't open the gate. I could only hope that the flock were still with lamb. I dared not go and check for fear of starting Belle once again on her mission to move sheep. Instead I sat in an armchair, cowered really, in the living room, waiting for eviction by my landlady and feeling that all hope of whatever it was that I was after was gone. The whole two months ahead ruined by this first morning's idiocy, like a delicate present clumsily opened, spoiled before it is even out of the box.

7

ON GOING DOWN TO THE SEA

There is a Nabokov novel (I can't remember which; either an early or a latish one) where the hero explains to his fiancée that he cannot marry her because he has a terrible secret. He is mad, he tells her. Actually insane. But secretly. He cannot bring himself to say more. His madness, he confides to his readers, takes a particular form: if he pictures himself walking in a particular direction, say along a straight road towards the sea and he comes to the end of the road, railings overlooking the beach, he is *completely incapable* of imagining himself turning around and returning the way he imaginatively came. So he is stuck. Unable to leave the dead end in his mind. It alarmed me when I first read it that Nabokov's character called this insanity, and dared not marry his loved one for fear of passing on the madness to his children. It sounded normal to me. I've spent hours of my life trying to get out of some cul-de-sac that my mind simply won't let me turn away from. Yet when I'm half asleep, in the state called hypnagogic (or hypnopompic if you are about to wake) everything is geometry. My hypnagogic world is purely shape and dimension, but not Euclidian or any other kind of spatial system I have ever come across. The place at the edge of sleep is some sort of geometry that things of this world cannot fit into, cannot relate to. Chairs and eggs and umbrellas float about, revolving and reorienting themselves, trying to make sense of the new space which bears no relation to their form, designed as they were to be useful things in the waking world. If I don't wake up, or fall asleep too soon, the forms sometimes get the hang of things and re-form themselves until they are chairs and eggs and umbrellas which belong there – but they are no longer recognisable as what they are except by their names. It is a great relief to me when they find their new shape in this other world I live in momentarily. I always feel that if I can get enough objects to reshape themselves I might be able to live there entirely and entirely abstractly. It's where I most like to be, this hypnagogic universe, for all that it can be strange and frightening. I think that it is in this other geometry that my books exist before they get written (and sadly, ineffectually translated into the world of Euclid). They begin as shapes I can't grasp. If I could get to them where they live, rather than having to adapt them to my waking world, we would all live happily ever after. 'We' being my chairs, eggs, umbrellas (&co), my books and me. The books being the very shape of everything in that world and me in it, and therefore needing only to be what they are (at last) to be what they are for (at last). As it is, there is only translation by a translator who barely speaks the language, the shadow on the cave, and the wrong shaped shadow at that. I am not at all happy to keep finding myself a Platonist, but my spatial troubles seem to make it inevitable.

What I really did want was to get to the sea. Going out two days in a row (especially as the first outing was so disastrous) seemed to go against everything I sit for, but the weather was wonderful and the pull of the sea was great. The Farmer had suggested I head for the coast at Lilstock. It was the emptiest beach, with a cliff walk and a handy nuclear power station just beside it. Not that this last was a selling point, only an additional way of knowing where I was going. What's more, there was an interesting little church nearby worth looking at. So I decided on a visit to the seaside the following afternoon. But as in my first walk, direction was a problem, this time not because I sensed there was a Platonically ideal way to go, but because there was an actual right way to go, and easy as looking at a map for a point less than seven miles away seems to be for normal folk, my capacity for getting lost is legendary.

Before the wonders of the worldwide web and the possibilities of instant research, I was inclined to think that I really had some spatial brain disability. However, I discovered that a lesion in the map-reading half of the brain was likely to mean I couldn't recognise things in my left field of vision. As far as I can know, I don't have any problem seeing the left half of the world, so I doubt that there are any lesions. My problem is more Nabokovian, I think. I have terrible trouble knowing which *is* the

125

left half of the world. I am left handed, and I'm always confusing left and right. It might mean that my brain hemispheres are reversed, or they might not be and it's the wiring that's different. Either way, playing a guitar or learning to crochet are hopeless tear-stained lost ambitions of the distant past. No one who knows me lets me tell them to turn left without asking me first to physically point in the direction I mean. 'Turn right,' I say, and point firmly left. 'Well, yes, obviously, I meant left.' I am not much of a navigator. Left means good, friendly, the right way (even if turning right is the correct way), right is alien, strange and not desirable. The words, left and right, and the directions I intend to give fail to match up.

Whatever the reason, my spatial brain does not seem to do the business that other spatial brains manage effortlessly. I just can't orient myself in the real world or by a map. North, south, east and west may seem like a good solution to most people, but just the mention of one or other of them sends me into a mental panic. My brain scrambles. The world becomes a tangled forest, a blank desert, a swirling void. Tohu bohu. Mind fuck. It's directly north, people say as if I had the faintest idea what they were talking about, for all the world as if roads don't turn corners. And, confusing left and right as I do, I can't possibly find my way on a map without turning it around to imitate the direction I will be taking. I have to imagine a little car going along the lines that indicate the road and then follow it with my finger as if I were in the driver seat. I cannot drive backwards or branch sideways in my imagination. Maps are a terrible but fascinating problem to me. I pore over them, tracing the route I need to take (I think) with a marker pen, trying to fix the movement of my hand in my mind as direction. But as soon as I put the map down, and picture myself in the car driving the route, I am lost. I could, imaginatively, get to the end of the stony drive that led to and from the farm, but then a great cloud formed in my head and obscured the way.

I have regular routes, of course, where I live, for places I go to frequently. It only takes two or three years to fix these in my mind, and then I'm fine. But I cannot deviate, and I cannot link two routes together. There is no connection between one destination I can get to and another. No overall plan into which they fit. I have to start from home to get to any one of them. Those maps that I have managed to internalise never combine to form a larger map of the general area. I can get to Waitrose and I can get to the dentist, but not *from* Waitrose to the dentist without going home first. I can get to the M11, and I can drive on it – if I didn't hate motorway driving – but even though I have been a passenger innumerable times, and a driver twice, I cannot make the slightest map in my head of what to do at the end of the M11, or even where the end is, to take me to north London. There is just a line for the M11 and then thick grey fluff like roof insulation until I imagine myself in West Hampstead, from where I can drive to several destinations having lived in North London almost all my life. As for south London, beyond Waterloo Bridge there is nothing, not even obscuring cloud.

I almost got to Lilstock without losing my way. I sang along with Handel on Radio Three and the sun shone, and focusing on the remnants of map in my head, I found my way to Nether

Stowey, to the main road and crossed it, passed signposts to familiar names on the way to my destination, and trilled, 'I'm all on my own and finding my way' to the birds through the open window. Then I got lost. I drove doggedly for three and a half miles beyond the signpost that said Lilstock was two miles away. I had glimpsed the sea at the top of a hill, gasped and cheered, and then lost sight of it. Then the sea was behind me. With my back to the sea, even I knew I was going the wrong way if it was the seaside I wanted. Though which wrong way is another matter. I drove on to a signpost and got out the map, turned it around so that the coast was behind me (the me in the tiny car driving along the road). Eventually, I found the name of the place on the signpost. I drove on to the place on the signpost and then stopped again and consulted my map. I re-directed myself, beginning from where I was now and going to Lilstock. A new route. At last I got to the parking place from where you walked a quarter of a mile or so to the sea. I parked. I breathed a great sigh. An epic journey had been completed. I decided not to think about how to get home.

There were two other parked cars. I walked along a cratered, stony path by the side of a field of grazing sheep until eventually it turned a corner and the sea appeared, so abruptly that it seemed to curtsey at me like a star waiting behind a rising curtain. Da *da*. The flattest, calmest sea. A sea pretending to be solid land. A sea concealing its nature and hiding itself until you turned that corner and it spread itself out in front of you, a bright silver grey expanse, sparkling but still. A desert with flickering bright spots, like mica glinting in the sand. The Bristol Channel, actually, on a clear, lovely day, and Wales in the distance cutting the horizon down to a side corridor. Then a breeze passed over the face of the water and ruffled the desert, turning it liquid, tiny waves rippling, making it look like a desertscape that looked like the sea.

The beach was another kind of desert, as if a giant had taken a microscope to the sand and transformed all the grains under the lens into boulders and rocks. Large stones tumbled on top of each other, smooth edged, but oblong or square, like great cobbles. Walking over them was difficult, they wobbled underfoot, perched unstably in crevices created by the uneven meeting of the stones beneath. The stones clopped against each other as they were disturbed, complaining and settling themselves down again. Several times I lost my balance and landed knees-first. My walking stick helped and hampered in equal degrees. Far off to my right, at the shore line, a figure stood still beside a fishing rod on a tripod. A dog ran around him or her, and barked distant and echoing. There was no one else in sight. I stumbled down to the sea, which even at its edge was barely moving. The whole world, sea, sky, cliffs, a palate of silvers and greys, bright and then duller as the white clouds shaded the sun. Even so, the glare made my eyes water. The only sound was the slight rustling of surf by the point off to the left, where the nature of the beach changed into great flat plates of solid rock, separated by muddy sand and tidal pools of sea water. To the right, on the cliff top above the angler was a square, squat building, not ugly, not beautiful. A series of cubes, anonymous and grey, and not entirely out of place among the squat grey stones I'd walked

129

over. It was the nuclear power station. This spot was particularly favoured by anglers, it turned out when I looked it up on the web. Fish caught here were huge, record-breaking in size and quantity. Something to do with the power station, perhaps, and/or the large outflow pipe beside me on the beach out of which flowed who knows what? Human or nuclear power station waste? Well, a big fish is a big fish to a fisherman. The man down at the end of the bay didn't seem to glow especially. Perhaps he didn't eat his catches.

Behind me to the left the back of the beach rose in a gentle slope to become stratified, sandstone cliffs that loomed over the sea. I walked up it and got on to the cliff path which went for seven miles above the beach to East Quantoxhead. Not that I was planning a seven-mile walk, just a little wander along the edge of the land with a farm field on my left (a single poppy waving in the wind) and beyond the field, the Quantock Hills, pretty as a picture, a postcard of hills, rising and falling above the wonky network of hedgerows separating the small patchworked fields that had not (because of their hilliness) succumbed to agribusiness and become gargantuan.

To my right was a seventy-foot plummet to the rocky plates of the beach and the sea beyond, livelier around the point, small waves breaking up into froth as they hit the cliff face. Down there, a white long-necked wader bird paddled in one of the pools (an avocet, the Poet suggested on the phone, making me think of the sweet yellow eggy drink I was allowed as a child to sip from a small glass at Christmas and not of white long-necked waders at all), and on the far side of the point there were two men also fishing, a deliberate distance apart from each other on the shore. Above the fields the sky was blue with just a few puffy clouds, but out to sea a darker bank of cloud was rolling towards the land. I could hear, and just about see, a sheepdog barking and gathering the flock together in the field by the car park.

And I was thinking all the time, as I do at solitary moments in lovely places like this, how *lucky* I am to be here, seeing this, doing this. Wind on my face up above the sea, the oystery smell of ozone, the sound of gravel crunching under my feet. A degree of shame: rich enough, free enough to have this moment. That actually was what there was to be thankful for. Thanks not to be hungry and destitute, and that for me working is nothing like being in an office or a factory all day, or a classroom, or, come to that, a field. What about people who live here, or are brought up with this? This is their normality, not a perfect moment. Are they lucky? Their pleasure in all this must be a much more measured sense of well being. Something to live with, a way of existing, like having a young vital body and not being old with a broken hip. What if the young noticed that all the time and were thankful? Impossible. Being so full of feeling astonishingly fortunate threatened to overwhelm the experience I was so thankful for. You would only want fleeting moments of that. But here again is that terribly difficult business of experiencing experience. I am so conscious of me being here, of being me here, not somewhere else, having this experience, that I lose my awareness of what is pleasing me in order to think about the pleasure. I am experiencing luckiness rather than what is actually happening.

Not that the sense of my great good fortune is entirely cerebral. It wells up and fills me like water rushing into an empty tank. It needs some sort of release. Gasping, or laughter is my physical response, but to feel lucky is to feel grateful, and not being religious means having nothing to be grateful to, nothing beyond process and accident that allowed this to happen, so there is nowhere to park the sense of good fortune. I have a great wish to say thank you, but there is no one, no where, no what, to say it to. Well, there's 'nature', of course, but I resist being grateful to the world itself for being what it can't help but be, or imagining that nature and I are in communication. Nature, whatever that is, is not aware and therefore does and allows nothing. I can't help feeling fortunate for a glimpse of it, for being able to walk in it as if it were something to do with me. But even the half-conscious sense that nature is 'doing' or 'allowing' for me, is at best nonsense and at worst a sentimental megalomania. And what about aspects of the world, the upshots of nature, that are intolerable? 'Allowing' disease, disaster, no end of suffering? If I am grateful to nature for this good stuff, must I be enraged at it for the bad stuff? Idiotic. No more malevolent than benevolent. This moment in the world is wonderful, but in general I don't feel at one with nature. I am quite apart from it. Alien to it. Mostly what I do is observe it and as usual try to name its parts. So I name the sea and then wonder what is the sound of the sea actually? I can hear it, of course, but how can I describe it? Obvious words, unobvious ones. All analogies. The sound of the sea is the sound of the sea. At least, this sound is the sound of the sea at this moment. The desire to name is the desire to capture, to hold for the future. Which is why animals don't need human language. And why I, having language, like it or not, find it impossible to experience experience directly.

The wind got up as the clouds drew closer to land. Had I had enough of this? Was the pleasure seeping away? It was less intense, and there I was thinking whether I should be thinking about going. The clouds dull the sky and my sense of gratitude fades. There's a certain chill in the air, and a tiny wave of bleakness begins to move inside me. I feel exposed. Out. Not safely indoors, surrounded by walls and warmth. *Stamina*, is the word that comes to me. I have none at all.

A couple of hundred yards into the drive home – turn map around, do not go back the way I mistakenly came – I saw a sign: St Andrew's Church. The Farmer mentioned it. I parked and got out of the car. It was a tiny stone building set in a quarter of an acre of tended garden dotted with old gravestones. The church was hardly bigger than a large shed, though with a bell tower at the top. On the wall by the entrance a plaque explained that this was a redundant church. It wasn't a phrase I'd seen before. The stone building that had existed on that site, in one form or other, since the eleventh century as a church was surplus to requirements. Unwanted, deconsecrated, left to rot. Redundant: such a forlorn designation, even if it is a simple, factual statement, and in this case, a technical term. But how redundant can a place be if someone has placed a plaque on it saying it is? A really redundant building would be a ruin. This wasn't. I tried the door and it opened. There was an altar at the far end (not very far – about twenty feet) with a pair of candles and a cloth on it; five rows of plain wooden chairs and next to the altar a table with a visitor's book, open and signed, including by one visitor who gave his address as Mars. Not entirely redundant, after all. Beside the visitor's book was a handful of leaflets with a picture of the church on the front and the title *The Church of Lilstock St. Andrew. A derelict church restored.* It explained that a church had stood on this site for many years before its entry in The Domesday Book: 'Ansger Coquus holds of the King, Lulestock. Bricsic held it in the time of King Edward and gelded for five hides . . .'

The King, William the Conqueror, had appreciated his cook, Coquus, enough to give him Lilstock. The present church was built by 1532. Its fortunes went up and down. In the fifteenth century the right to appoint a priest passed from local monks to Eton College. By 1554 it was in need of repair and the nave windows were 'greatly ruined', and in 1557 there was no priest. But by the nineteenth century 'services were held every Sunday, alternatively morning and evening, and there was communion four times a year. A porch and a bell-cote were added.' By 1881 the church was in ruins, and in 1980 it was declared redundant and deconsecrated. It became derelict. But in 1989, the local rector, the Reverend Rex Hancock came to the rescue. He set up a trust and acquired St. Andrews.

The leaflet continues, 'Out of his own pocket Mr. Hancock paid for the repair and restoration of the chancel, bringing the church back to life in 1993 as a habitable building and leaving it the place of charm, resonance and quietude which visitors find today. It is a Grade II listed building. Though retired Mr. Hancock still holds an annual service of thanksgiving there. The work of restoration was done by Arthur Booker, with help from his wife Tilly and their son David.'

Thanks follow to local businesses who donated timber, slates, the present bell in the bell-cote, and to individuals who donated their time and skill to craft the leadwork and make the altar cloth. So much effort had gone into reclaiming this tiny building for the once-a-year-service and the surprise of visitors coming on it by accident. Where the altar stands there was once a memorial slab which is now to be found at the rear of the bell tower leaning against the wall of St. Mary's Church, East Quantoxhead. It reads 'Here lyeth the body of Nicholas Luttrel of Honibere Esquire, who dyeth in March 1591. He lived 62 years.'

In the churchyard are the headstones, the engraved names smooth and flat, of Sarah Perrett, a lady in waiting to Queen Victoria, who came from Lilstock, and her brother Joseph, 'who worked for a time on land but was happy only when he could see the sea.'

Lilstock was never much of a metropolis. According to the leaflet, 'There were 11 households in the parish in 1563, 65 tax-payers in 1667 and 12 inhabited houses at the end of the 18th century. The population was 56 in 1801. It fluctuated consider-ably during the century, rising to 91 in 1811 and 94 in 1881, but falling to 48 in 1841 and 58 in 1901 ... in 1977 there were 5 inhabited houses. There are even fewer now.'

The annual thanksgiving service is held on Christmas Eve,

after I would have returned to Cambridge I noticed with a twinge of disappointment. I suppose you have no problem knowing who or what to give thanks to if you've taken the trouble to rescue an ancient church from redundancy and dereliction. I stood still for a while in the cold stone silence and looked around, breathed in the cold stony smell, looked at the cold stone walls and up at the dark wooden roof beams. There were several carved memorials on the wall, so rubbed out by the centuries that they were almost unreadable. One of them, made of slate was for a son and daughter of the Popham family, who died in 1713 and 1718; the other I couldn't make out. I turned to look back at the timber door, and saw, propped in the corner, a broom, a dustpan and brush, and a bamboo cane with a feather duster attached long enough to reach the beams across the roof space. When I looked back, I noticed the flagged floor around the altar was littered with autumn's leaves, blown in as visitors arrived and left the door open while they stood and looked around them, as I had. It indeed gave the place an air of redundancy, in spite of the white embroidered altar cloth, as if the dead leaves on the floor were the beginning of a new process of decay. Perhaps that was what the broom was there for, I thought. A visitor might want to give the place a bit of a sweep, spruce it up a little, keep it from encroaching redundancy. Very shiftily, and trying not to notice what I was doing, I took the broom and started to sweep up the leaves around the altar. When I'd got them all heaped into a pile, I scooped them into the dustpan and tipped them outside to blow around to where they belonged. Windblown leaves on the floor indoors made the place seem neglected and unkempt; in the autumn churchyard they were matter in the right place.

I was quite annoyed with myself for not allowing the unkempt to happen, for houseworking instead of just observing the early process of decay, but I enjoyed my sweeping. The bristles of the stiff brush scraped and squeaked across the stone flags, the drier leaves swished and crackled as they were dragged into a neat pile. I was performing a task, rather than just standing and looking; straightening up, making the place nice. Very bourgeois, downright idiotic, sweeping up in this place that had nothing to do with me just for some sentimental and domestic notion. On the whole, admiring as I was of the Reverend and his efforts, I was equally of the other party, and wished for things to be allowed to go to ruin if that was what was happening to them. A ruined old building is also a beautiful thing. A vanished old building, its present absence noted, is just as vastly rich a resource for thought. As is a vanished old building that no one now knows about. I really hoped no one would come in and see me. It was an act of tidiness, but to someone coming through the door I would look like a devout parishioner dusting and arranging the flowers at her local church. It would appear to be an act for God whereas it was actually an act for neatness. Which was bad enough. A human taking a hand in the battle of nature versus indoors. Sweeping away the leaves in this redundant church was an obsessively human act. I wouldn't have wanted it either misunderstood or even simply witnessed. I would not have wanted anyone to think that I was either giving thanks or tidying up. I do so hate the idea of being *good*. I looked at the long bamboo pole and then up at the rafters which could certainly have done with a dust, and decided enough was enough, either of sentimentality or compulsive neatness. I left the church and closed the door quickly behind me so that no leaves could blow in. The perfect little churchyard was surrounded by woods. The Farmer told me that in the summer she comes here to sit and listen to the nightingales.

8

ON SPIDERS AND RESPECT FOR SHEEP

Week 2

The following morning the Farmer was taking me round the farm on the quad bike. I lay awake fretting for most of the night. It was four-thirty the last time I looked at the clock. Worrying, dreading. *Not* because I didn't like the Farmer or because I didn't want to be shown around the farm and understand the layout of it better, and certainly not because I didn't want a ride on a quad bike, but simply because of the looming obligation to *do* something. It wasn't any imagined failure at socialising that kept me from sleeping. I know I'm perfectly able to be sociable when required. It was the fact of being *required* that sent the shafts of anxiety – painful almost – through me half the night. Something scheduled, something to be done, instead of nothing, no timetable, deciding what to do, or not do, moment by moment.

It was also about my notion of being alone. Being really alone means being free from anticipation. Even to know that something is going to happen, that I am required to do something is an intrusion on the emptiness I am after. What I love to see is an empty diary, pages and pages of nothing planned. A date, an arrangement, is a point in the future when something is required of me. I begin to worry about it days, sometimes weeks ahead. Just a haircut, a hospital visit, a dinner party. *Going out.* The weight of the thing-that-is-going-to-happen sits on my heart and crushes the present into non-existence. My ability to live in the here and now depends on not having any plans, on there being no expected interruption. I have no other way to do it. How can you be alone, properly alone, if you know someone is going to knock at the door in five hours, or tomorrow morning, or you have to get ready and go out in three days' time? I can't abide the fracturing of the present by the intrusion of a planned future. Probably I just don't want to die.

So knowing that I was expected to do something the next morning caused me to toss and turn the night away, and eventually to try out all the worries I could possibly worry about and then some I hadn't thought of before. It was a long night with the mind drifting into panic where none was needed. Didn't I want to see over the farm? Yes, I did. Didn't I like the Farmer? Yes, I did. Wouldn't it be fun, thundering up and down the hills and lanes on a quad bike? Yes, it would. But still I fretted as the night turned into very early morning. I ought to be silent, to be completely alone. Already a week had passed. I wasn't utterly, irredeemably alone. And now, four in the morning, my anxiety slipped into another gear and effortlessly my head was full of spiders.

I am a lifelong arachnophobe. They are always a consideration in where I am, where I want to go and how much I can relax. Spiders are a problem all year round, and in September and October in particular, when they come indoors to mate or do whatever they do in the autumn, they almost constantly worry at the darker corners of my mind. But at four in the morning they emerge from the corners of my mind and take up all the space available. It is my belief that I can actually summon them up by worrying I might see one. If I dare to think about them they will appear, malevolent, still as death or scuttling like an ancient evil up to no good. So I try very hard not to think about spiders, and therefore I do. Almost all the time. Naturally, in my right mind, I know that there are no end of times that a fear of spiders comes to me and no spider appears. Nonetheless, in my wrong mind, the permanently wrong part of my mind that is arachnophobic, I know damn well that my fear calls them into existence. The smell perhaps of spider anxiety having a spiderish come-hither pheromone. Or the thought itself magicking substance out of nothing. Dust conglomerating and developing eight legs and a desire to be in the presence of its creator. Me. Or they live, in shadowed places, behind things, underneath them, dark crevices I dare not look in case I find one, or worse, a nest of thousands. They're no fools.

As a child and young person I spent whole nights awake with the light on having seen a spider and watched it scurry away to lurk somewhere unseen. Eventually, I grew very slightly away from complete helplessness and found my larger, heavier seaside-scavenged stones useful for fighting back, at least making sure they didn't disappear and cause me even more terror. Hoovers are no good; the image of them alive, living inside the bag *that has to be emptied* is unbearable. They must be done for, but at a distance, by dropping something, or throwing something that leaves my hand out of it. My ex once gave me a blow torch, having got tired, ex that he was, of being summoned in the middle of the night to deal with a spider. But it was no good, apart from the damage and danger of torching the house, because even flame seemed to me to be connected to the gadget I held in my hand. Lately, though my instantaneous horror at the sight of them has not diminished, I am uneasy at ending their lives. It's an awful thing to do just because I have an irrational, demented fear of them. But I can't live in a place where I know a spider to be (yes, I know, I know, they're everywhere), and I can't touch them, not even with a tool that puts me at arm's distance. Someone once suggested using a soda-water siphon, and it almost makes sense. Really I need someone to deal with them. A friend of mine once said that the only reason for getting married is the cup of tea you get in bed in the morning (though that could only account for fifty per cent of contented spouses). For me, the best reason is to have someone to deal with the spiders. There are other reasons for living with someone, truly there are, but the *best* reason is that it goes some way to solve the spider problem.

However, in Somerset there was no one. I had a long fly swat. I walked around in a state of permanent high alert. I looked around every room before I went into it. I checked under the bed, in the cupboards, behind the curtains, under the pillows every night, terrified that I would find what I was looking for. And when I went to bed, I knew that I had not seen the one (at least one) that lurked in some shadow in a corner and was even now making its way towards the legs of the bed. If this sounds exaggerated, it is not. I don't know how I got the courage to go to Somerset by myself knowing that the spiders, the country spiders, for God's sake, were waiting. Actually, I don't know how I spent so much of my life living alone with no one to protect me from my terrors. I have a prescription for Temazapam for nights like this, and in the country every night was like this. Temazapam is mild as milk, but it blunts the pointy terrors enough for me to get to sleep. Who knows what crawls all over me when I've finally dropped off? I don't care to think about it. So, exhausted by the anxiety about my morning date, my mind turned towards spiders crawling along the floor and walls towards me, just in case I wasn't exhausted enough. Night-time and the irrational wear me out.

I woke and the sun was shining; the sky, sky blue. I got up when I heard the Farmer roaring off as she did every morning with two bales of hay on the back of the quad bike for the sheep. When she returned I would replace the fodder behind the driving seat. There was still that weighty dread of something I had to do. Right up to the wire. Paced about. It's impossible for me to work, read, or sit still while waiting for an event to happen. How much time in my life have I wasted waiting? Books not read, books not written, sinks not polished. Waiting is a full-time activity. It is an act that takes up all my energy and being. The idea of doing something to take my mind off an upcoming event is pure nonsense to me. Nothing must get in the way of hiatus. So great vacuums exist in time before something occurs – and then there's the getting over it afterwards. Hours, days, going over what happened, making it go away by draining it, squeezing the impress out of it by telling and retelling it to myself as a story, getting back to *nothing happening* (a condition I am inclined to call work, which it may sometimes, or may not ever, be); a difficult process that requires a considerable amount of nothing happening before it is completed and I can then get on with . . . more of it, I suppose. Though by then, it is quite likely that something else is due to happen. I really don't know how I've got anything done in my life, though it seems to be how I have to get things done. It is one of those mysteries like electricity causing a light to turn on but for no reason that can be understood by the casual observer, or even me, a decidedly uncasual observer. Not easy going.

About an hour later, there was a knock on the front door. I reacted like a soldier. Equipment ready, jump to it. My jacket and boots were waiting to be slipped into at the bottom of the stairs, and then I opened the door with what I hoped was a smile of pleasure and anticipation. In fact, now that the moment had come I did anticipate pleasure, though my smile felt like those awkward ones that stretch the politeness muscles. The social face that begins to give you pain after too long in the company of strangers. It isn't exactly shyness, this difficulty in spending time with, finding the right face and tone of voice to respond to, someone one doesn't know well. Unease is a better description. Ease does not come naturally to me. I suspect it didn't come naturally to the Farmer, either. But reticent people can't help each other. Of course, I can chatter endlessly to people I don't know under the right conditions: when I will not be in any relation to them for longer than a very brief period. Public readings, interviews, dinner parties, are all fine, but during none of those am I at ease so much as at attention. An hour on the back of a bike of someone who will be in some way part of my life for the coming two months is another thing altogether. Ongoing. The beginning of ongoing. Very difficult.

I clambered on the back of the quad bike, not a seat, but a platform of metal bars for carrying bales of hay, and held on tight. We were going to do a tour around the farm, not just for my benefit, but because it was necessary to go around once a day and check that there were no animals in trouble.

'The sheep get tangled upside down in the hedges sometimes and lie there all night.'

I remembered something I'd seen on the television. A sheep farmer, as gloomy a man as it's ever been my pleasure to watch, who blamed his temperament on the trials of caring for sheep, came across the corpse of one of his ewes that had fallen into a ditch some days before and failed to get upright.

'Sheep!' he spat contemptuously to the camera before looking down with disgust at the bloated body he would have to haul away and which would not repay its purchase or rearing costs. 'They die just to annoy you.'

I told this story to the Farmer, for all the world as if we were sitting next to each other at someone else's dinner table. An anecdote to smooth the contact. She barked a bit of a laugh, but the

145

Farmer was devoted to sheep. She didn't find them stupid or vindictively suicidal at all. They were quite sly, she found, and had the good sense to let the smartest among them go first and be in charge. And it was true; I'd been watching this from the sitting room window. Sheep don't follow like sheep, but like canny survivors. The gates between the sheep-grazed fields were opened in rotation to give the grass a chance to recuperate. When the gate was opened in the upper field opposite my cottage, the first sheep would notice pretty fast that there was now access to the greener grass that is always on the other side of the hedge, having perhaps enough brain to remember that it happened some mornings, or just smart enough to keep an eye out in case anything advantageous occurred after each visit by the Farmer. This first observant sheep walks through the gate as calm as midnight, while the rest of the flock appear to be oblivious, getting on with cropping the field they are in. Soon though, another sheep wanders, almost casually as if it were merely moving to a better grazing spot, nearer, towards the gate, and nearer still until, accidentally as it might have been, it crosses over. Soon a hazy line has formed. Half the sheep walk slowly through the opening, no rush, and settle down in a space of their own to chomp the new grass. The other sheep remain apparently uninterested, heads down, not going anywhere. But as I stand and watch (for half an hour and more) the line of sheep moving to the new field is maintained as one or two grazers just happen to manoeuvre themselves to be back of the queue, looking all the while as if their only interest is in eating. Then another sidles to the back of the line, and another. All unhurried, as if no plan had been made, but a regular procession go through the now well tried and tested gate, the stragglers unwilling to make a change, but eventually drawn, as if the line itself was a magnetic force or the increasing emptiness of their field pressed them to bring up the rear of the queue. Eventually all the sheep are in the next field. The whole process has a calm elegance. You could even imagine (if you didn't know how stupid sheep were) that they were doing what they had to do, helping the Farmer to help them, as it were, with the tiring business of providing them with sufficient quantities of food. Or maybe they are just dumb beasts and play an incessant unwitting game of follow my leader until the day they became lamb chops.

But, on that day, which I also watched, there was no gentle stroll through an open gate, the behaviour of both the Farmer and the farmed was altogether more urgent. The sheep chosen to go to the slaughterhouse, two year olds, were collected into one field and brought down to the sheep fold outside my kitchen window. The dogs bunched them together and the Farmer flapped her arms and shouted to get them all inside the small enclosure that held them tight, shoulder to shoulder. The animals shifted bad-temperedly, nudging each other to get more room. They had to wait until the transporter had been brought up and the ramp dropped. Then the Farmer swung open the gate and stood on the opposite side of it. The gate made a barrier to stop any sheep from skittering away up the field and the Farmer made a barrier on the other side, holding her arms wide to bar the way, making a corridor through which the sheep must pass, and shouting to direct them, alarmed now and jumpy, up the ramp and into the lorry. No choice. Manoeuvred into it. Not so smart. Just one at a time, popping gratefully out of the bottle-neck of the pen and into the narrow space that turned out to lead to the dark confines of the lorry, and then, if only they had had the memory to notice the process, to another darkness. Still, there was something edgy and jittery about them, and also about the Farmer and the driver of the lorry who must have done this hundreds of times but still looked just a little as if they held a guilty secret they were trying to conceal. Sheepish? Looked like that to me. The sheep perhaps could smell something, or see something out of the ordinary about the movements of the Farmer. Or nothing. Just me looking at a bunch of animals going to the slaughter and over-interpreting (because I must, knowing godlike what was about to happen to them), a perfectly understandable fidgetiness of creatures cooped up but without any conceivable foreboding of doom.

But watch the Farmer and her adult son on a different mission, trying to pick out a ram to send to a neighbour to impregnate his ewes, or a ewe with a festered wound that needed tending, and the sheep seemed quite as cunning – well, given the inevitable out-come, almost as cunning – as the Farmer herself. Again a group containing the individual to be isolated were run into the fold, then the ram or ewe had to be cut out of the mass and guided through a gate to a separate holding pen. Bella didn't help. She got wonderfully excited and wriggled into the pen causing ovine havoc, Farmer fury and sheepdog shame. Eventually she was hauled out by the collar and given a piece of the Farmer's mind while she herded the required but elusive ram or ewe through the gate, keeping the others out with her hands, pushing the desired beast with her knees, giving it an almighty shove and finally slamming the gate behind it where it found itself horribly alone. The other sheep were let out of their pen and herded back to their field. Then the son returned and climbed into the pen holding the ram or ewe, while the Farmer opened the gate of the pen next door that had held the other sheep. The son windmilled his arms and clapped his hands behind the sheep until it was at the gate of its pen and then the Farmer opened it outwards, making a miraculous narrow alleyway directly to the pigpens where sick ewe or stud ram was held, waiting to be cured or collected. The pens were a marvellous maze whose gates opened, closed, folded, and unfolded like a large construction toy to make, depending on requirements: corridors, open spaces of various sizes, separate channels or one large sheep pen. The ram or ewe being inveigled out of the flock fought and sometimes escaped capture sheepfully, more than sheepfully, doughtily, to remain part of a crowd. Though in the end the separation always happened. These separations were exhausting, fraught, and never worked smoothly. It was a joy, a fascination, a pity and a terror to watch the process, which could never be completed with calmness, whose very nature was agitation on both sides, but for which only one side could comprehend the necessity. And watch it I could just by standing at the correct window of my little cottage. Today, though, I had to go out.

Riding a quad bike on a hill farm where the hills were sometimes as precipitous as rock faces was alarming. Not for the Farmer, who seemed undaunted by any incline, but I was at least as fearful for my life as I was exhilarated by the tumultuous ride. We visited all the fields and I began, within my own spatial limitations, to get some idea of the lie of the land. It had been a good night for the sheep. None were found lying on their backs waggling their legs in the air or petrified, tangled in a hedgerow. We stopped to pick sloes for the sloe gin that the Farmer enjoyed. We went to a small wood on the common land that the locals had given up trying to protect from the deer who stripped the striplings put in to replace the trees they had destroyed. But, lately untended and overgrown, it was the best place to see deer, so we walked through it. The deer, of course, were much too smart to be seen. But as we returned to the bike and were roaring away, two young deer, a stag and a hind, soared into the air straight in front of us, over the fence the Commoners had put around the wood to keep them out, each taking a great balletic leap, challenging gravity and beating it easily, in order to get away from us. The Farmer shook her head in irritation at the impossibility of keeping the pests out. I marvelled at their performance. We went for miles around the farm and common land where the cattle grazed and wild ponies stole the hay put out for the cows. Through fields of nervous sheep, over dense bronze bracken, along narrow lanes and up and down steep green hills. We met the Farmer's daughter-in-law who invited me round to her cottage for coffee when 'I got tired of being alone'. She said she wanted to mate Pat, the dog with cancer, and her bitch 'so that Pat could have some fun, at least'. I wondered if it might no longer be his idea of fun. And even apart from his tumour, maybe in the world of dog, sex was more of a necessity than the fun it was for humans. For some humans, said the Farmer. Sometimes, I added. And the three of us laughed. Anyway, the Farmer said, his pills probably made him impotent and infertile.

We went on, riding through sloping fields and compact valleys surrounded by trees whose leaves were every colour of autumn from gold to scarlet. None of the fields was huge, all delineated by hedgerows tended by the Farmer and Commoners to maintain the boundaries and provide living space for wildlife. It reminded me of pictures I used to draw as a child of farms, hardly ever having seen any apart from in books: bold pencilled curved lines dipping and cutting across each other to form hills and valleys, stick trees with splodges of bright colour for leaves, bright green for the grass, brown for the soil, fat curvy clouds like cherubim thighs, dense poster-blue for sky, and V-shapes with turned-down ends for the birds dotted about. The Farmer would have seen her farm in quite a different way: problems, solutions, necessities, beauty with purpose, her glorious everydayness, her muddy domain. I saw it like a child's idealised picture of a farm. And the ride on a quad bike like riding one of the wild ponies. Not that I ever have. Not that I would.

When we got back the Farmer invited me into her kitchen for a taste of last year's sloe gin. Delicious medicine. She wondered what I did about living people when I wrote about them. When I asked, she said she was worried I'd write about her. I promised to show her anything I wrote and not to publish what she didn't like. She said good, but still seemed worried and distant. Back in my cottage I sat in the armchair and started to spiral into yet another panic. It was clear she was concerned at the idea of my writing about her and the anxiety grew that she would tell me to leave. It was an excessive response, little to do with the actual conversation we had had. But I felt I'd lost a subject – an important subject because she was so central to the farm, and intriguingly similar in reserve, though quite different in every other way, from me. She knew how to be alone, but possessed a rugged stamina I've never had.

I thought about how to write up my stay in Somerset without mentioning the Farmer, but to leave her out entirely seemed impossible. She and the farm were a unity, and my alienation from it was almost defined by the similarity and difference between the two of us. Here's the problem with non-fiction, life turns up such perfect situations and characters with which to illustrate an idea that it seems pointless to make them up. In fiction you don't have to. Call them Sandy instead of Carol and change their physical details, and you can keep real life pretty much intact. In non-fiction, imagination is required. Imagining for example, that there is a Farmer, a woman, older and much more attached to reality than you, who pricks your conscience and isolation with her sheer practical connection to the world around her. A figure who lives behind your house and gets on with her own life without more than the merest thought in your direction, but who represents for you an observing judgement on the evident uselessness of your life. How else are you going to get across the sense of shame you feel about the very satisfactory situation you have got yourself into? Someone's got to watch and judge, and God is simply not available to me in that form. So I needed to make up the Farmer. But the Farmer didn't want to be made up.

My anxiety at upsetting the Farmer and everything ending in a mess blossomed during the afternoon. I was convinced that another expulsion was about to be meted out to me. Getting thrown out was a repeated event throughout my youth, often, though not always, precipitated by my own action or inaction. Being evicted from our flat as a child, and twice expelled from school, of course. My fault, at least the second time, when I decided to take expulsion into my own hands and be actively bad. The first time I was asked to leave because my mother kept arriving at the school, angry and bereft, and making scenes. Essentially, my mother was expelled the first time. I was expelled from two jobs that my father found for me immediately afterwards. Once because I looked belligerent as I filled the grocery shelves, and the second time because the manager overheard me say I wanted to be a writer rather than the shoe saleswoman he was training me to be. After that I was eventually asked to leave the house of the woman who had taken me in, when my A-level exams were finished, because of my difficult and (again) belligerent manner. A second shoe shop fired me because I said 'fuck' in the staff room. A trendy dress shop gave me the sack because I read *Ulysses* (though anything would have done) under the counter when there weren't any customers. An Israeli café owner threw me out and banned me because he didn't like my unorthodox clothes or my response which was that I thought what the Israelis were doing to Palestinians was worse in the scheme of things than my choice of outfit. The macho Pamplona bull-running boyfriend of a woman I knew told me to leave their flat before supper had finished because I was a 'fucking feminist'. Some expulsions more serious than others, but for a long time, quite repetitive. I made a point in all of these exiles not to show anything but unconcern, but the truth was that the same cavernous sense of fear accompanied all of them, even the most trivial. Something bottomless lurked in the 'out' into which one was thrown. The possibility, I imagine, of being finally 'out', out of everything, everywhere, everyone, for ever, and the difficulty of comprehending where or how that would be. Lately, however, there has been a lull in expulsions. I'm less belligerent, I suppose, and I've withdrawn from the job market, and do not go about socially all that often. I haven't been thrown out of anywhere for more than two decades. But that afternoon I revisited my old world, reinhabited it as if I had never left, and as if I had not in any way changed, and the sense that another expulsion was imminent seemed as real and as terrifying as in the past. In any case, now that the quad bike obligation was over, I had to have something to worry about. It was one week since I had arrived.

I spent the evening reading Montaigne and a couple of essays by Thomas Nagel on Death and the Absurd, then took a sleeping pill and didn't wake up till nine-fifteen the next morning. One of the two ponies in the field outside my bedroom window was concentratedly scratching his haunches against the oak tree which, in the past week, had gone from deep green to a mottling of russet. This morning it was cloudy and, lacking any sun, the line of trees ranging across the top of the common were more manila than gold. I kept the curtains open at night, and the sense of the season moving along increased every morning as soon as I opened my eyes. Now with each night and each waking the quality of light and the state of the tree canopies told me about the passage of time and the truth about this season which, for all its rich colour when the clouds parted, was no more than a transition toward the loss of light.

9

ON ANATOMY

It turned out when I was eleven that I did have a condition after all. My mother had been found a job by a rabbi who was taking a great, and, as it emerged, inappropriate, interest in me. She became a housekeeper for an ex-tennis star and her businessman husband in their mansion in Hampstead Garden Suburb. To take a destitute woman and her child in and give them a home and an income would have been a *mitzvah* to the couple. It was certainly a blessing for the rabbi (still a trainee) who wanted to keep me nearby. Before that my mother and I were living in a bedsitting-room found for her by social services. She lay in bed and cried a lot. I had just started at secondary school where I went every day and pretended I lived like everyone else though doubtless everyone else didn't necessarily live like everyone else – no one suggested this; my mother was convinced that her catastrophe was the only catastrophe. Well, aren't we all?

For months my foot had been hurting. The pain increased as

I walked. I didn't mention it to my mother for fear of the result for us both of balancing another straw on top of her camel of disappointment. I passed a doctor's surgery every day on my way home from school, and one day I went in and asked to see a doctor. The receptionist looked at me oddly. I suppose it wasn't common for eleven-year-olds to register themselves with a doctor. But I was sent into a consulting room, and told the doctor my foot hurt. Quite soon (those days were before the NHS had silted up and been delivered the final death blow by Thatcher's scythe) a letter arrived addressed to me with an appointment to attend an orthopaedic clinic at the local hospital. By then, we had moved into the ex-tennis star's house. My mother was, of course, furious that I had gone behind her back. There was a row: I was making a fuss about nothing, I was selfish, what would the doctor think of her, didn't she have enough to do skivvying for them upstairs – this was her first ever job – but she came with me to keep the appointment.

My left foot was examined and x-rayed. We waited. When the doctor arrived he took my mother off on her own to speak to her. He came back and told me that I would have to have my leg in a plaster of Paris cast for at least six weeks. He didn't say what was wrong, or not, at any rate, to me. I was sent to the appropriate department and they wrapped my left leg in sheets of wet plaster from immediately below the knee to just before my toes began, incorporating a small metal rocker at the bottom on which to walk – or, rather, limp since it made me a couple of inches higher on my left than my right. I had to be on crutches at first. I was told to return to have the cast taken off in six weeks.

I cannot describe the pride I felt as I hopped crutchwise into school the next day. Crutches were better than a sling, better even than callipers. *And* I was suddenly a popular notice board. Everyone wanted to sign me. At home, or rather in the kitchen of the mansion where my mother wore her fingers to the bone and I hung out doing homework or watching television or reading, I was in deep trouble. The rubber ends of the crutches, and then the rocker at the bottom of the cast made black marks on the kitchen floor. She rubbed them away behind me as I walked and shouted at me. I was making her life a misery as if it wasn't miserable enough already, and in any case *there was nothing really wrong with me*. I wondered about that, because what better proof was there that I was suffering from something than crutches and a cast? But I supposed she knew what she was talking about, and that was what the doctor had told her when he took her to one side and which she now, in her rage, revealed to me. Even before that, when the kids at school asked what I had, I realised that it hadn't been given a name. I still couldn't stand four-square on my crutches in the playground and announce that I suffered from . . . I could have made something up, found a name of a condition in a medical encyclopaedia in the library, but I wanted my condition to be true. Real. Only things with names were real. Fantasy suffering wouldn't do, I ached for authentic suffering.

During those six weeks my mother got the sack. Not even God's blessing was enough to persuade the ex-tennis star and her stock-broking husband that my mother was someone they wanted to have in the house. There were awful rows, though they were very nice to me, apart from the husband mocking my apparently lower-class Yiddish (*baygle,* not *byegle* he informed me, trying to eradicate my grandparents' shtetl-ridden origins, and for Chanukah he gave me a collection of Kipling's poems – which I loved – in order to further effect my assimilation into a whiter kind of Jewry). We went to a bedsitter in Golders Green, found for us by the lovelorn rabbi, where I took up too much room with my clumsy left leg, and made too much noise walking on the floor so the people underneath would hear and complain and make my mother's despair even worse. I had a moment of inspiration. I called the estate agent where my father had worked before he disappeared into the blue and left us, months before, without any money, causing us to be evicted. My mother said he had vanished ('scarpered like a rat,' I think she said), but I asked the man who answered the phone if he knew where Mr Simmonds was working and I was put on to him immediately. He was surprised to hear from me, but not half as surprised as I was to hear from him. Just like that. So easy. We met, him and me and my big left leg, secretly at Golders Green bus station. That same week I had the cast taken off. I was to go back to the hospital in a fortnight. The next week I ran away.

'I'm going,' I said in the middle of a row.

'So go,' my mother screamed from the bed. 'There's my last ten pounds on the chest of drawers. Take it and good riddance.'

I was not an unfair child. I took one of the five-pound notes and left. I went to a long-lost cousin who I traced by going to the hospital where his wife once worked. It was my finest sleuthing moment. A melodrama ensued. My mother, having been told where I was, came that night and attacked my cousin's front door with a knife which she intended, she yelled, for me. The police came, I was put to sleep on the sofa with a spoonful of jam and phenobarbitone. My cousin had a young family, which I imagined I would join, because I did not want to go and live with either my father and his unknown 'other woman', or my mother. That a troubled little girl with troubled parents might not be just what a young family wanted in their house, didn't cross my mind. I had some notion that having tracked them down, I was theirs. It was only reluctantly and on a trial basis that I agreed to go and live with my father. (Some time ago I was telling this story to someone, a man in his sixties, who said, 'Why didn't you just do what you were told?' It was an extraordinary moment. It never occurred to me then or later that I was obliged to do that. In his world – where things were more stable if no less fraught in their way – children expected to be told what to do and to obey. They didn't 'decide' who they wanted or didn't want to live with. He was baffled that I might have refused to be with my mother and resisted living with my father. What did *want* have to do with anything? Mess allows in personal preferences, I suppose, that structure keeps at bay. He was right, I was a wilful child. I made a fuss. Sometimes it made life much more difficult, but occasionally it resolved impossible situations that my parents weren't equipped to deal with. Someone had to know what they did or didn't want.)

The cast came off. I was living with my father. Social services returned me back to the boarding school they had sent me to in order to keep me away from my mother, but which I had left, just before the ex-tennis star period, when my mother was asked to take me away. My foot still hurt when I walked, and hurt more the more I walked. I went back to the hospital. I have a strong image of the doctor giving me a very curious look; it seemed to me that he didn't believe me. He said the only thing left to do was to amputate the toe, making it sound like a threat. I said OK, if it would stop hurting, but he retreated from the suggestion when I didn't. I got the impression that I was making it all up. Looking for attention. I understood by then how I might do that. My condition was just that of being a difficult child. My father seemed to agree. Nothing more to be done. Let's see what happened as time went by. I supposed they were right, even though I was still in pain. I accepted the connection between mind and body at an early age.

I went back to the boarding school for a term and then it was the Easter holidays. I was fourteen. While I was at the grammar school, when my mother worked for the ex-tennis star, an extraordinary thing had happened. A boy in the sixth form had started hanging about with the girls I used to spend lunchtime with. Because I had dropped Latin I was automatically put in the lowest set of my year. The class I was with were losers, at least in the education stakes. No one bothered much about stretching us. I had my cast on, and although I was a plain, scrawny thing, and they were the most glamorous girls of our year (they knew exactly how to wear their berets folded in half and pinned to the back of their heads – so stylish. They taught me, but somehow the beret kept falling off or was at the wrong angle), they took me under their wing. I think they were sorry for me, being a bit of a clever, dull and twitchy fish out of their sparkling water. I felt

161

very honoured. I hung out with them, like a sort of mascot with my big white leg on which they had drawn hearts and arrows with initials, declaring who loved whom. I didn't have a heart and arrow of my own on my cast. I was much too preoccupied with my interior and home life, I suppose, to be thinking about that sort of thing. Sex had not crossed my mind, even though, with the glamorous girls' help I read, during our lunch breaks in one of the classrooms, all the right pages in an illicit and mucky copy of *Lady Chatterley's Lover*. It went over my head.

But this boy, not at all like my companions, in the lower sixth and doing sciences, hung around at lunchtime. Sort of mooched and mooned. I'd seen him about as I spent most lessons outside the classrooms in the corridor. The progressive boarding school had encouraged debate and queries by the pupils, and I was (and am) nothing if not argumentative. Eventually, a few weeks in to my grammar school experience, I only had to say 'But . . .' and the teachers would point to the door for me to go and stand outside it. I was something of a comic sight, I imagine, standing, day after day, outside classroom doors, with my big white leg covered with hearts and cartoons. The boy had stopped and chatted once or twice, even though he was older and off to university the following year.

One day, the leader of the glamorous girls, amid much giggling, gave me a note. It was from the boy – Derek. It said he loved 'you' and wanted to go out with 'you'. I gave it back to her and said I didn't think he was her type.

'No, he means *you*.'

I was flabbergasted. No one fancied me. Not even a science

sixth-former with thick spectacles. And I had my leg in plaster. Still. I met him that weekend at Trafalgar Square. He put his tongue into my mouth. I was more than flabbergasted. I asked him why he did that. He explained (although I imagine he was not very much more experienced in love's ways than I was), 'That's how you kiss.'

I could take it or leave it. But he had, it turned out, lost his heart to me in a way I couldn't possibly understand. I was not the sort of person people fancied and went out with. As for the L word . . . it meant nothing to me but family trouble. It was what people didn't do to make others unhappy; or did too much of and were cruelly disappointed. He was persistent; I went along with it. We went to a film or two and met in cafés in central London and I think, mostly, I just wasn't paying attention. Then I went to live with my father, and back to boarding school. He wrote to me all the time. We agreed to meet at Hyde Park on Good Friday and go on the Aldermaston March together. Three days and two nights. He was bringing a sleeping bag. Just the one. There was nothing I wanted to do more than go on the Aldermaston.

It was, of course, a secret. My father would not have permitted it. Derek never phoned me at home. I phoned him when I thought it was safe. Astonishingly, my father had agreed to let me go on the march. I told him I was going with a group from school. All girls. And a teacher. He thought it a stupid way to spend time, what did we think we could do about H-bombs and big political issues? But the young . . . they had their enthusiasms. I phoned Derek the night before to make the final arrangement of when and where to meet early the next morning. My father listened in on another phone. While I was lying in the bath having a secret cigarette, there was a knock on the door.

'I'm in the bath,' I called out.

'Never mind that, I'm your father. Let me in.'

I hurriedly threw the cigarette out of the window and sprayed some perfume around. Then, interestingly, after I'd unlocked the door, I got back in the bath. He came in and stood for a moment looking at me.

'You can't go tomorrow.'

'But . . .'

'I heard you. You're going with a boy. If you go, you'll get raped. It's out of the question.'

I made a point of not arguing about things at home. I sulked instead. But this time, I had a vision of Derek waiting for me to turn up and me not being there.

'I'll have to ring and say.'

He said I was not to get in contact with the boy again. I was too young to have a boyfriend. He gave me another long look, and then left. I spent the night in a kind of agony at the idea, not so much of not going, but of letting Derek down and him not knowing why. I think I sensed the power of an adolescent crush even though I didn't have one. Even so, I wouldn't try and phone him, I knew my father would be expecting me to, and I wouldn't give him the satisfaction of catching me out.

The next morning, I cried for an hour during the time when Derek would be waiting for me and finally realising I wouldn't come. Delicious melodrama but anguishing too, like the pain you feel for a wounded animal you can't explain things to. Later, I did what I had done every day during that Easter holiday, when I was barely talking to my father and the woman, Pam, he was living with, with whom I was at silent war: I set off to the Notting Hill Library, about fifteen minutes walk from Pam's house and newsagent shop on the corner of Holland Park Avenue. I took out three novels every morning, spent the day and much of the night reading them (while smoking out of my attic window) and then replaced them next morning. I was only a few feet from my door, when someone said hello. It was a man, in his early twenties I suppose. He had an American accent.

'Hey, would you mind listening to something?'

I didn't talk to strangers on the street. I ignored him. But he walked alongside me and kept talking.

'I work in the recording studio in Ladbroke Grove. I've written a song. You look like just the sort of person who would be able to tell me if it's OK.'

'Go away.'

'Aw, c'mon. I just want you to hear a song. OK. I'll sing it here.'

And he started to sing, quite loudly, standing in front of me and blocking my way when I tried to get around him.

I was fourteen, about three months off fifteen. I was not worldly. Most of my life was lived inside my head (or my solar plexus). My solar plexus was also the place where I felt the excruciating embarrassment of being full-throatedly sung to on the street with passers-by glancing and then studiously looking away. It's hard to explain now, but I would rather have been struck dead on the spot than be on a public street with someone singing to me. Now (one of the delights of growing older) I might join in or stick my fingers in my ears. Then, my whole unready ego screamed for it to stop.

'Stop it, please . . .' I begged him, as I would do later.

'Not unless you come with me to the studio and let me play you the song properly.'

I agreed. Anything to get off the street. I imagined a recording studio with people hanging about.

It was just a few yards from my house, in a basement. It was Good Friday and there was no one there. The American had the keys – he was the janitor, I think. He ushered me into the studio, one half wall of glass with recording equipment behind it, a fridge in one corner, a drum kit by the back wall, and a long, G-plan, Scandinavian sofa along the adjacent wall. When I was in the room, I heard the sound of a key turning in a lock. I looked at the man.

'I don't want you to lock the door.'

'It's OK.'

'I want to leave.'

He put the key in the back pocket of his trousers and smiled. Hey, come on. I knew what we were going to do, otherwise why had I come here with him?

'I'm fourteen.'

He laughed. I wasn't, he told me. I was nineteen, at least. He pushed me back, more playful than violent, down onto the sofa. I began to cry and repeated my age and told him I was – I sought out the word – a virgin.

'Hah, who are you kidding?'

I assured him. He said he didn't believe me as he pushed up my skirt. Knickers pulled down. A remarkable degree of pain. I didn't know it hurt. I have no recollection of being afraid that he would kill me. It was simply that I was in pain, not wanting this to happen and wanting him to stop. I pleaded with him to stop. When I cried out with the pain in my abdomen as he banged up and down on me, he panted, 'You really come a lot.' I didn't know what he meant. When I begged, he told me I didn't mean it. But I recall that underneath the pain and distress there was a voice rapping in my head that was almost exultant. 'That'll show him,' it said. I meant my father; I meant him making me let Derek down on the grounds that I would get raped. Eventually, it was finished. It probably wasn't long, but I had had no idea that sex took even that amount of time. He got up and went to the fridge. He took out a pint of milk and drank it down. I straightened my skirt.

'Want to hear my song, now?'

I shrugged. He put the tape on. I have no recollection of it. When it was over, he said he'd enjoyed himself.

'I've got to go home.'

'OK,' he said cheerfully. 'When we gonna meet again?'

I shook my head and told him my father would get angry if I met him. He asked for my phone number. I gave it to him. Then he unlocked the door and let me leave.

I went home and got into bed. There was blood on my knickers and I was very sore. I don't think I cried. I remember being in bed, that's all. I think I just lay there under the covers most of the day. He rang the following week. My father answered the phone and demanded to know why he wanted to speak to his daughter.

167

'My daughter is not allowed to have phone calls from men. She is fourteen years old. If you phone again, I'll call the police.'

He slammed the phone down, to my relief, and asked me who the man was. I shrugged and said I'd lost my address book. I must have dropped it on the street. I don't think my father believed me, but he let it go. I never told anyone about it until years later. Then, for decades, I referred to it as the time 'when I'd got myself raped'.

It was when I went back to boarding school, on the train, for the summer term, after those Easter holidays, that I decided that I would learn how to become one of the excitingly bad people, and at the end of that term, just as I had turned fifteen, that I got expelled. I had a letter from Derek months later. He had seen a film called *Portrait of Jennie*. It had made him cry. He had never stopped loving me. His letter made me cry, remembering again his being let down and getting no word from me, but I didn't answer it. I never heard from him again.

I was twenty-two before I went back to see a doctor about the pain in my foot. It had hurt all along, but that had come to seem normal. I was going to dance classes, walking around London. The foot hurt, but it always did. Lately, though, it had got worse. I went to my doctor. The orthopaedic specialist said that the bone in my second metatarsal was fragmenting. Lots of little shards were causing the pain. He would operate and clean it up, but it wasn't a cure, over the years it would get worse again. He was right, it did. But again, the pain was normal, until, suddenly, when I was fifty, it was decidedly abnormal. The pain was excruciating when I walked only a little way, more and different from the usual. I went to my GP. She looked back over my notes.

'Oh yes,' she said. 'You've had Freiberg's Disease since you were a child.'

'What's that?'

She didn't know, either. She looked it up and read out the description. I offer two medical descriptions below. I, of course, find every word riveting. You may not, and can skip it; all it says is that my foot hurt from an early age and the bone degenerated unto death by the time I was fifty. I wonder if the fact that the majority of sufferers are girls between the ages of eleven and twelve has anything to do with the ballet lessons I had from an early age, and the fact that I (and doubtless many others) disobeyed my teachers and was always going up on points without properly blocked shoes. Just a thought.

A. Freiberg's Infraction is a condition where the head of the 2nd metatarsal bone of the foot undergoes avascular necrosis (bone death due to loss of circulation). No one knows why it occurs, but repeated trauma is probably responsible to some extent. It typically occurs in an adolescent girl (less common in boys) who complains of pain and swelling at the head of the 2nd metatarsal with walking and running.

What does your doctor do about it?

X-rays show flattening of the metatarsal head in the early stages. If untreated, degenerative changes occur in the metatarso-phalangeal joint. Treatment in the early acute stage consists of a short leg walking cast followed by a foot orthosis to support the metatarso-phalangeal joints. Strenuous sports should be avoided in the acute phase. If the condition is discovered later in life, and there are irreversible degenerative changes, surgery consisting of debridement of the joint (cleaning and washing the joint to get rid of any debris) is often helpful in relieving pain. In the more severe cases, excision of the head of the 2nd metatarsal may be necessary.

B. Osteochondritis of the Metatarsal Head

In 1922, Dr Albert Freiberg described a pathological condition of the foot which affects the head of the second metatarsal. Freiberg noticed that this condition, now called Freiberg's disease, was most evident in tennis players, most likely due to trauma. Thirteen years later, Freiberg discarded his theory on trauma as a possible cause. In subsequent years, many individuals hypothesized that Freiberg's disease was probably caused by juvenile osteochondritis.

A GROWING PROCESS
Understanding Freiberg's disease requires knowledge of the ossification process in the metatarsal bones of the feet. Each of the metatarsals are ossified from two centers; metatarsals 2 through 5 have one center for the body of the metatarsal and another for the head; the first metatarsal has one center for the body and one for its base. Ossification begins in the center of the body during the ninth week of life. The center for the base of the first metatarsal appears in

the third year of life; the centers for the other metatarsal heads appear between the fifth and eighth year of life. Throughout adolescence, the epiphysis and metaphysic are separated by a narrow epiphyseal plate. The epiphysis ossifies to the metaphysic between 18 and 20 years of age.

EPIPHYSITIS

If during this time (when the epiphysis is still present), the blood supply is interrupted by trauma, epiphysitis occurs. It is believed that a micro fracture happens at the epiphyseal plate since it is somewhat calcified and vulnerable. This fracture could be due to endocrine disorder, trauma or infection. The exact etiology is still debatable and somewhat unclear. Trauma in the second metatarsal seems to be a plausible cause since it is usually the longest metatarsal in the parabola and excessive stress may be noticeable. In females, this condition is most often located in the second metatarsal.

Epiphysitis leads to aseptic necrosis, in turn leading to decalcification at the metatarsal head. Degeneration ensues, continuing for about one year from onset; this is then followed by regeneration that leaves osseous hypertrophy of the bone. Loose bodies are often found in the joint along with crepitus.

SYMPTOMS AND TREATMENTS

Early signs of this condition can be detected with x-rays; they will show a rarefaction of the metaphysic with sclerosis of the epiphysis. The distal end of the affected metatarsal is flattened, the shaft is hypertrophied and the head may appear somewhat fragmented. If diagnosed early, treatment should involve reducing stress on the *metatarsal. Padding of varying degrees can help to balance or elimi-nate stress under the affected metatarsal. Physical therapy can also attenuate the discomfort associated with this condition.*

If extensive osteophytic changes result and deform the affected metatarsal, it can also impinge on and affect the adjacent metatarsal. Surgical intervention may be necessary to remodel the joint. Surgery should aim to keep the metatarsal parabola intact to avoid transfer lesions.

So there it is. I had a condition all along. A real condition, with a name, and not even one of those evasive Latin names that means 'something wrong with the foot', but the name of the actual discoverer of the actual condition I had been suffering from since my childhood when I needed one so badly. Dr Albert Freiberg. *My* Dr Albert Freiberg, who had died eleven years before I was born, but who gave his name to the pathological state of my metatarsal. I wonder if anyone has biographied him? Of course, I prefer his *disease* to his *infraction*: infraction sounds too much like wilful disobedience to satisfy my youthful craving for the genuinely arbitrary misfortune of disability.

Clearly, the original doctor who looked at the x-ray must have diagnosed Freiberg's Disease. It was observable on an x-ray and he had put me in a 'walking cast' to reduce stress on the metatarsal. So how had it come about that I believed that he believed I was malingering? My mother said I had nothing wrong. Hadn't he mentioned the blessed Dr Freiberg to her? And when I thought he threatened me with amputation, was he actu-ally thinking aloud about *debridement* or remodelling the joint, and then decided it was too early? Was he not threatening me at all? But why didn't I have any more treatment? More interesting to me is that at the age of eleven, I was already prepared to believe that my body and its effects were a fiction. I understood figments of a needy mind. Though I felt the pain, I believed the look in his eye I thought I saw that said I was imagining it. In fact, it seems I was imagining the look in his eye. But I have never been ill since – physically or mentally, as it were – without an underlying guilt that I was fabricating it more or less unconsciously and undeserving of any treatment I received. Only open wounds or instrumental proof let me off the guilt hook. I welcome high fevers because then I feel that no one can accuse me of making it up. I love thermometers, I thrust them triumphantly under my loved one's nose to prove the physical nature of my malaise, even when there is no hint of accusation but my own. But I very rarely run a temperature these days, so I am not often completely satisfied with my state of unwellness. (My mother referred to having a menstrual period as 'being unwell', which was to be distinguished from being ill. Like net curtains pretending to be pretty rather than roller blinds which are plainly there to hide what is going on inside from intrusive eyes.) I am not just a hypochondriac, but a guilt-ridden hypochondriac. Is there a name for that? There ought to be.

It turned out, when, at fifty, I saw the specialist, that I was not only at end stage Freiberg's disease (which would have happened anyway with or without treatment), but that I had a Morton's neuroma on the same foot, which was causing the intensified pain. I won't trouble you with Mr Morton and his neuroma. Just an inflamed nerve that hurts like hell. If shoe pads don't help, it needs to be cut out and some or all of the nerve destroyed in that portion of the foot. Operation one didn't work. The neuroma grew back, the Freiberg's still hurt. Operation two was the major 'remodelling' of the last resort. Three metatarsals were cut shorter and held back together with titanium pins (£90 a go, my budget-conscious NHS surgeon informed me).

My foot, when it was re-dressed two weeks later, looked like butchered meat. I am not squeamish, but I nearly passed out when I saw it. It had lost all relation to footness, and had become a formless, swollen, bruised and bloody mess. I forced the weak-stomached Poet to look at it, because I couldn't bear the solitude of what I had seen alone.

'Look, you have to look!' I insisted, unravelling the bandages.

'No!' he screamed, screwing his eyes tight closed. 'I'll do anything, but not that.'

I was adamant. He screamed louder when he saw it.

Still, it had been taken to pieces and put back together again. The surgeon told me proudly of the creative work he had done. I had three months on crutches. Then another month or two on a single crutch. Luckily the floor I marked was my own. But life became very slow and hard work. The Poet looked after me like Florence Nightingale, and I only occasionally made him look at the bloody stump. After six months, when the surgical work had healed and my foot, though swollen, looked more like a foot, I returned to the clinic where the dressing nurse asked me if I was happy with the result of the brilliant surgery I had received, waiting for the delight and gratitude us non-payers should express.

'Well, if the result is supposed to be no pain, then – and I don't want to seem ungrateful – no I'm not.'

She turned and looked at me, quite surprised, rather cross. Then she left the room and about twenty minutes later returned with the surgeon. Actually, I had explained at every visit that my foot still hurt when I walked on it, but was told every time that it was early days. My foot had been taken to pieces, I mustn't be impatient. Today, however, the surgeon arrived and said, 'I gather you aren't happy?' I explained that my foot hurt when I walked, which was why I'd had the operation in the first place.

It turned out the early days were over.

'You'll have to adjust your lifestyle. At a certain age people have to come to terms with the fact that their bodies are getting older.'

Which was how he told me that the operation hadn't worked and there was nothing much more he could do. He was also telling me that as I was in my early fifties, pain and discomfort had to be put up with. It was a necessary part of being old. If it hurts, don't walk on it.

'Isn't fifty-three a bit young to become immobilised?' I murmured.

He clearly didn't think so. He'd had enough of me. He had done a beautiful job, as he told me after the operation, of redesigning my foot. All his skills and creative talents had come into play. He was rather angry.

'I'm not a miracle worker. The bone is necrotic. Dead. There's nothing to be done about it. We could excise it and replace it with a ceramic joint, but there's a high chance it wouldn't work. Better if you just re-organise your life to accommodate the situation.'

'How do I do that?' I asked, thinking that he must often have to say this, and that walking being not so much a lifestyle as a prerequisite for getting anywhere, he might have practical advice about the sort of adjustments needed.

It wasn't his job. He was a surgeon. He'd done what he did. He shrugged.

I left, brooding about being told that whatever my difficulties, they were mitigated by being old. There was nothing to be done about my foot, but it didn't matter all that much. This was my first experience of being declared redundant by age. It was quite a shock. It didn't matter much if I couldn't walk very far, because I was fifty-three.

And, in truth, in my particular case, it didn't. If anyone had to be told they couldn't walk far, it might as well be me. It couldn't have happened to a more suitable person. Very little life adjust-ment would, in fact, be needed. Who had set their face and their feet against the post-prandial promenade, the evening stroll, the brisk winter walk, the country ramble, the mountain climb, more stubbornly than me? Who had devoted so much energy to keep-ing still? If fifty-mile hikes across the Pennines were now out for good, no one was better placed than me to adjust to it. I've never woken up in the morning and thought that was just what I fan-cied. I was now officially entitled to sit on the sofa, and if I had to go out, to drive. In fact, driving hurt, changing gear caused too much pressure on my foot, but that could be overcome by buying an automatic car. Even less exercise. I may have had a tiny perverse wish to walk rise up in me when told that I'd just have to do without walks, but I was really disturbed only by what every ageing person must eventually discover: that growing old causes restrictions and that no one is outraged about it on your behalf. Will I have eventually (quite soon even) to adjust my lifestyle in ways that really matter to me? And will anyone care? Will they care when my eyesight goes and I can't read; when arthritis cripples my hands so that I can't write? And what if I can't even answer the door to the nice man from Waitrose, or the postman with the silk and cashmere wheat bags for my aching neck, that I won't be able to order on the internet because my fingers can't manage the keyboard, or over the phone because my clawlike hands can't pick up the handset let alone punch the buttons? Will the medical profession move heaven and earth to keep me reading, writing and shopping? Those things dear to my heart, which I really didn't want to do without. No, they won't, I saw, for the first time. Quite rightly, of course, in the relative scheme of things, when there are seriously physically impaired young people who need attention, and attention is rationed. But the shock was none the less shocking.

I recalled my months in St Pancras Hospital, the local catchment area psychiatric unit I was admitted to when I was twenty. Short skirts or vintage frocks from the Portobello Road, a predilection for scoring drugs in Notting Hill, and incapacitated by depression. I was sent there by a shrink who said I was to present myself immediately, do not pass go. I was in maximum suicidal mode apparently. I lived there for several months with a few other young people, depressed and manic. It became home. There was also a middle-aged range of patient. Quiet women and men who sat in the chairs around the wall in the day room and looked surprised to find themselves where they were. Then there were the old. Women, mostly, who were suffering dementia of various kinds and could not be accommodated in normal geriatric units. They were difficult, ranting, incontinent old ladies who had to be washed and dressed and who fought against everything that was done for them, so that the nurses lost patience and sometimes treated them more roughly than they should. Minnie was in her eighties, the picture of a sweet little old lady. I even have a sketch I did of her with her thin white hair pulled back into a neat and tidy bun, a shapeless cardigan perhaps once knitted by her, and big, lumpy black shoes that were never done up in order to allow room for her bunions or whatever it is that happens to the feet of the very old (perhaps I will find out). Sometimes she was just as she looked. 'Hello, dear,' she'd say as you sat next to her. And you could have a regular chat, or rather, she would reminisce about long ago and you would listen because it was as interesting as the radio. But sometimes, as the nurses said, she got the devil in her and shouted and screamed abuse at everyone and no one. She cursed us all, the foulest words falling out of her sweet little old lady mouth. She woke us up most nights, sitting up in bed and screaming, 'Open the windows, open the doors, let the firemen in!' She talked to herself half the night, or rather her mind spoke itself through her mouth, and she let out all her invective against everyone – she knew us all inside her head and hated us, even those she said 'Hello, dear' to and to whom she related bits of her life. 'Whore! No better than she ought to be. Filthy stinking down there. Does it every night with blacks, for money.' At night she loathed everyone. All of us got our share of abuse. In the morning, after she'd been put on the commode and had her hair done neatly, she'd be settled in her special chair in the day room and smile, toothless and enchantingly, 'Hello, dear, come and sit down. Let's have a little chat.'

Minnie. Several others, more or less the same. Mad old women. Reeking of urine or worse, unable to walk more than a few feet, and even then needing the support of a Zimmer frame. Awful legs, bumpy and knotted, hidden behind thick lisle stockings. Tits that sat on their thighs. Arms, in their sleeveless nighties, whose flesh hung down like swathes of window curtains. Pissed where they sat. Erratic, bad tempered, lost. No one ever came to see Minnie or any of the old women. And much of the time they didn't know where, what or who they were anyway. I liked Minnie. And loathed her. And all that happened in her life was about keeping her cleanish and dryish and sitting in her chair until she died. It seemed that you would have to have got your life very wrong, or would have to have been born into very wrong circumstances to become someone like that. But intermittently it dawned on me that, barring an early accident, something like that was going to happen to all of us. Some more fortunate than others, but essentially we were all going to smell, and our tits were going to swing, and people would keep us neat, if we were lucky, as they did when we were infants, until we did the decent thing and died. The problem was that, hard as I tried, I couldn't imagine *me* being Minnie. Of course, I knew that Minnie could never have imagined being whoever her Minnie was when she was young. But the idea that I was part of the great scheme of being young, ageing and dying, didn't help at all. Like not having any organs, Minnie was beyond my imagination except as someone else. And now, here it was, the fruit of my lack of imagination, squaring up to me. Eyeballing me, as tough as old boots. My new reality. I was amazed by the fact of finding myself consigned to the elderly half of the population. Now, it seems less impossible to be Minnie.

I have reached the age (rather early, I still think, in the manner of my particular generation) where the phrase 'only to be expected' comes regularly from other people's lips. Bits hurt. Stuff stops working properly. *Only to be expected. Nothing to be done. That's what happens, I'm afraid.* Somehow, I expected people whose job it was to mend things to go on trying to mend them, no matter what the age of the material they had to work on. Though, of course, I knew that the old are just not as interesting to work on, to listen to, to keep around, as the young. It may be that my generation invented that attitude – *hope I die before I get old* – but we have adjusted our view. Adjustments are possible, it seems.

On the other hand, it does seem to prove definitively that I do possess organs and conform to biological processes, just like everyone else. So another problem is resolved by time. Part of feeling like an empty envelope had been my consequent conviction that I was physically under my own control. It didn't seem to me to be possible to get the symptoms of age: extra weight, flesh losing its firmness and definition, memory depletion, digestive problems – if I chose not to have those things happen. I was convinced when I was younger that I could stem the tide, Cnut-like, simply by disbelieving in the process. The ageing of other people was simply a sign of their weakness of mind. The phrase 'letting yourself go' had a reality for me. It was a matter of choice whether one showed signs of age. Flabby, cellulite, knotted veins? Doesn't happen to me. I was thirty, forty, and even approaching fifty, and I looked and felt fine. It was my doing, I had no doubt, or rather my lack of expectation that anything should change about me over time. And suddenly, as if overnight, I was all out of my control. Not only did I have a full complement of organs, but they obeyed not me, but laws that were quite beyond my command. Suddenly I was impotent. *Process* had come to get me. There really was nothing I could do to stop my body deteriorating, or rather, doing what it had to do, as I got older in a way that now had a quite different meaning.

There is something else, totally inconsistent with the foregoing: I was shocked at my response to ageing because I had always imagined that I wouldn't mind – in fact I'd looked forward to it. A different way of being me. One of Peter Pan's (doesn't he come up a lot?) awfully big adventures. I am, after all, a woman of the Sixties and Seventies, the ones who put away all the nonsense about age depleting women, and I rather relished the thought of being a free-thinking free-living old bag. I remember my mother's body as a lumpish, ill-defined thing that she kept in check for going out, with a pointed bra that cupped her empty, dropped breasts, and a rubber encaser of her hips and stomach that was powdered on the inside before she struggled into it. She was often naked at home. I thought of her body as my mother's body, but now I realise that it was just an ageing body, and not a bad one at that for, as they say, her age. Sometimes, when she was asleep, I would gently pick up what I thought of as her chicken skin at her neck, and roll it between my thumb and forefinger. It was so tempting that although she invariably woke up and began to shout at me, upset, I suppose, that I played with her corrupting flesh like a toy, I could never stop myself from creeping up and trying again. There are pleasures to be had in the ageing body – I knew it even as a child. But the sight of one's own body losing its definition is, although strangely fascinating, not a bit pleasurable. As if someone is rubbing you out, the lines of your limbs and torso fade and mutate into a much more nebulous landscape. It isn't the wrinkles, it's the disappearance of proper edges that I find most disturbing. Also, simply, the fact that I am changing. I never had a weight problem, so I always knew that I was a size ten, slim, angular person. Sharp-edged. I catch myself in mirrors or shop windows, and I am aghast (not an exaggeration) at the person I see. Not me. Someone sturdier, rounded, not edgy. Of course. But it isn't me. Mirror, mirror, why are you showing me someone else? I've been one sort of person for nearly fifty years, how do I go about being another type altogether? And then there's the matter of desire. Of being desired. But that is another story, or rather, the same story, but a different part of the forest.

10

ON CAMELS

The second week in the cottage went just like the first. I went back to Lilstock once or twice, drawn by the sea. It roared on rougher days, and there was always an underhum. Either it was the sound of the nuclear power station doing whatever it did, or the dragging of the undercurrent. I worried a lot about the beach, whether to think of the rocks as giant pebbles or small boulders. And I brooded about what little I knew on the subject of fractals and mapping. The size of the rocks on this shore made it obvious how difficult it was actually to map a land boundary. Each up and down and in and out of each rock was or wasn't part of that line. I saw something far out in the sea. A hump. A creature, or just a mass of seaweed. I sat each time at the sea edge – or far enough from the edge of the waves not to get soaked – and thought that this sitting alone in front of the sea was exactly what I wanted to be doing. When I was fifteen, in the Lady Chichester Hospital in Hove, I spent hours doing it. It was deeper into the winter – December

1962 and January 1963 – an especially bad winter, and snow covered the pebbles on the beach. No one in sight. I sat for whole mornings and afternoons in the steely grey light, stared out to the horizon and waited for something to happen. In February it did and I left the hospital (where far from being expelled, they were holding on to me, unable to figure out what to do with me that didn't entail going back to either of my parents). Left for London. A new London, a new life. Everything different. Again.

But now, in Lilstock, I was in control, as much as one is ever in control (which is to say that unexpected fortune or misfortune on a large scale had not occurred for a while), and I looked out to sea with a somewhat less blank picture of the immediate future, but no less perplexity about all manner of things. I am calmer, but I really can't say that I know any more of what it matters to know about now than I did then, when I felt as knowing as an oracle (and perhaps was). My capacity for staring is about the same, but my sense that I have any idea of how or what to think has atrophied.

The Poet came on the third weekend and for two days everything changed. We were two people on holiday. We bought pheasant from the butcher in Nether Stowey and he made proper meals while I enjoyed them. We went to the sea and wandered about the beach, moving apart in different directions with our heads down looking for fossils and interesting stones. We had a blustery walk on the Lilstock cliffs which pleased me when it was over. The Poet strode off for seriously long rambles each afternoon while I sat in my chair reading. It was quite different from when he wasn't there, the being on my own but knowing he was

184

going to be back. Not at all unpleasant, on the contrary, but not really alone even when he was out.

We listened to music, watched TV, laughed as we do. We went further afield, the Poet having examined a map. We drove up to the top of Cockercombe and in the car park watched a man barking orders to people on cycles, a leader with novices, teaching them how to ride rugged terrain. 'There's an easy way and a hard way,' he said. Me, I'd go for the easy way, I muttered, disliking the pleasure he took in being in charge. 'You're not loose enough,' he yelled at the circling bikers. 'You've got a lot more work to do and I'm going to make sure you do it.' It wasn't raining, but a cold wind was knifing through my anorak. I didn't want to be there, at this high and beautiful place. Another day would have been all right. Now it felt cold and wrong. Bereft was the word I kept thinking. I could hardly have been less bereft, I told myself. I've been a bit bereft in my time (long ago), and this certainly wasn't. But *bereft* churned up from the place in me where it sits in waiting. I went back and sat in the car listening to the radio while the Poet walked for half an hour. I was much happier. Being out and cold is a kind of psychic exposure. Ridiculous, but a fact of my life. On Monday morning the Poet went back to Cambridge and I slid back into being alone.

Week 3

For a few days I gave up going for walks around the farm. When I felt impelled to go out through guilt or a sense that it was too weird not to mind having stayed in for so many days, I went to the sea, or into Nether Stowey for basic groceries and petrol, or all the way to Taunton for books and Marks and Spencer treats, and to wander about a high street full of multiples in case I forgot what W.H. Smith and Gap had to offer the world.

One morning I discovered with great pleasure that I wouldn't be able to make the trip I had planned to Taunton because the gate to the lane was closed. The Farmer and her son were on their quad bikes driving about thirty cows down the hill, towards the pens outside my kitchen window. Once the cattle were being penned in I went out with my mug of tea and greeted the Farmer. She said they were waiting for the vet to come and check the cows for pregnancy. She was very worried they might be barren due to some mineral deficiency in the soil. The bull hadn't been seen to be doing much, and last year there were very few calves, only about ten. If there weren't enough pregnancies this year it would mean serious loss of income. I returned to huddle and read Montaigne against the backdrop of the herd grunting and mooing. The Farmer knocked at my door in the afternoon. The cows were pregnant, after all. A great weight of worry had been lifted. About twenty-six were in calf and only five were likely to be barren. I made coffee and got out some biscuits to celebrate. I'd been quite worried. They were being left in the horse field for a while before being sent back to the Common.

The following day it rained continually. While I drank my tea, I stood at the window and watched the cows being fed by the Farmer's son. He drove the tractor up the field dragging a huge bale of silage. When he got to the top, he ripped the plastic covering off what looked exactly like a giant shredded wheat and released it from the spike that secured it to the tractor. He gave it a kick and slowly it began to roll down the hill, unwinding itself as it went, leaving a pathway of silage behind it down to the bottom of the field. The cows chased after the bale as soon as it began to move, some stopping along the way, others going down to the bottom where the silage was most dense. The gate to the upper field was open and they had spent the night there. When the tractor arrived the cows made their way through the gate to the lower field, except for one cow and four calves who ran up and down the length of the wire fence, anxious for food, anxious to follow, but apparently unable to get the point of the open gate. One by one – the cow first – they discovered it, until there was just one calf left. It ran up and down the length of the fence four or five times on its own before it finally got the message, lurched through the open gateway – one of the other calves looked up at it for a moment then carried on eating – and raced down the hill which was so steep that its back legs kept overtaking its front legs. It skidded to a halt and settled down next to its siblings to eat, at last. I'd been about to have a shower, but I had to keep watch at the window for the half hour it took for the cattle to get fed and the last calf to reach the lower field. One has some responsibility to one's surroundings. By midday, a thick mist had come down from the top of the coombe and surrounded the cottage. It was completely white through the windows. There was nothing in the world, just me in my isolation.

One evening I called M. in Lyme. It was near by – or nearer by than Cambridge – so I thought I might drive down and visit her while I was in Somerset. We were in our early twenties when we

met, in 1968, both of us patients in Ward 6 of the Maudsley psychiatric hospital. We'd had no contact in all the time since then,
until I published *Skating to Antarctica* in 1998 and got a card
asking, 'Are you the Jenny from Ward 6?' We met again, though
the negotiations took a long time, both of us protective about our
past and reluctant to put it at risk by encountering someone who
had actually *been there*. How dangerous suddenly to have discovered a witness to verify or deny our memories. Former inmates
don't keep in touch, as a rule. What I remembered was that M.
was as mad as a rat and that I lacked the talent for real madness
and was merely insolubly depressed. What M. remembered, it
turned out when we met, was that I was mad as a herring and that
she was just going through a difficult phase because the world
was all the wrong shape. Essentially, both our memories are correct. At any rate neither of us were very well or in harmony with
the world we both preferred to stay out of.

She sounded very cagey when she answered the phone. And
then astonished. She said she had feared when the phone rang
that it was Mad Bessie, who had once turned up at her house not
knowing that M. and I had known each other, and announced she
had read a novel of mine and that she loved me. M. informed her
that there was not a chance that her love would be requited
because I just wasn't that sort of person. Now Mad Bessie loves
M. because she cannot love me. Occasionally she asks her, 'How's
that bloody Jenny Diski?'

We talked uneasily about the Maudsley. Mostly we avoid confronting each other. We talk on the phone, make an arrangement,
break it. In fact, our actual memories of people and events are

remarkably similar, but our attitudes to that period are different. M. said that the time in the Maudsley was the happiest in her life, when she felt she could be completely herself and dive down in her bed with the covers over her head. She felt secure there, cared for. All the rest of her life has been a pretence at being grown up and responsible. She has an intense fondness for the patients and staff who we both remember. I have vivid memories but not exactly fondness. More of a nagging curiosity to know how it had looked through other eyes in that hothouse of permitted emotions. A kind of nostalgia for the only time I've ever felt that I was fiercely part of a group, but a strong distrust of that nostalgia. I recall the treatment, the doctors and nurses, and our fellow patients with a far cooler, perhaps more political eye than M. Why, I wonder? Because I was depressed and not mad? Because I have never got past a dislike of authority (which *they* saw as one of my problems), especially the multiply coercive, concealed as well as obvious authority of the psychiatric hospital ward and its agents? Because I'm more interested in the underlying workings of the institution than the indelible marks the place and people left on me? Because indelible marks considered in the present strike me as no more authentic or trustworthy than wistfulness? M. said it was because she is a nicer person than I am. Which is another way of putting it. She is more accommodating to the world, I think. Less resentful. Nicer, yes. But our great friendship in the loony bin was based largely on the fact that we were both spiky and awkward. Neither of us are *that* nice. With difficulty, after an hour of bantering, we made an arrangement.

'I don't like having visitors,' she said into the phone.

'OK, I won't come. What's that sound of people in the background?'

'Visitors. They're complaining about the cold. They've all got their coats on.'

'Haven't you got central heating?'

'I don't like having it on.'

'Then I definitely won't come. I hate being cold.'

'Come if you want. I'll put it on that day.'

'I don't know what the point is. It's just that you're only twenty-six miles away from here.'

'You might as well come. We could have a cup of tea.'

'It'll be a nice drive. I might as well come.'

We are, I think, really quite fond of each other.

We agreed a date. The night before, I phoned and cancelled. M. said she would come a few days later on the train and we could meet in Taunton. The night before, she called to cancel. It was a brief and rather satisfactory burst of communication between us. Enough for a while.

For the rest of the week I worked on being someone the Farmer might approve of. That is, each morning I got up at eight, had a shower (more positive than a bath), dressed for the outside world and went for a walk. I took the high road across the horse field to the leaf-carpeted path on the hill above the stream, or the low road along the watery lane at the bottom of the valley. Sometimes I went across the fields behind the farmhouse and through at least two gates. Occasionally I clambered up the steep wooded hill to the common, and then collapsed, gasping for breath and waiting for my heart to explode. Sometimes I took the gentler route to the common and sat on a fallen tree in a forest of bracken listening, when I finally figured out what it was, to the sound of leaves falling – just as much a disturbance of the thick silence as cows lowing in the distance, or a bird picking its way through the undergrowth. Once on the lower lane I heard a warm snuffling sound behind me and saw the Farmer on one of the horses from the field opposite my bedroom. The horse plodded along slow and dignified with the Farmer on top of her letting the animal take all the time she wanted. No hurry. It was the first time she had ridden in a year, she told me. She was feeling pretty stiff because of her arthritis, and the horse was old herself as well as in foal. She had got out of her field the previous spring and made straight for the most glamorous stallion on the common, in spite of being much too long in the tooth for that sort of thing. The Farmer laughed at herself and her mount, old and slow and stiff. But they both looked unhurried and contented to me as she waved and passed me by.

I tried to stay out for at least an hour, but my main aim was always to *have returned* from the walk; to get back, take off my outdoor clothes, put on my comfortable, slouchy, curling-up-in-the-chair things, and settle down at last in the living room, feeling I had fulfilled my obligation to the countryside. It was a kind of penance for the remainder of the day. Or a payment, a ticket to indolence, until the following morning when another fee would be due. Then I was free to be alone which, in some way I still cannot quite grasp, being out of doors did not permit. Aloneness means keeping still. I am a sloth, not a cat that walks alone. Metabolic? Idleness? Yes. Yes.

I went into Nether Stowey to get some petrol, and drove on to East Quantoxhead. On the way to Nether Stowey, I saw camels. Just a fleeting, peripheral sighting. Quite small, pale sand-coloured camels, long necks, humps (one hump or two?) grazing nonchalantly in a field next to the road, their heads appearing over the hedgerow like puppets. I had passed that field a dozen or so times during my stay and never noticed anything. By the time I had registered the oddness of it, I had driven past, and it was a single track road, not ideal for backing up. In any case, I was perfectly sure I imagined it. Llamas might have been reasonable. People farmed llamas, but camels were not really very likely. I'm not given to hallucinations, but I supposed that I had mis-seen something out of the corner of my eye. Or that I had better try and get out more.

I got to East Quantoxhead without trouble (I went the long way round, to Lilstock, since I knew how to get there, and then along the coastal road) and parked in the field by the church as the Farmer had explained. Then I followed a sign she said I would find that led to a path to the sea. I don't know how I followed it incorrectly. Later it was perfectly obvious which way the arrow was pointing, but I somehow managed to take the cross-country route, clambering across fences into private back gardens and a large down-sloping field planted with fir saplings in white plastic tubes which looked like a war cemetery. It crossed my mind to wonder how this could be called a path, but what did I know of country terminology? It began to rain and then it poured, sloshing down. Mud, wet grass, my hair plastered to my face and in my mouth by the rain which drained down my neck. Eventually, huffing and puffing and feeling that I had got something quite wrong, I arrived at the cliff top and the extraordinary vista of the beach below made out of great platelets of dark stone. Like man-made pavements laid in huge oblong tiles. I climbed down the rickety metal stairs set into the cliff and wandered delighted in the wild wind and bucketing rain. Even I can get pleasure from being out now and then. Sometimes bereftness is overwhelmed by exhilaration at the drama of being out in the wild and windy world. Though this was only the mildest of discomfort: the wind blowing my wet hair into my eyes and my fingers feeling a little chilly. I even found the proper path back to the car which took a quarter of the time. Radio 3 was playing Telemann's *Messiah* as I drove back, and the sun came out. A glory. I forgot to look as I passed the field where I thought I had seen camels.

The next day, inspired by the previous trip I set off to Cockercombe, feeling that I was quite getting the hang of this country thing. Out two days in a row. I hoped the Farmer had noticed. And then I hoped she hadn't.

It was bright but cold and the frost was still gleaming on the narrow road. As I approached the turn off to Cockercombe, there they were. Camels. Not hallucinating. Definitely camels. I carried on though and parked at Cockercombe. It's the highest point on the common land. A vast spread of bracken where you can stand and look out all over Somerset, stitched with fields and hedges. So I stood for a moment and took it in and then thought what a pity it was that there weren't benches set out around the countryside for those of us who had no wish to tramp about. I glanced behind me and to my right and there was a bench perfectly placed for looking out over the entire scene, hills, valleys, fields, and horizon. I was quite pleased with myself for summoning it up. First camels, now a bench. Soon I would furnish the countryside with everything I needed and it didn't. I'm very fond of camels. I used to dream about them when I was a teenager. Late one night, over hot cocoa laced with brandy a Great Poet interpreted my camel dreams as my quest for – oh I don't remember – a purpose, love, spiritual guidance, that sort of thing, I suppose. Not difficult, but the attention was pleasant.

There was a bronze plaque fixed to the back of the bench. I didn't have my reading glasses. I read:

In Memory of Alice Rose Reubens
4th July 1902 – 1st August 2002.

I thought how pleased she must have been to have lasted the full hundred years before dying, and that I might have a little walk after all in the knowledge that there was the bench to return to. I set off down the hill to have a think that resolved itself into thoughts about how to avoid the cowshit. The view was stunning but mostly, as usual, I concentrated on where I placed my feet and how far I should walk before turning back. No Coleridgeian striding along thinking up my finest poems. Not so much as a chapter heading. After twenty minutes or so, feeling pointless, I returned to sit on the bench, but when I turned to look at the plaque more closely I saw that Alice Rose Reubens' dates were actually *4th July 2002–1st August 2002*. She had lived just under a month, not just over a hundred years. I looked more carefully at the rolling hills, quilted fields, the knife-sharp horizon far off, low puffy clouds, pale blue sky, sunshine, the cloud shadow moving across the land.

On my way home I stopped in Nether Stowey and while my sausages were being wrapped I asked the butcher about the camels. She looked puzzled for a moment and then recalled. They'd been used for trekking by the sea and over the hills. She laughed at my surprised face, as if she had just seen the oddness of it. Sometimes the treks were several days long. They even did camel trekking hen parties. I visualised wild women in thongs on camels ranging the Quantock hills, and thought I wouldn't at all mind a trek on a camel.

I drove back and stopped by the camel field where two men were digging next to the house. The man who owned them lived up the track, not in the house, they told me. So I parked and walked up the rough track and into a field that was no longer a field but had been transformed into a suburban, domesticated garden. There were neat flower beds – hardy perennials on their last autumnal legs – immaculately clipped bushes, arranged symmetrical as you please, and a greenhouse. A caravan was parked at the back of the field, and in front of it on a platform three steps up from the ground, a kit-built wooden chalet with lights on inside, looking like a works office. As I approached, a small, elderly, bearded man came out to greet me warily. I told him I was a writer staying in Stillcombe and had seen the camels and wondered about them.

'They're my son's,' he said in a strong Scottish accent and invited me into a tiny living room with a wooden plaque over the wood burning stove: *The house may be small but the welcome is big.* He was watching TV and eating a sandwich. His wife was out. He didn't mind my interrupting his lunch, he said kindly, as he turned off the TV with the remote. His son lived in P. by the sea, about ten miles away, and the camels didn't trek any more because of the foot and mouth outbreak. Their enforced idleness had been so long that they would need retraining. My hopes for a Lawrence of Arabia moment in the Quantock hills faded, but he found an old brochure for me to look at. His son had been a great one for travelling, he said. I complimented him on the garden, he said he was sorry his wife wasn't in because she would have been pleased to hear it. The son or his son's wife came up every day to feed the camels, and he, the father, bedded them down every night. He didn't mind, he quite liked them, though the two llamas (I had seen llamas, after all) were mad, and raced round and round sometimes, shrieking like maniacs. They had been sent on holiday for three months (though I couldn't find out where llamas go for holidays) and were a bit better behaved. He and his wife had bought the field when they retired, from the farmer whose house was by the road. For a while they lived in the caravan, and then they built the chalet. They kept busy with the garden and the camels. He gave me his son's phone number and turned the TV back on as I left.

Rory had a broad Somerset accent. He was very happy to talk about his camels. Years ago, he had read a book called *Tracks* by Robyn Davidson, about a journey she had made across the Australian desert on a camel. Rory was thrilled by it, and set off for Australia to see the people who bred camels there.

'Aussie camels are sent to the Arabs for racing, you know,' he told me proudly.

He went from there to India, and then South Africa and drove with some friends from Cape Town back to the UK. Straight after school? I asked. No, he was about thirty then, he said, rather shifting my assumptions. He was now forty-seven, though over the phone he sounded like a much younger man. But not an ebullient one. When he answered the phone, before he knew who it was or what the subject of our conversation would be, his tone of voice belonged to someone living with regret. He had sighed hello, and then when he heard what I wanted to talk about he murmured, 'Oh yes, the camels' as if his heart might break. A cloud of melancholy hovered over our conversation.

'Life has taken a different turn,' he said when I asked whether he was going to retrain the camels and begin trekking again. I heard the voices of small children in the background.

'Yours?'

'Yes,' he said. 'We've got four now.'

'One for each camel.'

Rory grunted.

He told me how he had battled for months with the local

parish council to get permission to bring them over and start a camel trekking business. There was a good deal of local opposition to an unnatural intrusion on the environment. Camels are not a feature of the Quantock hills. Rory remembered one local man quite apoplectic about it ('Purple in the face, he was. I thought he was going to drop dead right there in the middle of the meeting.'). But Rory's determination and desire for camels in his life was formidable. The hard-headed businessmen of the District Council eventually overruled the parish council by eleven to nine because of the tourist attraction it would become. In the end, the locals came round to the camels and even approved of them. Rory went to Tenerife and brought four camels back to Somerset in a 1962 Bedford lorry, driving across Spain and then taking a boat.

'You didn't have a job?' I asked.

'Oh yes. I had a full time job. I'm an engineer. But the boss let me have time off whenever I was working with the camels. He reckoned it was better to know when he wouldn't have staff than keep losing them. I was reliable, you see.'

So Rory worked two or three days a week with the camels. It wasn't easy. Because he and his wife lived in P. he had to transport them there from his dad's field each time there was a trek booked. It was only a twenty-minute journey but it took about two hours by the time they had negotiated the lanes with the huge lorry and got the camels in and out and finally saddled up.

'It cost me three thousand pounds a year to insure them. And then it turned out I had to have a tachygraph installed in the lorry, plus an operator's licence which was five hundred a year, and I couldn't drive them until I'd gone on a course which cost two thousand quid.'

A small bubble of hilarity stuck in my throat. I tried not to laugh. Other people's difficulties aren't funny. But there was black comedy in Rory's doom-ridden voice with its unmistakable echo of Eeyore complaining that the wonderful house he'd built for himself had been carried off for firewood.

But the local vet seemed pleased to look after the camels.

'Did he know about camels?'

'Camels have the same sort of biology as any other cloven-hoofed animal. He's all right, the vet. He plays in a rock band.'

For five years Rory was taking around five hundred pounds a year on treks and doing fetes and shows. The camels were in big demand at Christmas for nativity plays, and they were regularly booked for parades in Exeter and Bristol.

'But it was terrifying, doing the parades, and going to schools. You were always anxious that they'd get out of control. The camels. The health and safety issues took the joy out of owning the camels, for me. All the crap of bureaucracy, getting permissions and that. But people came from all over the country for the treks. From London and the Midlands. There were people who wouldn't fly to go abroad on holiday, but they'd go on a camel trek in Somerset. We went along the coast, walking in a caravan by the edge of the sea. I loved it. The camels enjoyed themselves. There was something marvellous about a line of camels with the power station above them. I liked the strangeness of it.'

I asked how he knew how to keep them, and if they weren't unhappy in this climate.

'I wrote to Longleat to get information about keeping camels here, but they never wrote back. They seem pretty happy here. Well, they don't like the wet, but they go inside their stables when it rains. We put thick blankets over them in the cold. It gets cold in the desert. It's the rain they're not keen on.'

Rory and his wife Jane had their first child just as the camels arrived from Tenerife, then another one a year later.

'Jane made food for the treks,' he said. 'A packed lunch and dinner for each customer. Two meals a day. It was too much what with the kids and me being off looking after the camels a lot, and then the other two kids came along. The last one had just been born when the foot and mouth broke out. The camels were fine, but being cloven-hoofed, they weren't allowed to move from their field. The business died there and then, but the camels still had to be looked after and fed and insured and everything.'

Was he going to sell them, or give them to a zoo? Rory groaned a long, pained 'No, not if I can help it.' It sounded like something he had discussed before. He went on, getting fiercer.

'The oldest one's got an arthritic hip – you can hear it cracking when he walks. I've been thinking of having him put down, but I brought them over here and I've got an obligation to give them a decent life. I can't just get rid of them, they're my responsibility, and anyway . . . I love them.'

The way he said it, there was no doubt he did. Now he worked as a builder with a friend, renovating and converting old buildings into houses. He liked the work, it was a challenge. You've got to get on with the customers, give them what they want, but keep the old building looking right, but he'd been lucky so far.

So now that foot and mouth was over, was he going to restart the trekking business?

'No, I don't think so.' He breathed a sigh as deep as a moan. 'Before the foot and mouth thing, a friend of mine fell off and broke his leg during a trek, and he sued me. Well, I never felt quite the same again about the camel trekking business. It's like a mate of mine who built a human catapult machine. He used to take it around to fairs and fetes. Last year someone missed the safety net, maybe you read about it, it was in all the papers? So now he's being done for negligent manslaughter. It's too risky working with the public. I don't think I got the heart to do it again. I'm someone who's easily discouraged. I get downhearted. I had all kinds of warnings in the brochure, but the law lets people sue you.'

So the camels? 'They can live for forty years or more in captivity, I wouldn't want to be without them. They make my day when I visit them. What makes me really sad is that I can't have them where I live. I'd like to have them right here and keep them in a paddock by the sea and let them run around free in the sea air. In the mornings they could poke their heads through the bedroom window. That's my dream. I'm trying to raise money on the house to make it happen. I love them and I want them with me.'

The children were yelling in the background, and a woman's voice was calling. I thanked Rory for his time.

'No, it's great being able to talk about them.'

When I put the phone down, my heart ached. I looked at the obsolete brochure Rory's father had given me. It was bent and faded:

Bridgwater Camel Co. Animal Adventures in the Somerset Countryside.

Unique days out with exotic and domestic animals. Come and trek along the trails of the beautiful Bridgewater Bay. A rare opportunity to ride, walk with and talk to the animals in natural wild surroundings. The camels, namely, Tazruk, Atakor, Teifet, and Vera are chosen for their friendly temperament, while llamas Keaton and Mikey and the Hereford steers, Kooter and Mel serve as our mischievous pack animals who carry our picnic or barbecue food and shelter for groups of five or more. **This is no ordinary day out!** Animals also hired out for shows, fetes, weddings, plays, promotions etc.

In the middle was a form to be signed that said:

I the undersigned have read the Conditions overleaf and understand that Camel Trekking is an outdoor pursuit and can be dangerous.

Among the Conditions were:

You are advised to take out independent personal accident cover. The treks are NOT suitable for people with bad backs, severe arthritic conditions, pregnant women, children under 6 years old, people afraid of heights and people with grommets in their ears. These treks require an average degree of physical fitness and agility. Walking and riding is physically demanding though the pace is slow. You have been warned.

Camels are animals – although quiet, well trained and adorable they can still trip, fall, buck and bite, kick or just sit down without warning. Every effort is made to minimise these possibilities, but be warned.

Even so, I regretted that I was too late to sit between the humps of Tazruk and trek grandly up and down, over, around and across the Quantock hills.

11

ON BEING SHALLOW

Week 4

A note in my journal for 25th November. A month into my stay:

> *AM*: Put on going out clothes to go to Nether Stowey and get a newspaper, perhaps go on to Cockercombe. But it's very wet. I fed the birds outside the door while the tea brewed, and by then I'd had enough of out. I think I'll go into Taunton tomorrow. We'll see.
>
> *PM*: Dark and raining. Stayed in all day.

It rained for days. Incessantly, non-stop. Not that I minded. The two-year-old sheep (hoggets) had been collected and moved into the horse field ready to be taken to market. I watched them getting wetter and wetter with every day. The rain came down hard and vertical, like arrowheads. Thirty saturated sheep are a sight to see. When one of them gave itself a vigorous shake, it disappeared for several seconds in a cloud of waterdrops. They made me think of sopping, drenched woolly sweaters. My idea of hell. It made my skin creep. As a child I used to worry about drowning wearing a woollen sweater. Wearing the wet sweater, not the drowning, being the central cause for concern. I still can't bear to watch those English seafaring war movies with John Gregson or that nice man who died of throat cancer as captain where all the officers stand on the bridge in torrential rain, intermittently soaked by rollicking waves, drinking cocoa, wearing thick roll neck (roll neck!) Shetland jumpers with the scratchiest of duffle coats on top in case the Shetland wool wasn't hell enough. It makes my flesh scream. And I couldn't get over the sheep, covered in wet wool, standing there implacably day after day, munching grass in the pouring rain. I worried about the way they suffered. I worried more about the way they didn't suffer. I could have watched them all the time, worrying and wondering.

Another entry in my diary for that week:

1.12.03 PM
I'm in bed. Hibernating. This is the first day I haven't got up at all. I'm writing this in bed. I am completely cosy and content, but there's still a lurking fearfulness of not getting up, as if it might be the first stage of a decline into the chasm. It's what happened when I was nineteen and living in a bed-sit. I'd been

sacked [the shoe shop; swearing] and started to read *Anna Karenina*. Each morning (winter; paraffin heater) I stayed in bed longer, reading. Eventually, about halfway through the book, I didn't get up at all. Then I finished it and I still didn't get up. Then it was Christmas. I went to spend the holiday in the house of the woman who took me in when I was in hospital in Hove. By Boxing Day I was immobilized there. On my knees, bent over double on the floor of my room. Depression pain. My old shrink was called in and he sent me to the psychiatric unit of St Pancras Hospital. I blamed Tolstoy. There seemed to me to be not a single character in *Anna Karenina* who behaved decently for decent reasons. Including the self-righteous Levin. It mirrored, astonishingly I thought at the time, what I perceived about the world, or rather the people in it – including, of course, self-righteous me, though I wonder if I included myself at the time. I haven't read the book since. It may be that age and a lessening of depression would change my view of it. I'll get round to it one day, though if I was honest, I still fear a little that it was the book that sent me into that slump, and that it could again. Not rational. Well, it's a fear. Also staying in bed all day. I was inclined to think that the staying in bed also caused my decline into impossibility rather than the other way round. Not rational. When I had the last really bad depression, in 1984, I ended up sitting all day and night on my sofa, convinced that lying down would be the end. That horizontality would tip me over into irretrievable despair, not just the despair that people said (as people always say, and they're right, though it's not much help) would pass. It felt lethal when I tried to lie down. A sinking towards the final dark. I thought there must be something physiological about it, that lying down actually changed the arrangement and pressures inside my body and brain in such a way that endocrines and the whole chemical balance was altered and I would be deprived of the last drop of hope chemicals. I still think that lying down must do something. In any case, here I am in bed.

John le Carré was on the radio earlier talking about his despair. Iraq. Israel. The US. Us. Perhaps that's what kept me in bed: he was talking about having grown so much older and things being the same and worse, and the now inescapable knowledge we have that there will not be an improvement. He talks about Israel and America, but perhaps there's always an Israel and America and there comes a point at all times for people who don't have metaphysical or political faiths where the unimprovability of the world has to be faced. Despair is the nature of getting older. A sublimation of our own onrushing death. Probably. Though I'm inclined to think that the state of the world is worse than individual death. But I was despairing when I was younger. Very young. If depression is what I tend towards, then I've tended towards it for as long as I can remember. And is my being in bed now because of the incorrigibility of human beings any different from back then and my fury at *Anna Karenina*? And what about my sense that there is nothing I can do. Not just helplessness, but a knowledge that I just don't have any useful skills. And if I did, would I offer them? Or is the fact that I don't have the skills precisely my not offering them. It's still raining.

Week 5

On the 4th December there is a note:

> I haven't been out since – my trip to Cockercombe on 27th and
> meeting the father of the camel man. I now only half-heartedly
> feel bad about not going out. The continual rain allows me to stay
> indoors, so I delight in it. Sometimes I feel I'm going to bust with
> the pleasure of now: sitting, warm, alone, reading. But my dreams
> are awful. All about dispossession and having to find a place to
> live. Always packing too many things in too small a case. Having
> the wrong name. Missing the A level French exam and not being
> able to go to university. The sense of everything ruined and
> irretrievable.

Week 6

On the ninth the Farmer couldn't take it any longer and knocked
at my door to invite me for another quad bike drive up to the
common. Ozzy Osbourne had just fallen off his and was in a
coma. But the Farmer didn't do drugs or drink, though she was
very cavalier about attacking steep inclines. And the sun was
shining at last and the day deserved to be honoured. We
motored up to the common to look at her cows who were eating
the hay deposited there earlier by the Farmer's son. The
ponies – owned by Commoners but left to run wild – were
among the cows, eating the hay too. The cows seemed to accept
them. The Farmer laughed indulgently as she shooed them off.
She told me as we climbed off the quad bike that earlier she'd
discovered a ewe was missing. She had found wool littered

about, but not a single bone. What kind of animal eats bones, I asked. None, she said, perhaps the panther was back. We looked at the cows, the cows looked at us. The ponies kept their heads down in the hope we wouldn't notice they weren't cows. I told the Farmer that I was glad she had dragged me out. It was a lovely day, the view down and across the hills sparkled in the sunlight, the air was fresh – where it didn't smell, quite acceptably, of cow – and for the moment the farm was the best place to be in the world. She smiled. The farm was always the best place to be.

Week 7

Nonetheless, for the following seven days I stayed in, except for the occasional excursion to Nether Stowey for bread and peanut butter. I read Montaigne and Biencevenga on Montaigne; in between I listened to music, watched the television, slept.

Week 8

It was the annual carol service at Stillcombe church on the evening of the sixteenth. I'd said I would like to go when the Farmer mentioned it near the start of my stay. We went in her car. When she turned on the engine, the weirdest hooting, peeping and whistling began. It was the cassette player. The radio was broken and couldn't be turned off, so the Farmer chose enforced listening to a tape of the sounds of New Zealand while she drove through the Somerset countryside. It reminded her of the other best place in the world – the uninhabited island she had lived on with her sheep for a year. Exotic birds, tropical wind, crashing surf, during that drive in darkest winter through the wet country Somerset lanes. We laughed.

The old church was full. A leaflet explained that only a doorway which had been developed into a window remained of the original Norman building. The rest was bits and pieces – the chancel arch, the tower, the south aisle, the hagioscope, the font, the organ – were added in the 13th, 14th, 15th, 18th and 19th centuries. A proper old country church, which even had a drunken parson of whom it was recorded around 1800: 'Mr Reeks died last night in the horrors ... he killed himself by drinking'. Old landrovers and new 4 × 4s clogged up the little car park (not a 15th-century addition) and people squeezed out of their car doors, greeting each other, gazing up to the heavens to indicate the rain, acknowledging the visiting grandchildren, confirming that they would be at so and so's party tomorrow, next week, on Boxing Day. The Farmer and I went into the brightly lit, decorated church and suddenly I saw a community. The people the Farmer met at meetings. The Commoners who argued about the use of the common. The very old couple running their family farm from their unmodernised, unheated house without mains water. The retired townies who had bought property from farmers who had given up trying to make a living or had run out of descendants. The wealthy town dwellers who redeveloped farmhouses and barns as weekend and holiday cottages. The younger people who had bought ugly modern houses built by developers for the commuters who wanted the best of both worlds and thought they knew what that was. I hadn't seen any of this. But here it all was. A life-sized painting of country living, ancient and modern. There were lots of kids, come to stay with grandparents for Christmas. The Farmer's grandson and grand-daughter sang in the choir.

We sat in a pew near the back in the mixture of electric and candle light. The Farmer smiled and acknowledged people as they arrived, but with the reticence of a respected elder and a bit of a loner. I felt comfortable and a bit proud to be beside her. A black butterfly hibernating patiently by the window next to me was woken by the sudden warmth and light and flew drunkenly across the pews before fluttering up into the beams where it disappeared against the dark wood. The readings by the congregation were done almost exclusively by incomers, who, by the sound of their full, rounded vowels and projection all seemed to be retired actors. Not a single local accent was to be heard. The carols were strictly traditional. It was like being back in primary school as we stood to sing "Once in Royal David's City", "The Holly and the Ivy", "Silent Night", "Good King Wenceslas" and "Hark the Herald Angels Sing". The children in the choir sang "Away in a Manger" and the Farmer's grandson did his solo perfectly. He'd been very nervous. The Farmer and I smiled our satisfaction. It was the kind of service which must have been happening all over the country. I recognised the charm of it, the coming together of the community, whether religious or not, for this winter reiteration of social relations, and, except for a quiet pride in the Farmer's grandson, I was quite unmoved. It seemed to lack the sentimental power that old movies have over me. Somehow the separate reality of the individuals over-whelmed the symbolic meanings of the group activity. The underlying tensions were quite as evident as the interconnectedness. Family members disliking each other, incomers and locals, rich and not so rich. And Palestine, Iraq and all the rest of the suffering in the world going on and on while the readings and carols told us in our warm church that the world was saved. Still, like the Christmas assembly at primary school, I enjoyed the tunes. Perhaps Christmas carols are the last vestige of seasonality. We can eat tangerines and turkey all year round, but carols still only come out once a year.

The following day, just three days before I was to leave, I called into the farmhouse to thank the Farmer for taking me to the carol service and also for her kindness during my stay. She said I had been an unusual sort of visitor, but that I'd been no trouble and was welcome to return. I was very glad of that. I did a grocery order online to be delivered to my house in Cambridge the afternoon I got back. Emotionally, if not quite actually, I had already left.

What people always say about being alone for long periods is some variation on the theme of the immense and unimagined difficulty of having to confront oneself, a concealed self which lurks unnoticed below the requirements of everyday sociability. Coming face to face with yourself, is how they describe it. 'You really find out who you are', they say with a look of agonisingly acquired wisdom, implying an inevitable dark night of the soul. What I have discovered during those periods of being as alone for as long as possible, is that I am extremely good at passing the time, and taking pleasure in passing the time, reading, idling and pottering, rarely bored, hardly ever restless, sometimes miserable, often dissatisfied with myself and the world, without finding out an iota more than that about who I am, because that is pretty much what I'm like in company too. The agony of solitude passes me by, until, because social guilt and self-analysis are never far away, the lack of agony at being with myself becomes an agony of lack of self.

Why is being alone not excruciatingly painful, not a dread voyage of discovery of my unsuspected inner reaches, I brood? Where's the humbling insight into my deepest workings, the interior suffering, the anguish of the solitary soul faced with its own naked, unbearable image? Where is the suffering artist, imagination, creativity, anything? Where's the *through a glass darkly, now face to face*? The truth eventually dawns on me that this absence of painful confrontation with the shadow interior is, in fact, my moment of self-discovery. I find nothing more monstrous, chimerical, interesting, or elaborate than solipsism; certainly nothing substantial, just the echoing vacancy of a shallow vessel, an empty container, with nothing evident in it at all; its perfect hollowness is merely assuaged temporarily by inputs of reading, music or television. I hankered, when I was at home and subject to interruption and the (not excessively demanding) presence of others, for long periods of solitude 'in which to think', uninterrupted time when, at last reliably alone, I could 'be myself'. My agony is not what I find in the stillness of being alone, but what I do not find.

Again and again I strike out alone hoping that *this time* I will encounter something of substance, something deeper. But there's always the same nothing-very-much-there-at-all. A kind of reversal of that story where the brothers dig and dig looking for gold and find eventually that they have worked the land. In my version, there would be digging and digging and . . . nothing, no gold, no crop, no outcome. But perhaps that's what people actually mean when they talk about the difficulty of confronting oneself: the shock of finding nothing much there? I don't think so. Their tone of voice speaks of a discovery of something thicker and more intricate than blankness. They suggest that the busy-ness of their lives and thoughts covers up a profound inner complexity of being which silence and stillness brings into the open. For me, on the other hand, all the complexity of my outer-ness appears to be covering up is an inherent lack of inner person.

In Stillcombe drifting was as deep as it got. When I wasn't fill-ing my attention with other people's music or words, I was staring out of the window from my armchair without anything I could call thinking going on in my head. I *read* thoughts, noted them down with page references, and then waited for my own to come – as a result of what I had read, in spite of it, anything. But really there was only: what kind of day is it? Raining? Sunny? Windy? Mmm. The horses are there, or not there. The sheep near by in the upper field or not to be seen. My body warm, or in need of warming. Tea? Hungry? My mood – that wordless, thoughtless condition which functions without reference to what I would in spite of the evidence call my mind – is gloomy, easy, luxuriating in silence, anxious, joyful, despairing, or all those things in the course of a day (though always sinking towards dread as the hour of the badger arrives and the light inside drains away along with the light out in the world). Really, nothing that would distinguish me from the horses or the sheep or the wind except that I was conscious of my consciousness, could name my fleeting mood. Not much of a step up from the horses, sheep and wind to be aware of my shallowness and angst about it. Such anguish being not thought, but just an addition to the mood repertoire. All my mind could manage, apart from acknowledging the effects of the physical world on me and my shifting moods, were *chatterings*.

Memories, recent or so far distant as to be inherently unreliable, retold as stories, narrated or watched in the round, pictures and words, brief episodes leading to others. Add a great deal of insignificance: mentally rearranging the furniture, planning the next clothing purchase, wondering how long the cat is likely to live. Thinking? Sometimes it seems like thinking. You remember X, then the feeling that belonged to it, or rather the feeling you attribute to it; catch the echo of that feeling and then step across that stepping stone to the next memory, or the next episode and if you can get it, its feeling. Add conversations, movies, fictions. Just occasionally, you might, in the course of an hour or so, or an entire afternoon, suspect you had discovered some connected narrative, some series of events and responses that fed in to the being you had become. A pattern, a repetition, a process, an *explanation*. But like the burst of flavour of a single chocolate, the moment passes, what you thought you see fades and is forgotten or ungraspable. And even if it remains clear, what does it tell you actually, except that a story makes us feel some sense has been made of the episodic nature of time and experience? That arbitrary chance and the sense you have of personlessness in the watches of the night (and day) have been held at bay. Anything is better than those two possibly all important insights. All you can do with the results of this kind of 'thinking' is turn it into fiction and thank God you've found a way to avoid going to work in an office every day.

So my unsatisfactory thoughts about my unsatisfactory self had trickled on in the blissful Somerset silence. Time passing, the days rolling over into new days, the length of time left to me before I had to return shrinking so speedily that sometimes whole afternoons were given over to panic over the coming end of my sojourn and the nothing done. And I wondered about writing a book about what being alone is really like. About insubstantiality and emptiness. A book about these things – for why? To describe what is. To show. Show and tell. Why? Who do I want to convince, and of what? No one, nothing. In any case, as I imagined the book the blank pages which suit the subject so well filled with words; black marks smearing the white paper with the doing, looking, wondering, narrating that keep the underlying emptiness underlying. There is a sense in which every word I write is antagonistic to the only truth I think I have seen about myself in the world. Which is to hold still and silent until it's done. 'That passed the time,' Vladimir says. 'It would have passed in any event,' Estragon replies. That's the centre. Seeing the emptiness, not imagining it for one second to be more than emptiness, nothing more than nothing, and *allowing it*. Not to get anywhere, to achieve anything, but because there is nothing, actually, else to do. It is what it is. Empty. Nothing. It is not a position, not a tired old Sixties existentialism, nor a mystical way (though, of course, it is both). It's just the way it is inside. Why convey it? Why make narrative meaning out of it, when there is neither narrative nor meaning involved? Because it passes the time. Vladimir insists it would have passed with or without us. But doing, and the kind of doing that is writing, is an inability to come to terms with emptiness. In fact, an attempt to escape from it: to turn emptiness into substance – narrative, marks on a page. A fundamental lie. A failure at the core.

So I returned home and decided (again) that things and I were the way we were, and that things and I would go on being so, but I could at least stop fidgeting and keep still. (Another entirely novel thought struck me on the journey home: the fact that liking an article of clothing doesn't mean I have to own it. This seemed an extraordinary insight, and one that might well change my life and fortunes. It had truly never occurred to me before that liking some garment, loving it even, and having to possess it were two quite different things.) Back in Cambridge and in pursuit of keeping still and out of the way of things, I had a shed built in the back of the Poet's garden. I say shed; it's a one-roomed house really, twelve feet square, solid, cedarwood-clad, insulated, wired for light and warmth, plastered white walls, bookshelves. At the end of the garden, trains pass slowly enough to see the driver on their way to Kings Lynn, and in between, an apple tree, a wild flower patch and some new fruit trees. Arcadia, a hermit's cave, a writer's den. Actually, the back end of an urban garden, but it's somewhere else; I have to go there in the morning, it has its back to the house. It's an out of the way enough place to be on my own and quiet. And no need to walk, to take a train, or plane to get here, just up the garden path. I can fail to think here as well as anywhere far away, exotic or isolated, in the world. No need now to go any place at all.

PART THREE

ON DARKNESS

If one, settling a pillow by her head,
    Should say: 'that is not what I meant at all.
    That is not it at all.'

From The Love Song of J. Alfred Prufrock
by T. S. Eliot

12

ON BEING A TRAVEL HACK

And stay still I did. I hunkered down in my work-shed in the Poet's garden, didn't even go on holiday . . . until the following autumn when the phone rang and a commissioning editor of the *Observer* travel section asked me what and where I would like to write about for a special January issue of the magazine . . .

I *said* I wanted to spend a few days in the dark: brooding under the midday moon. A log cabin (heated, obviously) and maybe a sauna, in the far north, above the Arctic Circle. Lapland, say. That sort of thing. And I would, you know, meditate on darkness, on the loss of light in a snow-covered winter world where the sun never shines. Moody, solitary, dusk-driven stuff. *That* was what I said just off the top of my head, quite forgetting my resolve to stay still and, if I wanted the dark, turn off the light. Since everyone else they'd asked headed south to sun and sea, I was granted my not very well-considered wish.

Of course, given my new resolution, my answer to the travel editor should have been: thanks for asking, but I'm keeping still and staying in. It was what I had decided and what I wanted. A touch of Voltaire about it, I grant, though there are worse things to have echoing in your head. But alongside my wish, there was still a dormant, not yet quite quenched suspicion that some remote, strange place was required in order to achieve the perfect stillness, in which to listen to what it is I am always wanting to hear and hardly ever do. Not so much a wish perhaps as an irritation, a scratchiness of the mind and heart. I'd been in the far south during the summertime, when the sun never sets, making you wide, or rather, weird awake. Dreamy and fidgety – or as fidgety as I get – at the same time. What about life in the dark, I wondered. How would it be to sit in the dark, twenty-four-hour dark, in a snowy sunless world? What about that? Couldn't I get that by closing the curtains and keeping still? No, far off – strange – was also required. Because? Because the offer was there and I still didn't quite believe that I didn't want to go anywhere. I thought I'd better check it out.

I had never had my travel arranged for me before by a travel editor. It soon became clear that sitting still in a wood cabin for a month was not going to happen. Travel journalism is advertising for the tourist industry, and travel journalists are the means by which tour companies get to their public. It was naïve of me not to acknowledge this. Not, I was assured by the editor, that I had to give a glowing report of everywhere I went. But whatever the stated rules of neutrality of the press, I was

to be the guest of people wanting to advertise their wares
through me. Journalistic freedom is one thing, travel journalism is another. A curious moral no-man's-land. The paper got
everything free (except my services), so their negotiations were
implicitly based on offering commercial companies valuable
advertising. The idea of just going off somewhere and seeing
what, if anything, happened, began to look very unlikely. My
vague suggestion of Lapland, however, was a commercial
bull's-eye. The Swedish Tourist Board were particularly keen
to promote their part of Lapland, and tour companies in the
area had lately been started up by local people who were getting together to make an effort to bring more overseas visitors
in, having decided that tourist euros and dollars were needed in
addition to their regular source of income. An article about sitting in the middle of nowhere for as long as it took, looking at
the dark, might or might not be an exciting prospect for an
editor, but it certainly wasn't what the Kiruna Tourist Board in
charge of getting people to visit Swedish Lapland wanted. I
was given one week and a schedule which had me staying in a
different place, sampling the offerings of one or more companies, every day. As a sop to my wish to keep still and quiet, the
schedule was amended, after a lot of negotiation, to two whole
nights in one place (though it was up and off at eight a.m. the
second morning to get on with seeing everything on offer). My
daydream of daydreaming in the dark faded, but the thing was
arranged. I knew I'd made a mistake in saying yes, but it was
too late to get out of it. Then I was told that for half the time
I would be accompanied by a photographer. What else, after

223

all, is a travel magazine article for but lovely photographs? Not solitary, then, as well as not still. Well, a week wasn't long. At least it would be dark.

'Oh, it's never dark up here,' Per Nils laughed as he drove me from the railway station in Kiruna to his cabin in Övre Soppero forty miles north. 'We have the snow. Northern lights. The moon for two weeks of every month. In December, you can go deep into the forest in the middle of the night and see without a torch,' Per Nils said proudly. 'The south of Sweden where they have pavements and cities – that's where they go crazy in the winter. There is dark and madness. But they think we all walk round like this,' he put his hands out in front of him and shut his eyes like a child playing blind man's buff. There was no other traffic on the road and we weren't driving fast. Even so my muscles tensed ready to grab the wheel until the pantomime was over.

So, not still, not solitary, and now, it turned out, not even dark. Nevertheless, the following morning the sun didn't rise until eleven a.m., and then only barely. It remained just visible above the horizon, sidled west for an hour or so, and had disappeared by two p.m. By which time, the moon was high in the sky, and, Per Nils was right, it shone huge and brilliant: the snow dazzled in its glow, the stars, fat white balls of light, blazed, and the snaking aurora borealis added its weird greenish gleam to make the darkness startlingly bright. Snowlight. Snoonlight. It was too eerie to be a disappointment, even for someone who wanted blanketing obscurity.

Per Nils, his wife Britt-Marie, the first of my hosts, and everyone else I was to meet were Sámi. Lap, Laplander are Finnish names for them which they do not like. Sámi is their name for themselves in their own language, and Sápmi is their traditional territory, not Lapland – Finnish again. My ignorance of the Sámi people was total. But Britt-Marie was dedicated to teaching me and anyone else who would listen about the Sámi. This included teaching Sámi children, who like most of the children of indigenous people (or, I suppose, most children everywhere) are no longer learning traditional skills and culture.

Over a supper of reindeer stew (dark, strong, gamey and delicious), potatoes and lingonberry sauce (brilliant scarlet, slightly sweet, brightly sharp), Britt-Marie and Per Nils got me up to speed on what was most important to them. The Sámi are indigenous people of the Arctic Circle whose territory over the centuries has been carved into national borders by Sweden, Norway, Finland and Russia. Their traditional lands have been appropriated and reappropriated, while the Sámi just got on with their lives: which is herding reindeer. They are not a warlike people. They had their own language, their own reindeer-dependent way of life. But they had no written language, with the result, Britt-Marie explained, that no documents were drawn up, nothing on paper, nothing signed, so they had no legal rights as defined by literate society. Not like the Maoris, for example, in New Zealand. The Swedish Sámi have been given the right to make their annual treks into Norway, and the European Union insisted on their right to have their own parliament in Kiruna, both rights by gift rather than by right. In any case, everyone I spoke to said that the Sámi parliament did nothing but argue and split into factions without achieving any great benefits for the Sámi people. The members of the Sámi parliament became, in other words, politicians.

'We are not Swedish. We are Sámi,' Britt-Marie explained. She and everyone else talked about 'the Swedes' as a completely different group living in the same country. Colonisers, to their way of seeing things, who lack sensitivity to the needs of the Sámi way of life. In Stockholm they talk of the Sámi with a kind of amiable contempt.

'Ah, you are going to stay with the Sámi? Well, think of only one question you want to ask. You will have to wait such a long time for an answer.'

To the sophisticates of Stockholm, the people up north are slow, taciturn folk; small, outlandish people who live an ancient, unnecessarily difficult life in quaintly elfish brightly coloured clothes at the frozen top of the world. Certainly both Per Nils and Britt-Marie were short, and there's not very much beige or taupe to be seen, but it's hard to think of anyone less taciturn than Britt-Marie whose capacity for talk was gargantuan, and Per Nils' square, strong body was topped by a face scored with deep lines that looked as if they had been carved out by laughter. He seemed permanently on the verge of hilarity, even when he absented himself from the conversation by appearing to be asleep on the sofa while Britt-Marie expatiated on Sámi history and culture.

The Sámi people are reindeer herders; not nomadic, but transhumant. They have settled villages, several of which make up a single clan, where they live in permanent houses, but they follow the annual migration of their vast herds of reindeer, which head north to graze the same Norwegian pastures every May, and return to the Swedish forests in the autumn to eat the moss and lichen they forage for beneath the blanketing snow. Thousands upon thousands of animals saunter north and wander back south, like a tidal sea of ruminants, season after season. The clan, called a *siida*, is defined as a reindeer-owning group of related families and have cabins close together in the summer grazing land. In Swedish law, only Sámi are allowed to herd reindeer. Britt-Marie's *siida* in the Övre Soppero area owned about sixteen thousand animals, though when I asked how many she had, Britt-Marie looked severe and wanted to know how much money I had in the bank. It's an interesting question, because I've often wondered about that particular reticence, particularly recently, in a society that has become reticent about almost nothing else. Why, unless you are concealing income for tax reasons, not tell people how much you have in the bank? I've never quite got why that information is so secret. But then my idea of maintaining my privacy is to write books about myself, and make up others (also, you might argue, about myself) as a guarantee of self-concealment. Don't ask me about the logic of that, just believe me when I say it works. Ask me how many reindeer I've got and I'll tell you like a shot – and what more will you really know about me then?

Still, however disinclined Britt-Marie was to discuss her own reindeer holdings, she told me that a family needs about two hundred animals purely to subsist. A family of four should own five hundred or more to have a surplus with which to pay for the extras demanded by the modern world. (Houses, Swedish taxes, utilities, snowmobiles and petrol to run them, mobile phones, computers. All the things that need to be paid for with cash, not reindeer meat, skins, or tools carved out of antler.) Every man, woman and child has his or her own reindeer and infants are given their share of animals at birth. When reindeer calves are born, intricate cuts are made on their ears which indicate to which clan, family and individual they belong.

'The Swedish government is concerned about the troubles and rights of indigenous people everywhere except in Sweden. They don't like to think about us,' Britt-Marie complained. 'Now we can't survive just by herding reindeer.'

The value of reindeer meat is dropping because the Swedish company that used to buy the Sámi's surplus carcasses is buying Russian reindeer sold at knockdown prices to get into the market. And the Sámi are falling foul of EU rules about slaughter. They used to kill their own animals, but now, except for the ones they kill for their own consumption, the reindeer have to be trucked to abattoirs. Per Nils' normally bright face grew dark.

'It stresses the animal. Makes the meat bad. We have our way, our rules about killing the reindeer. Respectful, gentle. I was in Finland last year and in a restaurant I ordered Finnish reindeer,' he made a disgusted face, and flung something invisible but foul out of his fingers, away from him. 'I had to spit it out. It tasted bad. They don't know how to kill the reindeer properly. The animals are frightened, the meat is spoiled. And we have a very special relationship with our animals. We know them. Each one.

They help us to live. We care for them and kill them so that they die calmly. But if they will have a bad end, and we have to let them be sent in trucks for miles to be killed by machines, then we can't allow ourselves to care about them. It changes how we are with our animals.'

He shook his head.

'In Finland, they make jokes about us. They make that foolishness about Santa Claus to get rich tourists and they make us dress up as Santa's elves.'

Now the Sámi of this area around Kiruna have decided that the answer is to get tourists in. They want their money, but also hope that if people know about the Sámi and their way of life, there will be pressure on governments to take measures to preserve their way of life from the encroachments of modernity. Additionally, having their own *siida*-based tour companies means that old, lost skills, like skiing, carving, making clothes and shelter from skins and driving reindeer sleds can be re-learned, and young people trained in the knowledge that they will be able to earn a living from being Sámi without having to leave the area and depend entirely on modern occupations. The Sámi traditionally followed the reindeer herds on skis and selected young reindeer to be trained to pull sleds. The Swedish (not Sámi) tour operations offer visitors sled rides pulled by husky dogs. Dogs were never used by the Sámi. Britt-Marie disapproves. Moreover, in the last ten years or so Swedish tourists have taken to their Arctic Circle territory as a snow playground. They arrive at weekends and ride snowmobiles around in the birch forests. The Sámi used their ski tracks to make encircling paths in the forest around the herds, which the reindeer recognised and did not cross. Now the tourists' snowmobiles make new contingent tracks which confuse the herds who cross the traditional paths and wander in a much larger orbit. So skis are no longer efficient for patrolling the herds, and the Sámi too are forced to use snowmobiles. They need more cash to pay for them, their upkeep and running costs, they need cash to pay taxes, and they need to get control of a tourist influx that they can't prevent, especially with the super-chic ice hotel being blown by machine into existence every winter. So as well as reindeer herders they are becoming modern business people. The tourists (apart from the easy-riders) want the old ways, the Sámi want the old ways. Perhaps taking charge of their own tourism industry is the only chance for old cultures to survive. Perhaps also, I wondered, the old ways can't survive the lure of profit and the gaze of tourists, or even the gaze of indigenous people noting the gaze of tourists, without freezing into performance. Britt-Marie and others shrug distractedly in answer to my tentative question. What else are they to do? they say. They have to try. And, of course, it isn't my business.

Britt-Marie and Per Nils said goodnight and went home to their children in their house in the village. I stayed in the visitor's cabin with a wood-burning stove still blazing in the bedroom. Mark, the photographer, volunteered for the round turf hut fifty yards away, offering graciously to be the one that had to brave the icy open air to get to the cabin if he needed to use the loo in the night. I only had to open a door into the rigour of the unheated lobby and bathroom. Before they went, we checked the thermometer: it was minus twenty-seven degrees. That is very cold.

I have been in New York State when it was minus twenty. But this was colder, and I didn't know what I was doing here. I went out to see off my hosts. Just a moment in the cold which felt hard, implacable and shocking. Exhilarating more than shocking at that moment, knowing I was about to get back into the muggy warmth. Still, I stood a few more minutes out there after they left, feeling, at last, solitary in the night. This was the nearest I had got so far to my plan of keeping still in the dark. The snow gleamed, the stars hung low and bright in the gigantic sky, and the garish, dayglo green aurora borealis wiggled and waved like a Hollywood belly dancer, too kitsch for my taste. Darkness, as Per Nils said, was overwhelmed by other kinds of light than the sun, and although the silence of a snow-covered world was potent, as the sound of the car faded into the distance my hope of stillness was lost in ambivalent thoughts stirred up by meeting Britt-Marie and Per Nils, by the hard, cherished life of the Sámi people, by all the meetings and stories to come.

The next morning, over reindeer-blood pancakes sparked up with more lingonberries, Britt-Marie instructed me in the daily life of the Sámi with visual aids – particularly a large doll who stood in for Sámi babies, but had one grotesque lazy eye that remained closed in an uncanny wink, which Britt-Marie ignored in the enthusiasm of her exposition, but which I suspected that Per Nils quite appreciated. The morning wore on. The world outside grew a little lighter and then began to grow a little darker. My education continued. Reindeer ear markings. Symbols on birch and antler artefacts. Silver charms on cradles to keep the evil spirits from stealing the infants. Reindeer-skin clothing for winter herding. Firesticks. The ubiquitous knife carried on the belt of every man and boy that was used for everything, the survival machine. How to kill, skin, and preserve meat.

Just before lunch, a woman arrived with a message for Britt-Marie. She was a relative, a member of the *siida*. We were introduced and shook hands formally. Britt-Marie had just started to explain *joiking* to me.

'It is a special sort of song a Sámi sings when he or she is inspired.'

It turned out our visitor was happy to give an example. She was a short woman in her thirties, blonde and sturdy, though how sturdy was difficult to tell under all the layers of jumpers, and thick-padded outside gear. She placed herself about a foot in front of me, four-square, feet about eighteen inches apart, hands on hips, her head a little forward and her bright blue eyes intently staring into mine, and sang a brief tuneless song of repeated sounds: *loy-loy-loy* interspersed with what seemed like a few words in Sámi.

'There,' she said with a brisk highly satisfied nod when she had finished.

'Do you want to know what she sang?' Britt-Marie asked with a slight smile on her face.

'Of course.'

'She sang: "Twenty-nine Jennys can't compete with one Sámi woman"'.

The younger woman laughed out loud, with a broad grin of triumph on her face but held her pose, ready for an argument if I chose. But I had no doubt that she was right. And not twice times twenty-nine Jennys would have dared argue with the proposition.

'I go now,' she said, and spoke for a moment to Britt-Marie in businesslike Sámi.

'Thank you for the *joik*,' I said.

She nodded again and left.

Mark wandered around taking photos, fretting at Per Nils about wanting to take pictures of large numbers of reindeer. There were only a handful in his corral. 'Don't worry,' Per Nils said. 'You will see plenty reindeer.' But Mark was worrying. He was not having much luck taking photos of me. I don't like being photographed. And anyway, I'd spent the morning inside with Britt-Marie. He insisted, finally. Per Nils took us around in his car until Mark had found a suitable backdrop: an empty straight road, a wood of birch trees, street lights and frosted snow. I did as instructed and stood stiffly here and there along the road, in the woods, walked toward and away (my preference) from the camera. I was not capable of relaxing, as I kept being instructed, in front of a camera lens. The cold was astonishing. The previous night I had needed, try as I might to avoid it, to pee. I had opened the door on to the unheated front lobby where the bathroom was and met a wall of iced cold that felt like an explosion. The dying remains of the wood burning stove kept the room behind my back still warm. I hadn't really taken in the degree of cold until then. Now, standing having my photo taken, though bundled up in layers of silk underwear, cashmere jumper and windproof jacket, the cold made itself known to me again. Frozen air without a hint of moisture burned my face, pained my nostrils and

233

the back of my throat as I breathed in. No wind, just palpable air, completely dry, completely arctic, iced steel, like inhaling knives. Per Nils, acting as chauffeur, stood and watched.

'It's very cold,' I wailed, watching the white words cloud the air.

Per Nils made an equivocal face.

'Mmm, cold. Yes. Not *very* cold.'

This was not what I meant at *all*.

Lunch was thick reindeer slices roasted on birch twig skewers over a roaring open fire in the centre of the traditional circular hut. My hosts had built it on their land to show tourists how the Sámi existed when they lived out in the forest with reindeer. We sat on reindeer skins and wrapped the blood-dripping chunks of meat, crispy on the outside, in flat bread. As delicious as a steak sandwich can get. Very, very good. And washed down with lingonberry juice without which, in some form, no meal, I now understood, would be complete. The fire blazed and crackled. Bits of bright burning ember floated up towards the open top of the hut passing through the metal rack on which reindeer meat could be laid for smoking, and out through the hole, lighting up the morose, darkening sky. I was content in the warmth, scented with burning birch wood and a mini-fireworks display. I would have been happy to stare into the fire and follow the embers for the rest of the week. Daydreaming, staring. But we had places to go and things to see, so I was ordered back to reality and Per Nils kicked snow into the fire to make it safe. When we left, my face and front was suffused with warmth, but the backs of my thighs, I noticed as I got ready for an outing, were frozen, numb and white like dead meat with the cold. I hadn't bothered with long johns. I put some on before we went out, after slapping my thighs like a penguin to get the circulation back.

Britt-Marie took us to the local Baptist church which doubled as the area's hotel for Baptist pilgrims and a community restaurant. It was something we had to see, she said. And so religion reared its head. The Sámi originally had a shamanistic religion, a belief in the spirits of natural things in their world that could be summoned up by incantation and drumming when advice or forgiveness was required. There were copies of the drums the shamans used (reindeer skin, birch wood), but only two of the original great drums were known to exist, one of them – of course – in the British Museum. No one I spoke to could (or would) give me very detailed information about the old religion.

'Oh, we've forgotten it,' they insisted, and as often as not looked away as they began to talk about another topic. Even Britt-Marie, the loquacious pedagogue of Sámi ways, did no more than show me examples of a drum. When I asked specifically about the spirits and their stories she said she didn't know. 'It's what we have lost,' she said. 'We don't know any more. It's forgotten.'

Swedish Lutheran missionaries began to arrive in the eighteenth century. They burned the drums and burned the shamans at the stake. Being, as ever, a peaceful people, not given to war, the Sámi converted, and Sámi society went the way converted indigenous societies so often go. By the middle of the nineteenth century, Lars Levi Laestadius, a Lutheran minister and botanist who had grown up in Swedish Lapland, found Sámi life riddled with 'misery and alcohol' and brought about the Laestadian Revival, an especially grim, pietistic form of Lutheranism that emphasised humanity's inherent sinfulness and the horrors of eternal damnation, demanding confession, penitence and a rigidly conformist morality of its believers. The Sámi people produced two generations of stern Christian puritans who drew a veil over the old religion, and enforced sexual abstinence outside Christian marriage, teetotalism, and dumb obedience to parent and pastor. It was, Britt-Marie said, a very strict way of life to be a child of her parents' generation. Now, as everywhere, people were questioning the old ways (the *new* old ways) and looking back at the Sámi past. But if they were rediscovering the spiritual beat of the old life, they seemed to be keeping it to themselves. It was impossible to tell if the evasion I found when I asked for details of their shamanistic religion was really ignorance or simply none of my business. I got the feeling that it was more private than lost. Why not? No more my business than the number of reindeer in their bank account, and why risk another sort of destruction of their ways, by anthropologists and psychologists this time, perhaps?

But the world is a very small place. No disdain for cliché can dispel that truth. The Baptist church Britt-Marie wanted me to see was built by a powerful new movement in Sámi spiritual and social life. It is the same one that takes us to war against unbelievers, calls The Other 'terrorist', and makes felt sincerity the mark of truth. Evangelical fundamentalism is a new force among the young. Happy-clappy believers in the Bible's literal truth and the power of being born again in Christ have arrived and converted the grandchildren of the Laestadian moralists. Britt-Marie and Per Nils, the intermediate generation who rejected their parents' Victorian values take different sides. Britt-Marie is keen on this energetic new smiley religion that incorporates the nice cosy bits of the old life with a new cement of belief in redemption for the faithful, while Per Nils keeps his wary distance. He drove us to the Baptist church and then waited outside in the afternoon dark. When I asked if he was coming in, he shook his hand at me. 'I don't care about God,' he murmured, rolling himself a cigarette. 'I don't care for this,' he waved the back of his hand at the building we were about to enter, and at everything and everyone in it. Britt-Marie was unfazed. So long as he gave lifts, Per Nils wasn't required to take on her project in its entirety.

We were greeted by the minister whose inclusive, non-judgemental smile was no more than a whisker away from a smirk. Have I made it clear? I don't like belief systems and even less like those that peddle self-righteousness. I have no doubt the minister was a sincere man, but I am not as impressed by the idea of sincerity as the sincere seem to be. He took us to see the chapel. The whole place had been built by believers, with rooms and saunas (strictly his saunas and hers saunas) for groups from all around and far away to come and benefit from a northern baptism.

In the corridor I was transfixed (the precise word) by a large poster on the main notice board. It was a coloured drawing of

Christ being crucified. Called, I think, *The Agony Of Our Lord*. In this case *agony* meant what it said, in the most modern sense. Not so much a struggle as intense pain. All around the edge of the central drawing, with arrows indicating which part of the torso and limbs were being detailed, were inset diagrams of the physical events occurring in each part of Christ's body during his time on the cross. It was, literally, an anatomy of crucifixion. I've since looked up that phrase on the web and found an article on the website of the Holy Trinity Greek Orthodox Church in Tulsa, Oklahoma, taken from the *Journal of the American Medical Association* (JAMA Vol. 255 No. 11 March 21, 1986) called 'On the Physical Death of Jesus Christ'. It explains the physiological results of flogging, carrying the cross the two and a half miles, nails through the wrists and feet, and hanging on the cross. Diagrams just like the ones on the poster show in cross-section the route of the nails into the nerves and musculature; the distortion of the rib-cage is pictured constricting the ability to breathe; an abdominal section depicts the route and perforations of the major organs made by the spear in the side. The article has a concluding pro-resurrectionist paragraph which did not, presumably for reasons of space, appear on the wall-poster of the church in Övre Soppero:

> Thus, it remains unsettled whether Jesus died of cardiac rupture or of cardiorespiratory failure. However, the important feature may be not how he died but whether he died. Clearly, the weight of historical and medical evidence indicates that Jesus was dead before the wound to his side was inflicted and supports the

traditional view that the spear, thrust between his right ribs, probably perforated not only the right lung but also the pericardium
and heart and thereby ensured his death (Fig 7). Accordingly,
interpretations based on the assumption that Jesus did not die on
the cross appear to be at odds with modern medical knowledge.

The poster skipped the theological conclusion and just dis-
played the evidence of agony. It was an interesting interpretation
of the doctrine of Christ suffering for our sins. When these guys
said suffering they meant *suffering*. Gory, gaudy physical suffering. Something you could get your eyes and teeth into. All the fun
of the post-mortem, and the comic book and oh, imagine, go on,
you know you want to, imagine the pain. The true religion? I
don't know, but truly a religion for our times.

The chapel turned out to be the underside of the sado-
masochistic lip-smacking. Kitsch to the point of pain. A gaily
though badly painted *Sound of Music* backdrop of lush mountain
pastures and a waterfall led the eye down to the baptismal bath.
Baptismal swimming pool actually, eight-foot square and neck
deep. In my mind, I recall leprechauns and garden gnomes hanging their rods over it, hoping to catch a soul or two, but perhaps
my memory is jesting with me. The changing room for baptismal
bathers was a miniature Swiss wooden chalet – I am not making
this up – beside the pool. Glass windows, with flowery curtains
that could be drawn by those changing into bathing suits showed
the inside with a little table and chairs and the walls painted with
trompe l'œil shelves and kitchen appliances. It was the hut
Goldilocks found in the woods, the Seven Dwarfs' forest home.

239

Heigh ho, heigh ho, it's off to God we go. Human beings had to crouch to get through the small door (Alice in Wonderland?) and then, changed in order to *change*, they exited through a door that led them directly down steps into the baptismal water, where, I suppose, the minister waited with his everlasting smile to greet them in the name of the Lord. Theme park Christianity had taken over from authoritarian Lutheranism, though I dare say it was as authoritarian in its way. The young, according to Britt-Marie and the minister, were joining in droves. The Arctic Circle as everywhere. Born-again true believers are running the most powerful countries in the world, why wouldn't they be up here, too? They incorporated Sámi life into this nonsense by building everything out of local wood and reindeer antlers. They 'respected' Sámi life and adapted Christianity, as missionaries have always done, to local customs and rhythms. But in the end the bad faith of bad faith shows through in the tawdry tat, and disrespects the aesthetics of the people it is converting. It was more depressing than sitting in the dark for a week could ever be and not, absolutely not, what I meant at all.

The next day on our itinerary read in brisk military fashion:

> Out to Nils Torbjörn Nutti in Jukkasjärvi. Britt-Marie will drive you there. A small village outside Kiruna. You'll meet Nils at about 10.00. Going out with reindeers to see the reindeers in their winter habitat. A visit to the Jukkasjärvi church with its famous altarpiece sculpted by Bror Hjört and the organ made out of birch

and reindeer horns by Lars Levi Svonni. In the afternoon there will be a visit to see the site where the ice hotel is being built. Nils will take you there. Transfer to Giiron Siida, Håkan Enoksson, snowmobile tour to Buollanorda, dinner and accommodation in Lavvu.

There were too many words with which I was unfamiliar for me to get much of a picture. Place names and people's names were hard to distinguish – was Giiron Siida a place or a person? Ditto Håkan Enoksson. Mark and I admitted to each other that another church visit was one too many, unique altarpiece and organ notwithstanding. Mark had already been to the ice hotel a year or so before, stayed there and taken photos, though we perked each other up a little by hoping that seeing it being built would be more interesting. For him a photo opportunity; for me, an ice hotel being built. The snowmobile tour of Buollanorda (where ever that was) sounded fun, and then it was off, presumably in a car, to Lavvu for the night (where ever that was). But *what about sitting still under the midday moon and brooding quietly?* To me, low-blood-pressure, slow and slothful creature that I am not unhappy to be, the itinerary didn't describe a day, but a couple of weeks' activity. And even then I would cry off most of it and beg to be allowed to keep still where I was. Apart from the fun ride on the snowmobile, of course. And all in the charge of a businessman who wanted to show off his wares. I'd thought all these things before I left and teetered on the edge of cancelling the whole thing. Now I'd committed myself, it was a matter of doggedly getting through it. Doing what I had to do, getting out

241

of it what I could, and finding some space for being on my own in the snow and dark. Apart from the fun ride on the snowmobile, of course.

Jukkasjärvi was shrouded in a wet, dove grey mist when we arrived. This was not weather, but the effect on the whole area of the great machines that were manufacturing snow out of the dry air and electricity, and blowing it out to build the ice hotel. The church awaited us in the tiny square where the handover from Britt-Marie to Nils Torbjörn was to take place, and the wooden offices of *Nutti Sámi Siida* (the tour company) was the only other building. Nils Torbjörn Nutti (the man, Nutti being his *siida* name) came out to greet us. He looked very businesslike, rather severe. Perhaps shy, or maybe fighting a resistance to servicing outsiders. Still, it was his business.

He took us to his office and over coffee we all thawed while he told us how for the five years from 1989 to 1994 the winter weather had been very bad. In the Arctic Circle, among reindeer-herding people, this means not enough snow – as indeed was the case this year; at any rate, it was late in coming. The reindeer need a deep blanket of snow covering the ground. It keeps the moss they eat warm and alive, and they nuzzle down through the deep snow to chomp on it, fresh and nutritious, throughout the winter. If there is only a light covering of snow, the ground freezes, the moss dies, and is anyway inaccessible to the reindeer: there's nothing their big, soft, wet noses can do to break through the ice. They starve. If they starve, the Sámi starve, so Nils

Torbjörn and everyone else had to bring the weaker animals into the corrals and feed them for those five years, and probably this year too. The feed cost money, and even with nurturing the more feeble ones the reindeer died in large numbers, so money was already short. A circle of desperation. Then the Ice Hotel arrived. Rich folk from around the world were charmed by the ice-sculpted rooms (ice reindeer coming through the ice walls), by the vodka bar made of ice, the glasses made of ice, movies shown on a screen made of ice, the beds made of ice. Very few lasted an entire night in their ice room – there are proper warm cabins available for those who give up after an hour or two of being charmed and frozen. In the morning the hardier tourists are rewarded with a hot toddy in bed. Advertising companies arrived to film two minute commercials that took weeks to make and all the talent of the world's greatest directors and designers. The previous year some fashion glossy did a shoot there, and for several days Jukkasjärvi (church, wooden offices, square, reindeer corral, scattered houses) was honoured with the sight of a gaggle of supermodels slipping around in high heeled ugg boots (possibly I made that up) dashing from one warm sanctuary to another. At least Nils was told they were supermodels. In the first place he didn't know what they looked like, and in the second, bundled up, they didn't look like anything.

'Everyone looks same in fur and down jackets. Couldn't see faces.'

Then multinational businesses began to send their executives on incentive weeks. Ice hotel a rugged but luxurious treat, and then the trials and tribulations of nature to mirror the rapacious, icy world of commerce and bond the warriors of capitalism. They needed someone to organise outward bound activities, sled rides, nights in the wild. That was when outsiders brought in husky dogs, because business people neither knew nor cared about the authenticity of their experience. Five thousand rich people a year were arriving in Jukkasjärvi. Nils Torbjörn saw that local people could make the money that was flying around instead of the Swedes and/or European consortia raking it in. He started his company offering all sorts of short and longish trips and vicarious ethnic experience (experience being the key word in eco-tourism).

'For us it is stupid things, but they bring money,' he said, not happy about his English but vastly better than my Sámi or Swedish, and looking at me taking notes dutifully – the useful idiot and enemy. I felt like both and wanted to feel like neither. The various *siida* got together and formed an organisation of mutual interest. Their tours would counter the influx of outsiders taking the money that the Sámi needed, and if they were authentic, it would also keep old skills alive – in some cases, re-establish them, because young people would have to be trained to be guides. Nils Torbjörn and his colleagues were well aware of the risk they were taking with their ancient existence, but the world had caught up with them and their ancient existence was being eaten away by the effects of modernity and global warming. It was, he made clear, a matter of survival and survival is something the Sámi know a good deal about.

I was part of the chain of necessity, a link to the thousands of rich newspaper readers who want authentic experiences for a few days, and are prepared to pay large sums of money to feel that they are living a life in nature with those who know how. It's the twenty-first century version of big game hunting. Just like big game hunting, it preserves the game (or the ethnic group), but at a peculiar price of turning them into *faux* domesticated creatures, managed, kept within bounds, allowed to survive so that the big white hunters can come and play. In the case of indigenous peoples, it makes museums of culture in the way that the round hut built by Britt-Marie and Per Nils next to their house was an exhibit, built purely for visitors to sit in and imagine they were living a natural outdoor life. It was better than losing everything and an entire culture seeping into modernity and disappearing. The Sámi people I spoke to thought so, hoped so, and I just don't know. But then it's not for me to say.

13

ON BEING VERY COLD

And so began the coldest and one of the longest twenty-four hours of my life. I may have mentioned before that I dislike being cold. I always have. As a child I huddled next to the radiators in the flat and the corridors I played in, most of my games being suited (or adapted) to keeping as close to a source of warmth as possible. Cold is always bleak. The twin of dereliction. I swathe myself in bags filled with wheat hotted up in the microwave; I take baths to suck the warmth deep into my marrow then wrap myself in oversize cardigans that entirely enclose me to keep the heat in. Even as I write, in May with summer promised in a blue sky and apple blossom, I feel my feet beginning to chill and stop writing this to reach for a pair of cashmere socks. There is no contentment without warmth. Cold is a kind of internal desert, a terrorism enacted on me by the world. I can't account for it, except that I was born and bred with central heating or that I was born and bred for central heating. Someone suggested to me that my devotion to smoking was an addiction to the warmth of the glowing tip and the inhaled heat of the smoke. It doesn't sound that far-fetched to me.

But while I intensely dislike the cold, I also hate being constricted by too much clothing. Light loose tiers are fine, but I can't bear fitted, figure-hugging, tight layers that make movement difficult and me always aware of being swaddled. Feeling bundled up, just thinking about it, makes me want to howl and rip everything off. Ideally I require a warm, very warm, room; light, comfortable clothing in a pleasing fabric (cotton, silk, unscratchy wool) that hangs loose, and perhaps something pliant and easy that I can drape over myself for extra comfort. A soft shawl or a fleece blanket, say. A duvet is perfect. But that would require me to stay in bed or at least curl up on a sofa. Not at all an idea that fails to appeal to me; indeed, I have just described my most desired condition, but some of the time it's impractical. In Jukkasjärvi it turned out to be impossible. Bundled up is what it takes not to have bits of yourself fall off you if you are going outdoors for any length of time, and it seemed that I was.

Nils Torbjörn took us downstairs to a basement room full of shelves and racks of clothes. He sized me up and handed me a pile of garments: all-in-one snowsuit, two pairs of socks, lined fleece and reindeer skin gloves, boots and hat. I began to unzip my windproof jacket and was wondering about the decorum of taking my trousers off in front of Nils and Mark.

'No, no, put on over.'

I pulled the insulated snowsuit over my trousers (which were already uncomfortably over my long johns) and then, tucking the bottom of my windproof jacket down inside, struggled to get my arms into the top half and shrug it over my shoulders. The restrictiveness of the layers of fabric made me want to scream. Nils looked impatient. I found the zip and after a good many failed attempts managed to engage the two sides of the zip and close the suit over everything I was wearing (cotton jersey vest, silk thermal long-sleeved vest, big baggy cashmere sweater, fleece scarf, cotton knickers, silk long johns, cotton moleskin trousers, two pairs of cashmere socks) which I had thought more than enough for any kind of weather. It was, in fact, as Mark said (also struggling into his snow clothes), as if we had been wearing nothing but lawn cotton pyjamas until now. Simple bending was already impossible, so I dropped to the floor to pull on two pairs of woollen socks as thick as my fingers and coarse as pan scrubbers over my own two pairs, and then dragged on boots which were soldered rubber, calf-high, double-felt lined and zipped up underneath the trousers which were then zipped down and poppered at the ankle. Then I was stuck, lacking any kind of mobility, mummified into clumsiness that made me incapable of re-arranging my own body to raise myself up from the ground. I flopped into laughter. I was already finding it too difficult being a human being trying to survive an afternoon of cold weather, and I hadn't gone out yet.

Nils watched my performance with a look of great weariness on his face. This was the kind of thing he was letting himself in for. Eventually, he bent down and offered me a hand up. It had taken over twenty minutes to get this far. He picked up the hat and gloves that I dared not lean down for. The hat was reindeer skin lined with thick fur. It flapped down over my ears and buttoned under the chin, to keep the ears from freezing and the hat from flying away. The front had a fur flap that was turned up against the crown. I had a lot of trouble with the button on the chin which seemed too big for the buttonhole. I might have been a toddler. My shame was complete when Nils buttoned it for me. He looked down at my gloves but I pulled those on briskly (well, the first one was brisk, the second took a while to get on with my other mittened hand), zipped and popped them closed at the wrist to show that I wasn't a complete incompetent. Nils didn't look convinced. In the end I was kitted out in a devilish black and red outfit (designed, I suppose, to be visible in the snow, but making me look more like a boy racer than I could have imagined beyond my fiftieth year), my face enclosed in a scratchy fur halo and my feet encased in boots that made me walk lifting my legs with great deliberation like a post-war movie robot. Mark was a little more adept at dressing himself, but not much. We stared at each other. He was a tall and entirely shapeless ball, I was exactly the same but shorter. I don't know how the supermodels had looked, but it was clear that any hope I might have harboured of becoming a vintage glamour model was gone. The issue of vanity, for all my ever-increasing years, is never far away. It wasn't just the photographer waiting for a great snap of me for the colour magazine; even on my own, in a bathysphere, I would have despaired at the sight of myself. Whatever inner beauty I may possess is not of the slightest interest to me. Outer beauty is what I mind about. In temperate climates, even with the effects of ageing and the loss of skin-deep beauty, a degree of *outer* outer beauty can be achieved by a large enough expenditure on clothes. Not in Jukkasjärvi. A large enough expenditure can keep you warm. Better to look like a dumpling than die of cold, you might think. Maybe.

On the way to the start of our sledding adventure, we stopped off at the church. Mark and I suggested that we might give it a miss, but Nils was very firm. It was one of the sights of Jukkasjärvi, and part of the tour. It had important art and artefacts and tourists liked to see it. We did as we were told, and stomped a little unwillingly in our cold weather gear towards the church. But Nils was right. This was not a born-again horror, but an enchanting wooden pale-green painted interior. The famous altarpiece was a triptych painted in the early twentieth century by Bror Hjört in the colours and primitive style of Rousseau, a delight of bold blues, reindeer blood reds and sunburst yellow telling the story of the conversion of the Sámi people by the black-suited moralist Laestadius. But telling it, surely, with tongue in cheek, in the gaudy colours and emphatic outlines of a cartoon. The smaller, central panel was a portrait of Jesus in a garden of brilliantly tropical trees and flowers such as neither Palestine nor Jukkasjärvi could provide. He carried a chunky cross and fat drops of blood red sweat dripped juicily rather than agonisingly down his torso. The panel to the left showed Laestadius, his arms upraised in rhetoric, explaining how all the drinking, whoring and greed must stop, while a gaily dressed Sámi family (and a reindeer) stood obediently in a group and listened politely to his words. The panel to the right of the redemptive Jesus showed the same people after they had accepted Christ into their lives, as happy and holy as ticks. No longer an awkward solemn group but leading proper socially productive lives, sure of their final welcome into heaven. A couple (married, obviously) cuddle in the foreground, doubtless in preparation for making the next generation of Christians, while a child leaps gleefully behind them, probably at the thought of a maths exam, and an old man looks on, the picture of contentment, or maybe just glad to be nearer the end than the beginning of all this positivity. Laestadius in full Victorian high collar and waistcoat kneels, giving thanks for their miraculous salvation and the simple happily ever after of it all. The church, covered in painted Sámi symbols of their world and made out of the raw materials of their lives – birch wood and reindeer parts – was built in 1905 by the Lutheran church by way of an apology for the wrong-doings of the murderous early missionaries. I would have been happy to spend an hour or two sitting there, taking in the silence and the scent of wood and the lightness, but time was getting on. We were summoned outside.

Nils took us to the small corral behind the square to begin our reindeer sled adventure. A dozen or so reindeers looked up, faintly interested as we walked through the gate. Two young men in traditional Sámi clothing, the same colours as the triptych, topped with bright red, embroidered short capes, were leading reindeer towards us.

'Would you like to take your reindeer and lead him out to the sled?' Nils asked.

'No, thank you,' I replied, thinking it a much better idea if one of the young men who looked like they knew one end of a reindeer from another dealt with that sort of thing. Thinking too that

251

his question was a question, and not simply a polite form of words.

'You have to, it's part of the experience,' Nils-Torbjörn said, ditching politeness for proper Sámi forthrightness, and handing me a halter with a huge-antlered, fat-nosed animal attached to it and not quite far enough away for my liking. I started to explain that I was an urban person who liked to keep still and watch things . . . but he had gone off to catch his own reindeer for the trip. Up close – very close, too close – my trotting, not walking, reindeer kept catching up with me although I explained to it that I was supposed to be leading it and therefore it was supposed to be following me. A fully adult antlered reindeer is an enormous creature. The size, say, of a small pony or one of those dogs that's the size of a small pony, but with a multiply-branched crown of antlers that reached well over my head, though its lower parts were exactly and distressingly level with my eyes. Eye injuries, eye loss, is common among reindeer-herding Sámi. I had no trouble understanding why. The reindeer, unlike me, was trained and knew that a trip was in the offing. It did what it knew it had to do and made for the gate of the corral. Finally, it led me, trotting in its own inimitable knock-kneed way, through the gate and to the sleds that were waiting. The young men harnessed my reindeer to a sled that was just a wooden platform with low sides on two wooden skis and extending shafts to which the animal was attached. A reindeer skin lay on the bottom of the sled. Nils instructed us. It was best to kneel, rather than sit, that way we had more control over the reins. We were going through the forest and across a frozen lake to a clearing in the woods beyond where we would have lunch. Then we would come back and visit the ice hotel. At which point I put my foot down. No ice hotel. We didn't need the ice hotel for the article, and it got enough publicity, I said. Could we please be let off that visit? We were. Nils didn't mind so much if we didn't get to the ice hotel. He continued to explain about the sledding trip. The sleds would be roped together for the first part of the journey through the forest, because the track was narrow and very winding and it was best if the lads were leading us. It was fine by me.

We set off with a powerful jerk of the tow-line through which it was easy to feel the twang of energy of five reindeer raring to go. We entered the forest almost immediately, a dense mass of skinny, snow covered birch trees with gracile branches extending in all directions, a network of delicate and sometimes wayward scaffolding. The ride was bone-shaking; the sled had nothing in the way of suspension, just the wooden ski and thin layer of platform between the ground and me. Traditionally this would have been fine, several feet of snow providing its own suspension, a smooth glide through the magic forest. But this year at least there weren't several feet of snow, there was barely a few inches. The forest path undulated with stones and tree roots, hillocks and humps. My knees and shins couldn't take kneeling through being swung this way and the other; I wriggled into sitting position, hanging on to the sides of the sled for dear life as it tipped and tilted around curves, rattling alarmingly, juddering my vertebrae enough to make the phone number of my osteopath spring urgently to mind. The frost sparkled prettily and I had never in my life sped through an untouched forest powered by reindeer, but all I could think about was how much it would cost to set my back right, if it could be done.

Alarming, adventurous indeed, as this was, we were at least travelling in a nicely tied-up convoy. I could devote my energy to ducking and diving to avoid the low hanging branches and twigs that would otherwise have put out my eyes, and trying not to be tossed out of the sled and break my nose, my neck, my skull against one of the beautiful tree trunks. But as we came to the end of the forest, and to the edge of a frozen lake, about twenty minutes after the start, Nils waved the convoy to a halt, stood up in his sled and announced that now he would untie the reindeer and Mark and I would take the reins and be in charge of our independent beasts. It was very simple, he explained, the animals would follow each other across the lake, all you have to do is pull on the left rein for faster, and the right for stop. Make them know who was boss. That was all there was to it. My reindeer, like every horse I have ever ridden (two), knew immediately who was boss and began a slow, insolent saunter when I jerked the left rein, stopping regularly to investigate the ice to see if it might not yield up a tasty morsel of moss, and raced his best mate over the agonising humps (no smoothing machine for this ice rink) or, when we got to the other side and more intricate, lethal birch forest paths, hurtled between the frozen birch trees as I tightened my grip and hauled back on the right. Who would have believed that such galumphing beasts could run so fast? Who would have believed that trained animals could have such a good time and care nothing for the welfare of the precious goods they towed within inches of murderous branches and crippling tree trunks?

I renounced any pretence to authority and just clung on. All I lost was the respect of my human guides, and dignity (not much of that left anyway after the dressing room interlude).

Soon, though, more than my dignity was threatened as my left thumb began to disappear. It grew cold and then numb and then number, until finally it didn't even figure as a phantom digit. All my anthropological and arctic exploration reading boiled down now to the symptoms of frostbite and the crucial role of the opposable thumb in the making of homo habilis and therefore sapiens, and therefore me, and how would I ever write or type or turn the pages of books again? Right-handedly, but I am left-handed and can do nothing except knit right-handedly. I don't mind the idea of becoming an old lady who knits, but not to the exclusion of being an old lady who reads and writes. Nils stopped us a couple of times to see if we were all right but I felt idiotic complaining of the cold. Finally, though, I confessed to my lost thumb. He looked anxious and told me to take my gloves off and enclose my numb thumb in my closed right fist. While I was doing this (and everyone waited) he looked at my gloves.

'The lining . . . inside . . . not right . . .'

I hadn't managed to put my glove on properly. Not even that.

'Just the leather covering the hand. It's no good. Freeze.'

I thought something was wrong inside my glove, but it was too hopeless to complain about uncomfortable gloves among these maestros of discomfort. I nurtured my thumb back to pins and needles and finally full-blooded feeling, and we set off again and eventually – after another half hour – we arrived at a clearing in the woods and Nils Torbjörn's lunch facility. The reindeer were parked and we were led, sore-backed, sore-arsed and emotionally jangled into another circular Sámi hut, like Britt-Marie's but a soft variety, genuinely a tent, made of birchwood uprights and tanned reindeer skin. In the centre a fire had been set (I expressed my gratitude to my host for good forward planning) and was lit by one of the lads. It was soon blazing and we lounged (in as much as it was possible to lounge dressed rigid as we were) on a carpet of reindeer skins, not as soft and luxurious as you might imagine, my skin prickling as the heat from the fire began to thaw my frozen cheeks. Once the fire was blazing, lunch, brought in Tupperware containers on one of the other sleds, was heated, and soon we were gorging ourselves on reindeer soup (delicious and a kind of getting my own back), flat bread and lingonberry juice. We relaxed and Nils Torbjörn spoke of Sámi life. Once again I was told about joiking. Mark, who had missed my joiked humiliation back in Övre Soppero, said he'd like to hear a joik, but Nils explained that people joiked only when the spirit was on them. They couldn't joik to order. Mark wondered how the spirit of the lads was and after a fractionally encouraging look from Nils, one of them diffidently agreed he might manage to joik. Nils looked pleased. There was a silence for a few moments while the lad composed himself, or summoned the spirit up, and then the almost familiar *loy-loy-loy* and tuneless chant echoed in the vaulted space of the tepee. We were rapt – spellbound by the warmth, the smoke, the cold, wild journey and the young man's light yearning voice. It was very short. He wasn't much in the mood to bare his soul to strangers, and when he stopped I felt a little ashamed at encouraging him to draw it out of himself just for our entertainment. But it was beautiful and appreciated. We thanked him and said so. He looked shy, more than shy, like a startled creature and disappeared inside himself for the rest of lunch.

Much too soon, as far as I was concerned, it was time to hop back on the sled and give rein to the whim of my reindeer. But really, even for me, it wasn't half bad. A bit chilly, but another glorious, not-quite-in-control ride over the iced top of the world, exhilarating, now I had abandoned hope of control. Leaving the forest and arriving near the paddock, my reindeer lost it completely and made a break for it, racing his friend in front for home. There was some shouting from behind, for me to get a grip on the reins and slow him down and for the reindeer to behave, but neither of us could. My animal overtook the one in front and for a few outstandingly alarming moments I was eyeball to antler with Mark's reindeer who was flinging his head about in fury at his defeat. I do remember the excitement of danger, the thrill of uncertainty, but I recall with even more pleasure the relief when the lads finally got hold of my reindeer's halter and brought him to a standstill so that I could get back on my own two quite shaky feet.

It was as well that we cancelled the ice hotel visit because we were only just in time for the handover to our next host, Håkan Enoksson, and the thrills of a snowmobile ride and a night in Lavvu.

'You are spending the night in *lavvu?*' Nils asked, looking quite concerned.

'Yes, is it far?'

He shook his head.

'Where we had lunch. That is *lavvu.*'

Spending a night in a tent in minus twenty-seven degrees, a tent in any weather, was not something I was aware I had agreed to do. Not something, in a million years I *would* have agreed to do. I know my limitations and that is well beyond them. On the other hand, I was now at the mercy of my hosts.

'Perhaps it'll be a centrally heated tent,' I laughed weakly, stunned actually at the prospect of the night ahead and trying to bank down the panic. Lavvu was not a place, unless the images of hell I now had counted as a location.

Nils shook his head sympathetically.

'A fire in the middle, perhaps, before you sleep. Very cold. Hard night.'

14

ON MOVEMENT AND STILLNESS

The night was young. It was a moonlit and sunless mid-afternoon as we set off in Håkan's mini-bus to his father's house half an hour away, to pick up the snowmobile. Håkan wore round rimmed spectacles and had a mild, thoughtful look, as if his mind, or the better part of it, was elsewhere. An intellectual perhaps, a dreamer. So in the car I asked him about the old religion, whether anyone still practised it, if it was really forgotten. He kept his eyes fixed on the empty road and murmured that he didn't know anything about it. There was a silence. After a moment, to cover the awkwardness he added:

'Some people, perhaps, are shaman. Privately. I don't know. It's all forgotten.'

The relationship between privacy and tourism is going to be a difficult one for the Sámi, I think, who have as clandestine a place within them as I had when I was a child.

'About this tent we're sleeping in tonight,' I said, getting on to a subject that concerned me very closely.

Håkan told us the plan. We would pick up the snowmobile and equipment from his father's house and then travel to the *siida*'s corral. It was an hour or so from his father's house. An hour (or so) on a snowmobile in this weather suddenly seemed very different from a treat. I'd thought it was to be a quick turn round a lake for the tourists. A ride, not a journey. We were exceptionally fortunate, Håkan said, because tomorrow we were going to witness the annual parting of the reindeer. Usually it happens later in the autumn, but because of the mild weather (mild!) the reindeer were failing to get at the moss. No moss, to them, meant it must be summer and they had already begun to head for the grazing up in Norway. Seven thousand reindeer had been collected in a large corral and tomorrow morning they would be herded into a smaller space and then into the even smaller separating corral where each family would pick out its own animals by the marks on their ears and separate their own herds to take them into the forest for the rest of the winter where they would be looked after by the family members. It was also an annual accounting, a chance to check numbers, as well as each animal's health, to castrate the males destined for slaughter the following year, spray the new members of the herd with a splash of dye in the family colour, and inject them against pests and diseases. Usually, it took two or three days. It was clearly a very special time in the year of the Sámi, and that was what we would be participating in tomorrow.

This evening we would go to his brother's family cabin near

the corrals, have a meal, and then Håkan, Mark and I would spend the night in a *lavvu* erected by Håkan at the edge of the main corral to keep watch in case the animals were spooked or wandered outside the boundary line. I could see that we were indeed remarkably fortunate to be allowed to witness the parting of the reindeer, but all I could think of was that I had to spend the night in a tent in a field of seven thousand reindeer at minus thirty degrees. There was, I acknowledge, just the merest shimmer of excitement; a faint flutter of thrill vibrated through my nerve pathways. Here was my sense of adventure: a segment of me as thin as a slice of prosciutto. It did exist, but barely. I tried to encourage it; like the man in the Jack London story, *To Build a Fire*, I nurtured my tiny spark of excitement, cupped it in my hands and blew gently on it, but it went out rather than glowing and growing as I kept remembering with unwelcome clarity the times in my life when I'd been camping. At school once a year; on a trip to Morocco in the early Seventies (when we discovered, at the end of the month of sleeping in an elementary boy scout tent that a perfect whitewashed room with a real bed in it was as cheap as a campsite); for a short while when my daughter was little, we camped sometimes on Dartmoor and in a field in Wiltshire where – bizarrely – a man in the next field boiled lobsters and sold them for a song which made the discomfort easier, before I decided enough was enough.

It was the mornings that came back to me with physical clarity. That bleak chill, opening the tent and being hit by damp, disinterested air. The shivering wait for the kettle to boil on the primus stove, slowly, very slowly, so that at least I could have a cup of tea; getting into yesterday's moist clothes without a bath or shower and *never getting warm*. The fuss and bother of taking down the tent, and being instructed by some man or other how to fold it just so in order to fit it into its bag. 'No, no, like this. Come on we'll have to start again.' I don't care. I don't want to know. Nor about tent pegs, poles, ground sheets, fly sheets or how much is left in the calor gas thingy. I want to go home. Even an unheated 1950s bathroom was better than this, though only just. Why, when houses and ways of waking up warmly in them had been invented (the latter not until the early 1970s when huddling over a paraffin heater to get dressed and losing brain cells to the fumes became a thing of the past), would you sleep in a field and wake to bone-chilling dewy morning air? Why would you choose to be cold, damp and miserable? Other people love it, I know, but to my very core, I don't get it. They revel in the smell of morning grass, the fresh and invigorating chill of night blowing away, the freedom from the daily round of domesticity. I never liked any of it. I can't remember ever wanting to be invigorated rather than warm and cosy. I want lavender and jasmine in my bath, not eucalyptus and peppermint. Nor do I want a revitalising shower with needlepoint sprays stinging me into vivid consciousness. A bath has everything: warmth and comfort. It is not good to be too far away from a bath. Except cold ones. At the progressive, vegetarian, nature-cure boarding school that the London County Council sent me to in order to develop my potential, we had a cold bath and a designated half-mile walk every morning before breakfast. It is perfectly true that we were astonishingly healthy, but there is more to life than not having a cold. Indeed, suffering a sore head, runny nose and shivers in bed has a kind of charm, bestowing a sense of being nurtured, even if it's only by yourself telling yourself that you can't possibly get up in such a state. Never being ill just meant that we never got a day off school or time snuggling in bed daydreaming and reading on our own in the dormitory or the blessed isolation of the sick bay. The daily morning price of not having colds was far too high. Camping was, on balance, worse than cold baths and morning walks. I didn't like it when I was twelve, and I put my foot down around the age of thirty-two since when I haven't done it.

As you get older, if you are fortunate, you get to make choices. I chose to stay home rather than go away if it meant tent-life. How did it happen, then, that aged fifty-seven and having decided that I am what I am, and can, being what I am, stay home, stay still, and be what I want to be, I was about to spend a late autumn night in a tent with two strangers (three as it turned out, and a dog), two hundred miles inside the Arctic Circle? How did I come to be so far from what I wanted and who had brought me here? I had, of course. And it would have been so easy to avoid. *Just say no.* Do you want to go away and write about darkness and the north? No, thank you, I think I'll stay where I am and make things up. Sit in my study in the early hours of the morning, listening to the silence of a sleeping world, in a small pool of light. Or imagine it. Why did I say yes to this? Perhaps, after all, I am a fidget. Or perhaps I'm just a girl who can't say no. Or maybe I do it so that I can write about how much I don't like it. Maybe, being a lifelong moaner, and finding life enchanting now, I need to create opportunities to exercise my moaning skills. Whatever the reason, we arrived at Håkan's father's house where the old man greeted us and showed us where to put our cases and decant only the essentials for the night and day ahead. Yet again we put on bulky layers of insulating clothes in readiness for the great outdoors adventure on which we were about to embark, and Håkan handed me a short, waist-length, thick, scratchy wool hooded cape, crimson red and brightly embroidered with blue and yellow patterns, to pull over my head to lie on top of everything else.

'You will need this on the back of the snowmobile.'

Håkan hooked a wooden trailer on runners to the back of the snowmobile and packed it with supplies and the makings of the *lavvu*, leaving a space at the back for Mark, who climbed in and huddled with his precious camera equipment under a blanket of several reindeer skins. Håkan's collie dog ran barking circles around us, thrilled at the coming trip. He was ordered into the trailer and settled for a moment on Mark's legs, rather welcome as an additional source of warmth, but as soon as I sat on the pillion seat, he got up and leapt on to my lap, large, heavy, damp but throbbingly warm. Håkan shouted at him to return to the trailer, and I lost something quite like a security blanket when he obeyed.

It was a joy-ride. The most beautiful journey I've ever made, most mythic, most magical, most bone-shaking. It was dark, apart from the moon and starlight. The engine revved into life and we drew away from the small clearing around Håkan's father's house and into the forest where the trees concealed much of the sky, and the moonlight and stars were replaced by the headlamp of the snowmobile blazing forward on to the path ahead of us. We crashed through the forest as fast as swerving along the narrow, bumpy track would allow. There was too little snow for the smooth ride snowmobiles are intended to provide. My bones cracked and rattled as they had in the reindeer sled, the metal and mechanics were no more forgiving than wood and reindeer. Even so, I didn't care as I held on to Håkan's waist and looked over his shoulder at the beam of the snowmobile headlight which revealed the birch forest track, no different from the sort we had sledged through that afternoon, to be, after all, a glittering fairyland labyrinth. Every lit-up twig on every branch of every tree was a glistering white, stark, frosted finger pointing urgently in every direction, making an intricate latticework which sparkled, twinkled, actually dazzled the eyes, as if the forest had been sprinkled with a layer of diamond dust. Though it seemed perilously fast to me after the reindeer trip (which was already more than fast enough), Håkan went relatively slowly because of the trailer and his novice passengers, but still the twists and turns of the path made us tilt from side to side as if we were taking corners on a TT racecourse. Occasionally, Håkan shouted a warning for me to duck out of the way of an overhanging branch or to hang on tight as we bounced even harder than usual over a stump or rocky part of the track. In between the forest were ice-rink lakes on which Håkan let out the throttle and we raced at fifty kilometres an hour and more over the frosty surface, under a suddenly wide open, absurdly moonlit, starstuck sky.

When, during the flight back home toward my proper life of southern ease, I wondered why the Sámi people are battling to continue to live their incredibly hard life, I remembered that snowmobile journey when I became Hans Anderson's little Kay, whisked off to the world's end by the Snow Queen, and fell into an enchantment at the beauty and bleakness of the frozen wilderness. Even I, with a shard of the devil's mirror in my eye making my view of the world so cold and cynical, looked at this world and saw the glory in it. It was little Kay's job to rearrange the ice to spell the word *eternity*. The girl, Gerda, saved him, but did he need saving? Wasn't solving the puzzle of the ice a proper life in its own way? He was rescued by love. Well, I don't know. I've never been able to feel it was an entirely happy ending. At any rate I gazed, astonished, at the icy night around me as if I had just been born, and understood perfectly that a person might devote their life to simply looking at and being in this landscape whatever the hardship. It was a fleeting epiphany. Even as it was upon me, I knew it wouldn't last.

We had to stop in the middle of a lake to let Mark take a picture of me from the back with my arms out wide. The cape was flapping and blowing behind me in the wind, and, with the hood up, from Mark's angle I looked like a broomstick-riding witch in black silhouette. I instantly saw myself as he had, stark and witchy against the headlamps in an otherwise empty world. For a while I held my arms out to make a static silhouette that he could photograph, but then it got too cold to be modelling and I wrapped them firmly around me under the cape. Enough. Photographers are perfectionists. They will put up with any discomfort for a picture. I am neither a photographer nor a perfectionist. Also, my face was suffering, burned by the wind and cold. I had a fleece neck warmer that pulled up to cover my mouth and nose, but it wasn't nearly dense enough to stop the rushing, ice-cold wind, as sharp as broken glass, from reaching my face. Every fifteen minutes or so Håkan stopped, got off the snowmobile and inspected Mark's and my face by shining a torch directly at us to see if there were any signs of frostbite. It gave a sense of seriousness to our adventure. It wasn't quite a fairy tale game.

Eventually – it either took much longer than an hour, or seemed as if it did – we arrived at Håkan's brother's cabin, among several others belonging to family members. It was basic. Two bunk beds and two camp beds, for Erik and his wife Eva, their two small children, and Håkan (though not tonight); a wood-burning stove at the centre by a small table and four chairs and a tiny kitchen area (fridge, sink and calor gas cooker) by the front door where the wet outdoor clothes hung. I was shown to the single wooden outhouse about fifty yards away for a pee, made especially urgent by the ups and downs of the snow-depleted journey. I was given a flashlight to use inside. On the way we passed the insides of the reindeer that Erik had slaughtered for supper and for the following days. Håkan apologised that we had missed it.

'It is very interesting how we kill our animals.'

The snow was darkly bloodstained all around and under the blackened heart, liver and intestines, and other nameless bits of viscera laid out neatly in a row. The meat was up, out of the way of predators and the dogs, on a rack built on stilts. Another smell mingled with the crisp smell of ice. The recent death hung in the air and bloodied the ground, not hidden, but a fact, indeed the point of Sámi life. It was, after all, what the Sámi and the reindeer were all about. It was a serious thing to do, but there was nothing sentimental about the necessary sacrifice of one of the creatures in their care for the feeding of the family. Not even a sacrifice but part of the quid pro quo for the continuing existence of both parties.

For supper Eva had prepared vertebrae stew. Like oxtail, but more lumbar than tail. Huge segments of backbone stewed in their own juices and eaten with relish by everyone. After the meat had been cut off and eaten with the carved knives all the adults had attached to their belts (Mark and I used regular knives and forks, having no side arms of our own), the glutinous connective tissue and marrow was sucked from the bone until it was bare and dry. The bowls were stacked high, and the juice was soaked up with flat bread. No lingonberries, this time. This was basic and serious fuelling up by people preparing for two or three days of great physical labour, but the way they relished every mouthful, wasting nothing that could be cut or scrapped or sucked from the bone, was also some sort of respect for the recently dead creature we were eating. Even so, I had to decline a second helping – the food was as delicious as ever, but I stared at the picked white bones on my plate with astonishment that I could have eaten so much.

'Eat more. Eat more,' Håkan insisted. 'You need the nourishment for the night.'

Erik, like his brother, was a thinker, quiet and watchful. He was the head of the family and in charge, made final decisions and had the respect of all the family and clan. He and Eva owned a large number of reindeer, but Håkan, as he explained, had fewer than any of the other adults. In his youth he had not been so committed to the reindeer-herding life as his brother and therefore hadn't received many from their father, who put most of the family herd into Erik's care. Those Håkan had didn't thrive and multiply because he didn't pay enough attention. He had wanted to travel and see the world. Now he realised how much the Sámi life with reindeer mattered. He was trying very hard to build up his stock of reindeer. Erik looked on approvingly as Håkan explained this. The prodigal brother had returned and was making amends, but he was also planning to bring in tourist euros and dollars to support his entirely reindeer-dependent brother and sister-in-law. Eva was small and strong, and a little daunting with her energy and canny pixie face and fierce, black vigilant eyes. She had cooked the meal and paid attention to the children's behaviour while Erik, who had killed the reindeer, sat on a chair in front of the stove looking softly through its open doors into the fire, and smoked. There was no tension here, but it wasn't a simple division of labour. Eva had her own reindeer, a lot of them. In fact, she was the only woman in the *siida* who actually worked with the herds, handling them and physically caring for them exactly as the men did. It was her choice, Erik said. As a child, Eva told me, she had loved caring for the animals and wanted only to be a herder. Such passion is appreciated by the Sámi and she was trained by her father just like her brothers. After dinner Håkan went off to check on the herd and build the *lavvu*. We drank coffee and Erik spoke to me, almost dreamily, about how he and Eva loved the reindeer and wanted nothing more than to live the old and, they hoped, future life where the relationship between them and their animals was the whole point of existence. There was a special bond between human and reindeer that made life worthwhile. He and Eva were, he seemed to suggest, married to each other through their reindeer and their pride was in teaching their children how to live the reindeer life. Which was all wonderful and very moving, but Håkan returned and announced that the *lavvu* was ready and it was time to go. I left Erik and Eva's cabin, full of love, respect, quiet thought and warmth, with immense regret – and not only because I dreaded the al fresco night ahead.

It was another half a mile on the snowmobile to the corral of myriad reindeer and our night's accommodation. When we stopped there was the *lavvu,* and just beyond it the massed dark shapes in the night for as far as the eye could see that were seven thousand grazing reindeer, mostly still, a few walking dreamily to and fro in search of a better patch of moss. They snorted and snuffled, filling the air with their warm breath and soft animal mumblings, the only sounds apart from our own, but they kept a semicircle of empty ground, a few yards, between the nearest of them and our *lavvu* at the edge of the corral. It was quite eerie, the underlying silence of an empty snowy wilderness, their shadowy forms and low, gentle gruntings making the world around us theirs and us *other*, a handful of interlopers. It wasn't at all clear to me what exactly was to be done if something frightened them and they stampeded. Håkan, even on his snowmobile was not going to have much effect on seven thousand panicking reindeer, I imagined. As we approached the *lavvu* we spoke in undertones, advised to keep our voices down by Håkan in case we spooked them, but we would have done anyway. It wasn't just that I didn't want to scare the reindeer and make them (and me) panic, it was also that I didn't want to disturb them. There they were, the great herd, being reindeer, doing what they do.

Whereas I was not doing as I do. There were four of us sleeping in the *lavvu*; Håkan, Mark, me and Per Erik, a young man from Norway who was related to Håkan's family and come for the parting of the reindeer to learn the work. He was lighting a fire of birch logs on the bare soil at the centre of the circular tepee, six or seven feet in diameter at the bottom and open to the sky at the peak above so that the smoke could escape. A carpet of separate reindeer skins lay over the rest of the lumpy, snow-covered earth and there was a six-inch gap of open space all around the bottom, between the edge of the tent and the ground, which was, Håkan explained, 'to let the fresh air in'. I have never been a great one for opening the bedroom window at night. In my darkest moments during the previous few hours contemplating my night in the *lavvu*, I had not imagined that there would be six inches of nothing between me and the icy outside air, as fresh as fresh could get. Once, when I was a fifteen-year-old hitchhiking failure, I spent the night on a roundabout on the A1 in two inches of snow. That time I had an illicit boyfriend and a single sleeping bag between us. I had laid a web of elaborate lies to spend the weekend away from the psychiatric hospital in Hove to be with him. I was young, very young, and in love. This time, too many decades on to be amusing, I had just the sleeping bag, and not a nice modern down-filled, nylon wind-proofed affair, but a padded cotton thing such as I'd only seen in army surplus shops. Håkan also supplied us with two wool blankets. We took off just our boots and otherwise fully dressed, including our hats, climbed into the sleeping bags which had been arranged in a circle around the fire. The cold blasted my back, while faint indications of warmth began to reach my front from the fire which was being carefully built up by Per Erik and Håkan. I felt like a hapless child being kept alive by the adults. In effect, that was exactly the situation. Hapless and being kept alive, anyway.

Håkan nodded to Per Erik who opened a food box and brought out bottles of beer. I declined mine. Nothing seemed less comforting to me than cold beer. But I was cheered to see Håkan pull out a half bottle of brandy from his pocket, and pour it into birch-carved cups which I didn't decline. We sat up, leaning on our elbows and drank, staring into the fire, getting just a little drunk. In a kind of panic, Mark and I talked of another world. Photography. Was it art? Susan Sontag on the subject. Annie Leibovitz. Susan Sontag and Annie Leibovitz living together. Gender politics. The conversation got more and more remote from where we were; we chattered as if we were at a dinner party in London, giggling and joking, gossiping about lives as far from here as it was possible to get. Håkan and Per Erik drank their beer and brandy and stared quietly into the fire while Mark and I babbled and finally ran out of nonsense, or became aware of the silence of our companions and where we were in the world. Then there was nothing left but to settle down and get on with the night. Each of us alone. There was one thing left to do, it turned out. Having let us run out of evasive conversational steam, Håkan this time drew from his magic pockets four short lengths of twig with the bark removed.

'I made these for us. Toothpaste and tooth brush. Here. Very good. Keep them also for the morning.'

He showed us how to rub the twig between our teeth and get them fresh and clean. There was no doubt now that we were on the nursery side of the *lavvu*. It was after midnight.

'We must sleep now. Tomorrow will be very hard.'

I swallowed a Temazapam I had taken care to bring with me. Sometimes on sleepless nights at home, or in spidery autumns in the Quantocks, I take half and it's enough to get the mind to stop racing and fall asleep. An hour and a half later I swallowed a second pill and wished I had opium, barbiturates and chloroform for chasers. Not that my mind was racing; it was numb with disbelief. I lay awake, turning over and over, one way and the other. Back to fire and freezing face and front, or front to fire and freezing back? Each time, the other way seemed preferable. But finally I decided that it was better to lie facing the fire on my implacable, bumpy patch of earth, softened not at all by the reindeer skin, because then at least I could watch the flames instead of having to close my eyes tight against the searing cold on my eyeballs the other way. Closing your eyes if you can't sleep is a kind of pantomime. Better to keep the eyes restfully unfocussed on the rhythm of the fire. The mind drifts, and for whole seconds at a time you can forget where you are. The dog came in and sniffed around each of us, eventually snuggling himself up against Per Erik who remained deeply asleep. I could have done with him at my back, but the dog was no fool. So there we were, the five of us.

Four of us asleep and one awake. Wide awake. Not keeping vigil but desperately unable to achieve unconsciousness, listening to the strange tocking sounds outside and remembering that Håkan had explained how reindeer have two bones in their ankles that click as they walk so that they can be followed by their young or the members of the herd behind them in a snow storm or at night. Click, click, click. Coming closer. Snuffling up against the *lavvu* now that it was still and silent, making an investigation. Not interesting. Click, click, click. Moving away, back to the herd to sleep or find more moss or think, or whatever reindeer do in the middle of the night.

It's a truism that as you get older time speeds up, but I have now developed a theory that if you want to live for ever, or to seem to, then you should take up residence in a *lavvu* because, even at fifty-seven, a night without sleep in what amounts to out-doors at thirty or more degrees below freezing, causes time to move with such glacial slowness (I use the phrase deliberately: ice and time are kissing cousins) that the lifespan of the mayfly would seem to be Methuselan. Most of the night I perched on my elbow, staring at the embers of the fire in the centre of the tent. A better woman than I might have meditated on the nature of existence, but I spent the night willing the fire not to go out and watching time creep, observing the singularity of each minute as it passed by. I noted every fraction of every second of every minute of the seven . . . six . . . five . . . four . . . three . . . two unimaginably cold, inconceivably long hours I had yet to live through until morning would free me from my wakeful isolation. I have experienced before the exceptional loneliness of lying awake while others, or the other sleeps. I lived through all those long, miserable promiscuous nights (the night being miserable, not necessarily the promiscuity) when I was very young and thought I ought to sleep with anyone who wanted to sleep with me (gratitude, practise). And there I lay in their wrong-smelling beds next to their wrong-smelling bodies, in the wrong place with the wrong person who was deeply unconscious, without hope of release until morning. Those dawns were grim. Now, it felt the same, without the promiscuity – unless my being there was a kind of promiscuity. The others were asleep. If you can, it's the best thing to do. I had wanted to be alone, but this wasn't what I meant. Not what I meant at all.

But I wasn't entirely alone, not all the time. Every hour or so Håkan opened an eye, as if part of him had been alert all along, and reached out to put another log on the fire just as it threatened to die and deprive me of the last glimmerings of warmth and comfort. I wouldn't have dared do it myself; it would have felt too much as if I were participating in rather than enduring this night. He glanced at me stark-staring wide awake, and smiled sympathetically. I smiled madly and he nodded before going back to sleep. Twice he got up and patrolled the corral. Mark woke up once or twice and groaned with cold. He looked round and saw me sitting up.

'Still awake?'

'Mmm.'

'Ugh,' a grunt of fellow feeling before pulling his sleeping bag and supplementary blanket over his head to stop his face from freezing, and returning to blessed unconsciousness. And twice I had to get up to pee. I don't think I've ever urinated in a more beautiful setting, but the getting there was a struggle. At moments like these you realise how much better it is to be a man. *Pace* feminists, but this is the hard core, down beneath the rhetoric, truth about biological gender. Getting out of the sleeping bag, finding the right boots, the right feet of the right boots (barefoot was unthinkable), putting them on, doing them up, finding ditto gloves and ditto hands of the ditto gloves – all this was a cross-gender bore. As was crawling over Mark, trying not to wake him or set bits of myself alight and opening the *lavvu* with as little blast of outside to the inside as was compatible with getting out into it. Just thinking about those preparations took an hour or so of steeling myself mentally each time – which at least passed a couple of hours in practical thought.

Outside there was a short walk under the unbelievable star-spattered sky to achieve a decent distance from the *lavvu* and a safe distance from the reindeer. Then the real drawback of being a woman came fully home. Just two zips was all a man would have to release to reach his penis and point it away from him in order to empty his bladder. If he wanted, he might have the additional glory of writing his name in the snow and sending a message to the stars. Well, naming and signalling are optional male extras I have always been prepared to forgo considering the drawbacks that come with the territory, and, these days, surprising numbers of men remember to put the lavatory seat down, or even, I understand, sit down themselves to pee. What no man would have to do to empty his bladder (oh, the denial and wishing it away as I felt its pressure grow during the vigil hours) was what I had to do: take off my gloves in order to unzip my all-in-one insulating suit, pull it down to the waist; unzip the windproof jacket underneath, find the button and flies of my trousers beneath, after lifting several layers of jumpers; undo the trousers and then wriggle down the whole half-shed assembly of knickers, long johns, snow suit, down as far as the bulk would go towards the ankles. (Remember the temperature.) The startlingly beautiful stars indicated not a cloud in the sky, nothing to keep the world warm – and there I was bare-arsed, bare-torsoed, bare-legged and bare-handed and bare-faced in the middle of an empty, endless, freezing universe. Because I was a woman needing a pee. The pain of the icy night wind, of course, and the awkwardness of balancing in a constricted squat made the bladder resist. I wondered exactly how many minutes it would be before frostbite and hypothermia set in. But listen to the silence, the animal mufflings, see the slow-moving lazily curious shapes appear from and disappear into distance and night, moving in to investigate and then shrug at this new activity in their ever-present world. Even the painful cold on my naked skin was a spectacular experience. A momentary staying still, small and alone, in the midst of vast numbers and vast space. Not dignified, for sure, but it was a sacrifice easily made. Staying still and quite remarkably alone. Peeing on the ground in the middle of the night in the midst of a herd of reindeer inside the Arctic Circle. Who would have thought it? Naturally, peeing itself was a struggle – my legs tangled in the clothes, trying to keep the urine away from me and my clothes and not to fall over. Then remembering how men seem to manage with just a quick shake as I semi-squatted, semi-tottered, and waited for the drips to stop before performing all the unzipping and pulling off and down in reverse, on and up, layer after layer, zip after zip, gloves back on, a farewell to the night and the stars, and au revoir to the reindeer and then back to the tent. Don't wake anyone (the first time I tripped over Mark and did wake him for a nanosecond), get back to your place, take off your gloves (more zips and poppers) and boots (zips and buckles) and struggle yourself back into the sleeping bag, spread the blankets on top, shush the dog who wakes up and starts to take an interest, and settle back down – noticing that already there was just the slightest pressure in my lower abdomen.

I have no doubt that there are many people who adore essential, bang-up-against-nature kinds of experience like this. I commend Håkan's *lavvu* to them.

Nonetheless, I survived the night, stiff and sort of mad with lack of sleep. Håkan declared it morning at around six o'clock and began to bank up the fire. He speared some salt fish on birch skewers and set them close to the embers. A pot of water was put to boil on top of the burning logs. He looked at me in a kindly, gentle manner and pulled more marvels from his pocket.

'Here, eat this,' he said, handing us each a dark lump of something fibrous and shrivelled. 'We call it Arctic Root. It tastes like shit but it will give you energy.'

I was too tired to taste anything, and chewed it dutifully waiting for an electric jolt to set me to rights. No surge of power rippled through me, but perhaps it worked in a more subtle manner than the pharmaceutical Speed I knew in my youth and needed now, and kept me somewhat sustained during the day. At any rate I didn't die of weariness and misery, and I'm happy to put it down to Arctic Root. Nothing else seems likely to be the cause of my continued existence that day. (Returning to Cambridge, I looked on a herbal remedies website and discovered that Arctic Root, aka *rhodiola rosea*, providing salidrozid and polyphenols, was the remedy du jour, high on the top ten best-seller list. Naturally I bought a large bottle of capsules – which don't taste like shit – and continue, so far, to survive the memory of that night.) We folded our tent after Håkan took it down and then he put it back in the trailer in the steeliest of grey dawns.

This time, the shapes arriving in the murky light were human and mechanical. The families came on their snowmobiles and pickup trucks for the day ahead. Men, women and children, everyone was there, mostly dressed in serious modern cold weather clothing, but some of the younger men wearing tradi-tional bright woollen embroidered jackets cinched in at the waist with a hefty leather belt with their hand-carved knives, blade curved behind them, attached at their hips. The men swung into action, riding their bikes in standing position and the round up began. Mark and I rode, a burden that slowed him down, in Håkan's trailer as he and the other wranglers, along with men, women and children on foot, dogs running, people shouting instructions to each other and making whooping noises at the alarmed reindeer, spread out in a mysterious pattern, began to surround the herd. I couldn't make any sense of the sudden swerves and complete changes in direction of the snowmobiles, criss-crossing each other, the furious yelling, dogs barking and racing here and there according to orders whistled or vocalised by their owner. It seemed chaotic, like a carnival, or a mechanised dance put on for someone who saw the whole picture from above. But the faces were so intent, almost angrily concentrated in the silvering dawn, and somehow after fifteen minutes seven thousand reindeer, at first alerted and trotting, then panicked and whirling together to find a way around the noise and pressure, ran in the desired direction which was into the smaller, though still sizeable corral. The rest was done on foot. A snaking line, men and women, held a huge length of white material, some strong woven fabric, as high as they could reach, shaking it violently at the animals and shouting. They formed a moving white wall around the back of the herd and shooed them forward. The line curved tighter and closed in, so that the ever-contracting wall and hollering people pressed the entire, running, fearful reindeer herd towards a narrow passage where, after seventy or so beasts had been funnelled through, the gate was closed and the remaining animals allowed to run free and return to grazing calmly, utterly forgetful of the terror in which, only moments before, they had been caught. My job in all this was to stand out to one side of the snaking wall, along with the children and old people, and head off the stragglers and escapees. This was done by flapping the arms up and down (quite a good way of keeping warm) and hooting. I was not a confident flapper, but it turns out that even the most desultory of flaps will persuade a wayward reindeer, or – as I discovered to my very great relief – several hundred wayward reindeer in a breakaway mini-herd coming your way to change its collective mind and get back into the crowd. It was almost miraculous. What masters of nature we humans are.

In fact, this was a situation I had been in before, improbably given my inclinations. Once in the dying days of the Seventies, I visited a friend who had rented a cottage in Wiltshire. We had supper and smoked a small joint. Then she suggested a walk across the adjacent large ploughed field where, at the other side between two oak trees, there was a huge boulder, indented at the top as if some giant had pressed a fist into it when it was still half-molten. This, my friend informed me, must have been some Neolithic monument to female fertility, a vulvic altar. Being between the oaks, and the boulder not being from thereabouts pretty much clinched it, apparently. I didn't argue. It was the Seventies, I was stoned and what did I know about large rocks between oak trees? We climbed up and stood on top of it, to feel the vibes of ancient powers, I dare say. Dusk had fallen as we'd walked across the field and the light was failing fast. It isn't likely that we lowered our voices as we discussed where the rock might have been brought from. Slow shapes appeared out of nowhere, looming and then lowing. Cows. Bullocks. Geldings. I didn't know. Bovines, anyway. They got closer and then formed a crowd, pressing tightly up against the rock. Their rock, as they might think of it, in their field. Several of them pushed their noses against our legs. I felt the dampness of their breath. I am a city-bred person. This was too close.

'No,' said my friend, country-wise, who earlier in the day had said things like ah, the smell of fox. 'Don't worry, they won't hurt you. We're the masters here.' Likely this was the dope talking, she wasn't usually given to such extremes of hubris. 'Look,' she continued, 'all I have to do is raise my voice and they'll scatter.'

'I don't think . . .'

She gave a series of loud whoops that gave me quite a turn, but had much more of an effect on the herd of cows or whatever they were. As a single unit, they wheeled around and began to stampede. They thundered off into the darkness up to the other invisible end of the field. The ground actually shook and I could feel it up high on the vulvic rock. It was a sight and sound I knew only from cowboy movies and watching *Rawhide* on TV, starring the boyish Rowdy Yates played by Clint Eastwood before he became the Man with No Name. The thunder of their hooves died away.

'Jesus, what have you done?'

My friend looked a little surprised herself. We decided to go back home before the farmer had us arrested for ruining his animals' milk or meat or whatever it was we exploited them for, but just as we had stepped down from the woman-worship-rock and were walking back to the gate, the ground began to tremble again and an ominous, truly terrifying low roar began to increase in volume. The cows, reaching the end of the field had wheeled around and were coming back, not one bit slowed down or over their fright. The earth was dry and corrugated, difficult to walk on, let alone run away from a herd of cows. The shadows broke through the dark and came hurtling our way. A fast moving convoy of twenty or thirty juggernauts of deadly hoof and muscle.

'Umm, we're going to die.'

I meant this completely sincerely. It was clear that I had come to the end of my life, and I felt idiotic that I was to die, run down by a herd of cows because I'd thought I was a master of the universe. I pictured myself found face down in the dry earth, my spine shattered into splinters, and felt curiously embarrassed. I'd always hoped for something lingering and calm, certainly not so silly a finale. 'She was run over by a cow, you know.'

'Don't worry,' my friend said. 'Keep still. They won't touch you. They'll come towards you and then they swerve away.'

I wasn't impressed by my friend's certainty about the natural world any more.

'Just don't move.'

It wasn't difficult. I was paralysed with fear. I stood very still and dug my fingers into my friend's arm. I felt it was the least she deserved. I recall that she dug her fingers deep into mine also, but later, after the event, she said she had remained calm and serene and most certainly did not clutch me in terror.

And it was as she predicted. This bloody great mass of flesh came, maddened with fright, rushing uncontrollably towards us two young women standing in the middle of the field, and one by one, as they got to within a foot of us, they peeled away to right or left of our bodies in their path, like air in a wind tunnel or water streaming around a rock. At the bottom of the field they came together, turned and proceeded not to trample us to death again as they raced up to the other end once more. It can't have been good for them. Surely their milk was sour and their meat tough. We walked quite slowly to the edge of the field – my friend advised me not to run, what worked when we were

283

standing up probably wouldn't if we were lying on the ground having tripped – and after another joint and a good deal of recrimination on my part, we went to our beds to sleep the sleep of the reprieved and never spoke of the incident again.

As it was with cows, so, it turns out, it is with reindeer. The seventy or so reindeer trapped in the small circular separating corral like a rodeo arena, wheeled round and round at top speed, having nowhere else to go, while the group of men and Eva, who had been waiting, stood inviolable in the dead centre, observant in the eye of the whirlwind. Here's a bit of traditional knowledge you might find useful one day. Reindeer herds run anti-clockwise. Always. Except when they are out of control. A clockwise running herd is disturbed and dangerous. At the first sign of the running circle reversing, everyone piles in, flapping and hooting like crazy to get them circulating properly. It seemed to me that either way, they ran incredibly fast – lethal in the small, cramped space of the separating corral – but so long as it was anti-clockwise, the men in the centre spotted the reindeer belonging to their family by the marks of its ears and leapt out into the whirling throng to grab hold of that particular animal in the midst of all the turmoil, the thundering hooves, the dust and the white, smoky puffs of breath of seventy frightened beasts running as fast as they could and getting nowhere.

There was a choice of holds: you either threw your arms around the thick neck in a kind of ardent hug, or you opted for grabbing the beast by the antlers. Either way, you hung on tight, very tight, and wrestled the complaining, writhing reindeer towards one of several gates that led off from the circular barrier to your family's paddock, arranged like spokes on a wheel around the separating corral. That is to say that *they* did. Having been persuaded by Håkan to stand for a few moments inside the corral, at the edge near the gate (no, thank you, I won't stand in the middle), and finding yet another species of hoofed beast that had the unexpected decency to change direction rather than trample me to death, I decided that I had had enough adventure and joined the women, old men and children of Håkan's family paddock. This was cowardly and lazy, but looking about, it was only Eva, Håkan's sister-in-law, and recognised by all as an exceptional reindeer herder, who got down and dirty in the circling frenzy. It crossed my mind that:

a) I didn't have to prove that I was one of the boys

and

b) I didn't have to learn how to be a Sámi reindeer herder because I was not a Sámi reindeer herder and neither my hosts nor I expected me to become one

and

c) I've never willingly joined in anything: sport, singalong, religion, and I still didn't want to join in.

I was a watcher, a very very tired watcher, and that was what I was going to do.

A massive fire burned in Håkan's family paddock by the gate to the corral, made from seven-foot lengths of log piled six or more deep. There were benches and portable chairs all round it, and people not actually wrestling the reindeer sat around the fire, chatting and watching what was going on; commenting, laughing, talking to the tiny bundled children, some jumping up to do their tasks when one of the wranglers arrived through the gate attached to a furious reindeer. A tiny old woman with bright pink cheeks, belted into a fur coat, sat by the fire facing the gate with a large chart clipped to a board on her lap. Her daughter sat beside her, helping ('She cannot hear so well these days.'). When man and reindeer arrived, he shouted out the name of the owner within the family; the daughter repeated the name in the old woman's ear and the old woman called the name back loud and clear to check she had it correct. Then she marked the reindeer down on the chart as belonging to that individual. Every man, woman and child had the slashes against their names totted up at the end of the separating. From all around in the family paddocks the sound of Sámi names being shouted and then repeated, rang out like song and echo, mingling with the thudding of hooves and the crackling of the fire. Every bone in me ached and everything that was not bone was molten with tiredness. I sat by the fire and watched, an outsider in every way. Not belonging and not up for the adventure of pretending to belong by participating. The older men and women by the fire laughed at my weariness, though the younger women were more understanding. I would have been warmer running around with the reindeer, risking a lost eye or a broken foot, but I was stuck in my determination to remain a non-participant observer. It was a resolve by then. I would not move. I froze – except for the bits of me increasingly burned by the fire: my knees, hands, and most of all my face. The wind whipped the smoke from the fire directly into my face. I moved to the other side of the blaze. The wind changed direction. My eyes stung as if acid were being dropped into them, they wept and closed, red with rubbing and irritation, Mark said. My throat rasped and I choked on woodsmoke, but I was *not* going to move away from the fire. I wanted heat at any price, and I wanted to keep still.

'Ah ha,' the fur-encased old lady laughed. 'We have a saying. The smoke follows you. It means you will be rich.' Or so her daughter translated. What she probably said was 'Who is this idiot?' I smiled and smiled, self-deprecating, acknowledging my idiocy, my lack of Sámi-ness, but remained where I was stubbornly, as if my life depended on it. It felt as if it might. I had a powerful sense that if I moved even slightly I would simply collapse like a puppet with cut strings, as if someone had severed all the connecting nerves and muscles in my body. But although I declined to wrangle reindeer, and brought shame on myself and my kind, Mark upheld the honour of southern wimps, put down his camera, and for a while became a veritable Sámi, fearlessly shouting, 'It's one of ours,' as he was dragged across the corral floor. Håkan grinned proudly at him, and I cheered, but one or two of the younger men gave him a bit of a sideways look.

One woman jumped up each time an animal came through to inject it against blowfly, while another sprayed the yearlings and calves in the family colour, but it was the men who, in pairs, wrestled the big males due for slaughter next season to the ground and secured them with a knee in the neck. One man then

ON TRYING TO KEEP STILL

lay full-bodied across the writhing creature while the other took
an instrument like a pair of spatulate-ended pliers and closed
them tight over the reindeer's testicles, holding them there firmly
for several moments before releasing them and then grabbing a
hacksaw and cutting off the great crown of antlers; a sign, I suppose, to recognise the geldings, but there was always a bit of a
swagger as they carried away the branching trophy and threw it
with studied casualness into the pile, ready for carving. A sweaty,
dangerous business, though the women looked on from around
the fire and laughed as the men were tossed about by the struggling animals (and sometimes thrown off, grasping their own
testicles). Finally, the castrated male was allowed up and ran
through to the other members of the family herd quietly grazing
in a paddock beyond.

Twice, I glanced behind me to the far end of the paddock and
saw Erik, Håkan's brother, leaning over one of the animals. I was
alerted by a silence falling around the fire, the jokes ceased, the
chatter slowed to a murmur. In the frozen, silvery air the distant
figures of Erik and the reindeer he stood beside looked like an
old, silent film. Erik seemed to have his arms around the reindeer's neck, and remained slightly bent over when the beast
slowly sank, as if its weight had suddenly grown too much for
him to support. It dropped first to its knees, paused for a second,
and then lay itself down carefully on the ground. Erik went with
it, still holding it, on to his knees and waited there a moment until
the back legs had stopped juddering. Then bending over further
he began intricate sweeping movements, and I realised that he
was skinning the dead creature. One of the women noticed me

gazing at the distant, silent pantomime and explained that the reindeer was found to have a broken jaw, probably having run up against a tree during the round-up. It couldn't survive, so it had to be slaughtered. There is a special cut that severs the nervous system so that the animal loses consciousness instantly. Erik was exceptionally skilled at killing reindeer without frightening them. It took about an hour for Erik to peel away the skin and turn the dead reindeer into cuts of meat. Everyone knew it was happening, but no one spoke about it. It was necessary, but it was a serious event. The slaughter and butchery happened at the far corner of the paddock, furthest away from the gate through which the other animals arrived. Erik's calm and deliberate manner was his natural mode, but it was also to keep the other animals from growing fearful. His movements were slow and considered, and he created a strange silence around him as if he had turned the sound down. Once they were released from the arms of their captor, each healthy reindeer loped, grateful to be free and as light-footed as a reindeer can manage, to join the increasing gathering of the family herd in a small collecting paddock at the far end. They all had to pass the dead animal, but they were eager to join their companions after their traumatic handling, and nothing in Erik's manner caused them to notice him and wonder at his work. Though surely they must have smelt the spilled blood. When Erik returned to our end of the paddock, he looked solemn and exhausted. The others around the fire nodded at him and made room for him round the fire, acknowledging the weight of the duty he had had to perform.

Behind us, beyond the collecting paddock, was a mountain,

grey in the distance when the work started at eight a.m., rose pink as the sun came up at eleven, and fading into a delicate pale blue by two p.m. with the sun setting and the moon standing proud over its stepped peak. Come sundown (or lunchtime as you and I know it) they turned on the spotlights, mounted high on poles in the centre of the corral. Brilliant white work lights hazed down, illuminating the thick dust dancing around the reindeers' legs and revealing a heavy white meringue of their massed breath hovering just above their heads, iridescent at the top like the silver lining of a cloud. The scene became all the more like a rodeo, this time for a movie lit by a great director – Peckinpah, perhaps. The spectacle made me gasp out loud. And still it went on and on for hours. Each new group of seventy or so reindeer was herded into the corral, wrangled through the gate where the capturer called out the name of the owner, the old fur-wrapped woman by the fire called back the name to make sure it was correct and made her mark on the accounting sheet. This would go on for two more days until every one of the seven thousand reindeer in the large corral was separated into its family herd. The God of Genesis made the world by dividing and naming; creating order out of chaos. It was a very long day after an even longer night, but by the end I felt I had witnessed the world being put into order.

Even so, enough was enough. Shamelessly, when asked if I was going to stay in Håkan's *lavvu* that night, I begged for a bed off the ground and with walls around it. My discomfort had already been noted and it turned out arrangements had been made to rescue me.

'And a jacuzzi?' Håkan asked.

I laughed and said that tonight anything even remotely approximating a bed would give me the greatest contentment. I asked for nothing more. I'd even sleep with a pea under the mattress. But first there had to be another magical, frozen ride back on the snowmobile. This time I wanted to be in the trailer covered with reindeer skins and warmed by the dog, in the hope that it would jolt less and allow me to gaze idly about. So Mark rode pillion and dodged the blinding twigs, and we bounced and bumped across the ice and the forest trails. Halfway back, the careful but exhausted eye of Håkan missed one large root in the middle of the forest path and the snowmobile in front of me crashed on to its side throwing Mark and Håkan to the ground. The trailer just came to a sudden stop. An interesting moment this, especially for someone who so longed for silence, darkness and stillness. For a heartbeat or so I achieved all three of my desired conditions. One of those split-seconds which seems, while the brain takes stock of a new and surprising situation and its implications, to last half a lifetime or so. There was complete silence, complete stillness and complete darkness. No one moved, no one spoke, the engine died in the middle of the dense forest, away from the world, in the freezing cold. Almost immediately I leapt out of the trailer and ran to see if Håkan and Mark were all right.

During the 'almost' before *immediately* and while I ran the half dozen steps to where they had tumbled, I imagined both men injured, pinned by the bike, perhaps, unable to walk, unconscious or worse. I remembered that my mobile phone had refused to work as soon as I left Stockholm, and hoped I could find Mark's phone if he was not conscious and call – who? I didn't have any numbers of people who might be nearby and know where we were. I would try 999 and 911 and hope one of them put me through to an emergency service somewhere or other. And tell them we were where? Oh, somewhere between Håkan's father's house and his *siida*'s corral. As if I didn't know that the Swedes knew almost nothing about the Sámi way of life. And while we were waiting, assuming anyone could figure out our position, how would I help my bleeding and broken companions? Had I ever done the First Aid course I'd been thinking about doing since 1971? No. I'd watched a lot of medical television programmes which equipped me only to watch more. And what if Mark's phone was damaged or didn't work? Even if my foot worked properly, how could I walk in this weather to find help, and which direction would I go in. Look at the stars? I would die of hypothermia staring at the stars before I have the faintest inkling of what they could tell me. Two things were going on in my thoughts in those few seconds; one of them quite surprising. A rising panic of course at what might have happened to my companions and my ill-preparedness to be of any help to them; but underneath that a kind of calm suffused me. It was the feeling you get when you have no alternative but to manage. I remembered it from long ago, hearing that my father had left us ... finding my mother grotesquely mad ... getting expelled. That moment past which the unimaginable had actually happened. It didn't mean I was any more useful. It just was what it was. I remembered it. You'll manage somehow – or you won't.

Mark and Håkan were fine, if a little shaken. The machine wasn't damaged. We heaved it back to upright and set off again. Håkan was apologetic but what he wasn't saying, very kindly, was that it was all my fault for demanding to ride in the trailer. The snowmobile was better balanced with a lighter person on the back when there was so little snow to stabilise it, but Håkan hadn't wanted to insist. I was pitifully good practice, at least, for the tourists Håkan and his people were going to bring into their daily lives. It never crossed my mind. Things don't when you have no idea about the world you are passing through.

15

ON THE SOFA

Håkan wasn't teasing about the jacuzzi. He drove us in the mini-bus from his father's house to Kiruna, the town that contains the Sámi parliament which no one thinks very highly of, as well as the Swedish iron ore mine that has contracted and utterly changed the traditional herding land, and is part of what threatens the Sámi way of life. Kiruna was the favourite place of no Sámi I spoke to. But overlooking the station was the Hotel Rallaren where Håkan had arranged for me to spend the next two nights before I returned to Cambridge. Mark and I were the only guests. It wasn't really open yet. The old wooden building had been restored by Jan, who was half Sámi, half Swedish, related on his mother's side to Håkan, and his Finnish wife Kirsi. Jan was still working on the hotel, finishing the tiling in the sauna, fitting the cupboards in the downstairs bedrooms.

Upstairs was ready, a bedroom each for Mark and me, a cen-tral sitting room with a table and a sofa, and a bathroom with a

power shower, a basin below a lighted mirror and a large bath
that bubbled air through the water. Jan and Kirsi had made the
hotel of my dreams: simple, plain, comfortable, beautiful and
airy, and, with no other guests, silent. The beds were hand-made
by Jan, their solid wooden head and foot boards polished and
minimally carved with a geometric shape echoing the joints that
held them together. I had the promised jacuzzi, but not for as
long or as pleasurably as I would the next morning. The bed,
with its cerulean blue linen throw over the duvet, was on my
mind. I just got clean and warm for the first time in two days.
The floor of my room was polished wood, and the timbered walls
were painted a soft white, the cupboards a pale dove grey. I lay in
bed in my plain, calm room. It was like resting in a cloud. The
snow was falling through the street light when I closed the curtain
and the silence was total. I held on to the pleasure for as long as
I could and then I slept for ten hours, waking up from time to
time to wonder where I was and for the gratification of falling
back once again to sleep.

The next morning Mark left and I was completely alone in the
hotel. The day was my own. Kiruna was outside, but it would
still be there for me to visit the following day, before I left. After
breakfast (reindeer blood pancakes in Kirsi's café), I went back
upstairs to the empty top floor and the long, low sofa in the sitting room. I spent the day on it, reading, writing, just sitting and
staring at the white wall opposite or the snow falling lazily outside. I wrote notes about the previous two days, made sentences
of reindeer and forests and people who were confronted with
having to open up their world in order to keep it going. Took

experience and turned it into words and staccato phrases. When I was hungry I went downstairs to the restaurant and Kirsi made me a salad for lunch. Then I returned to the pale silence and the sofa, scattered now with books and notes and the duvet from the bed. I have one like that at home.

EPILOGUE

Back in Cambridge, and on my own capacious sofa some weeks later, the phone rang. It was a producer from BBC Radio 4. They were planning a series of short stories to be read by an actor on the subject of the old worldwide *post restante* system. They were commissioning six travel writers to produce fifteen-minute fictions on the subject and would I do one of them?

For reasons that must now be obvious, the idea of being thought of as a travel writer surprised me. But I said yes, because, as has also been established, I'm a girl who can't say no. Or perhaps because the novelist in me wanted to see what the travel writer would write. This is the story I wrote:

Star Stuff and Nail Parings

If a confession is an apology then this was neither. It was just a clarification in the form of a letter popped into an envelope and addressed to herself, last name only in capital letters, to: Poste Restante, The Main Post Office, A Town As Far Away From Here As It Is Possible To Get. She was a writer of fiction. Let's call her Daphne. She wrote novels long before she became the travel writer she is now mostly known for. It wasn't at all clear to her what a travel writer was, but it had come about that she was one. These things snowball. Loving stillness and silence, it occurred to her one day that she would love to be in the blank, extraordinary landscape of Antarctica, so, it being inordinately expensive, and lacking a rich husband or a handy inheritance, she arranged to pay for the trip by writing something about it. Next, being partial to vast empty spaces and the clackity clack of train wheels on rails, it was a railroad journey around America that took her fancy. And lo and behold, it was official, she was a travel writer.

It was while Daphne, as we have decided to call her, was on those trips that she found herself wondering what the experience of experiencing where she was actually gave her that she couldn't get from other sources – books, films, TV, photographs. Silence and stillness she could get most readily and most effectively at home, where with the door closed, the phone off the hook and the blinds drawn, things were as quiet and peaceful as they could get in advance of the grave. And there was no effort involved in getting there. Mostly what she experienced on her actual journeys, aside from dreary airports and wan hotel rooms, was her anxiety to be experiencing something. Like everyone else she took photographs and wrote diaries: snatching at the here and now of where she was and hoarding images of it up for the future when she would no longer be there and it was no longer then. As a result she was always focussed in advance of herself. Never quite where she was supposed to be going when she got there. A very wearing way to exist. Travel was more a fear of the future and oncoming death than a paying attention to the present. Moreover, the air of Antarctica was filled with the nerve-shredding shrieks and abominable smells of a million penguins jostling for prime position, and even apart from the penguin throng there was not the slightest chance of being left solitary in such a lethal and environmentally policed environment. Just try wandering off alone towards the whiteness wilderness and see how fast your minders came alongside to herd you back into the group. As for the train around America – it was invariable that just as some astonishing visual beauty, the Rockies, the bayous, Grand Canyon, came within view, the sun would set. Somehow, the United States or the railroad had been geographically arranged so that all the best sights were reached at dark, no matter which direction you went in. And as for the peace and quiet – have you ever tried to be silently alone with a trainload of chatty American citizens with nothing much to do for the next three days?

Anyway, Daphne didn't like going out. Having reached, somewhat to her surprise, her mid-fifties, she had done with wondering where in the world she belonged. She found it was perfectly possible to declare that where she belonged was indoors, at home – it didn't need to be sought out, no voyage of discovery was required. And she had had her fill of experiences. It turned out that after the first few decades, one experience is inclined only to remind you of another you've already had. In any case, why all this desire for new experience? Death was the most novel experience she would ever have, but why book ahead? Before that culminating event, there was the new experience of ageing to look forward to – the pull of gravity on her flesh, organs wearing out, joints creaking to a halt. All these experiences could be had in the comfort of her own home, her own particularly and personally arranged environment. Such new experiences as she was absolutely obliged to have were going to come to her, whether she liked it or not. She didn't even have to go shopping these days – body and soul were kept ticking over by a nice man from Waitrose who arrived once a week to deliver what she ordered from their website. So why would she schlep around the world looking for things to happen or to see? The need to earn a living was the only compelling reason she could think of. People, these days, were prepared to pay her money to go away and write about far flung places for those – like her – who preferred to stay at home.

She came to an important conclusion. Knowing from her fiction writing how relatively easy it was to conjure up places to which she had never been (the fourteenth century, for example; the landscape of insanity), and also knowing how often the destinations she actually went to disappointed, she decided that it would be much more satisfactory if she stayed still, and using a mixture of conscientious research and free-floating imagination, made up her travel books.

It wasn't that Daphne wanted to trick her readers, only that she had come to realise that neither she nor they greatly benefited from her actual presence in the places she was paid to write about. Unfortunately, for some reason – pedantry, convention – people such as readers and editors cherished the notion that in a travel writer actual presence guaranteed authenticity, and authenticity (whatever that might be) was what everyone seemed to be after. 'She's been there, you know,' carried much more weight than 'She's read everything about the place and seen all the multi-million-pound BBC documentaries.' Quite why this was, Daphne couldn't grasp, when in her experience, other places were exactly like their descriptions in books and depictions on screen, and if they weren't, they weren't in a way that was a dismal let-down. Still, even though she was confident that her fictional travel writings were quite as valid and certainly as interesting as if she had been where she said she had been, Daphne felt she had some obligation – pedantry, convention, she too was a creature of her time and place – to give people something of the authenticity they craved – so long as it didn't require an actual, physical journey.

The solution came to her when, as she was preparing for a month-long though hypothetical journey around Burkina Faso, her agent suggested that he could keep her informed about the negotiations on her new contract by writing to her care of *poste restante* in the towns she would not in fact be travelling to. Daphne agreed to the plan. It didn't matter that she would never receive the letters, she could say that they missed her in each place, or had simply not arrived. As to their contents – well, she supposed that her agent and publisher would agree to what they would agree to whether he heard from her or not, and nothing could be finalised until Daphne put her signature to it. She gave him her itinerary and then thought about the letters that would arrive and sit waiting in the pigeonhole marked, let us say, M, for collection. Wasn't this a modicum of authenticity? Letters written to her, her name on the envelope, anticipating her arrival at the main post offices in Ouagadougou, Fada-Ngourma, Tenkugogo, Boromo, Bobo-Dioulasso and Ouahigouya. *They* would be there, her name would be clear and present in the very air that she would have breathed, even if she was not. Her existence would be established in those places. There is such a person, she will be here, the letters themselves would proclaim. Postmasters and mistresses having looked at the name and put the envelope into the appropriate pigeonhole would expect a Daphne M. to turn up, wait patiently in line with her passport in her hand and ask for her mail, and when she didn't arrive, they would wonder from time to time if she would be coming; perhaps, some of them, the more conscientious ones, might even be anxious for her to arrive before the four week deadline after which the letters were returned to sender – or most likely just dropped in the dead letter sack and thrown on to the local rubbish dump. If people noticed your name in a place, and they would have to in order to put the letters in the right pigeonhole, they were thinking about you, and that was as close to *presence* as a person could get without actually being there. Wasn't that what people who crave fame want? To be thought about in places from which they are absent, by people who do not know them? What better hope do any of us have for an afterlife, for posterity, when all is said

302

and done, but that someone, sometime, somewhere, might think of us by name when we are physically nothing more than dust? God himself promised Abraham, not an actual life hereafter, but that his *name* would be remembered by future generations. If it was authentic enough for Abraham just to be thought about when he was not present, it was authentic enough for Daphne.

But she had to admit that perhaps not all her readers possessed the same sense as she had of the virtual reality of a name. There were, she knew, people who had a very literal attitude to presence and absence. And it was also true that her agent wouldn't find it necessary to send her a letter everywhere she planned not to go. Unfortunately, she was not quite so much in demand as that. Daphne decided, in fairness to the pedants, that it was important to be present in a pigeonhole at each town she was not going to go to. Clearly, the solution to the problem of achieving a presence in every place on her virtual journey was for Daphne to send a letter to herself *poste restante* to all the towns and cities on her route. The problem of her more literal readers who demanded the physical attendance of a travel writer in a place, took rather more thought to solve. The answer came to Daphne, as good ideas so often do, while she was in the bath. She was cutting her toenails and as she watched the tiny crescent moons sink slowly to the bottom, she thought idly how each paring was potentially a perfect replica of herself – at any rate it would be to a geneticist for whom nothing human was alien. She was star stuff, she was toenails, she was hair clippings and dandruff. And there it was.

For her forthcoming book on Uruguay she would post herself to each place she planned to write about, a nail paring in Baltasar

Brum, a single hair pulled from her head in Mercedes, a pinch of dandruff in Dolores, a flake of dried skin from the sole of her foot in Carmello, all sealed in otherwise empty envelopes addressed to Daphne M., at the main post office in each town she was planning not to visit. Let anyone dare to say she wasn't present in the places she wrote about. Bits of her that might just as well, with the help of science, have been all of her, arrived, stayed a few weeks, and left, just as she would have done. Who dared to suggest she didn't travel?

After that, Daphne stayed home in the most delightful way. The only going out that was required in preparation for her trips was to the library from where she brought home piles of useful titles for each place she planned to visit. The expenses for travel and hotel accommodation easily covered the cost of the books and videos she bought. The nice man from Waitrose delivered all manner of delicacies that had been flown in from the part of the world she was not in but should have been, and Daphne curled up on her sofa, sampling exotic fruit and vegetables, sipping coconut milk or oolong tea or rioja, and watching or reading about the land and life of the tropics, the Far East, or Southern Europe. And in all these places, town by town, according to her travel schedule, letters with bits of Daphne inside rested, *poste restante*, in their pigeonholes, patient as milk, waiting to be collected. Except for this one letter, an explanation, not a confession, sent to Daphne M., Poste Restante, The Main Post Office, A Town As Far Away From Here As It Is Possible To Get.

ACKNOWLEDGEMENTS

I would like to thank the organisers of the Wellington Readers and Writers Festival for taking me to New Zealand and making my participation in the festival so enjoyable. My gratitude also to the *Observer* for enabling me to travel to northern Sweden, and to the Kiruna Tourist Association for organising it. My particular thanks to Per Nils, Britt-Marie, Nils Torbjörn, Håkan Enoksson, Anna Sarri and Pär Svonni for tolerating my equivocation, though I hope they know how lucky I think myself to have met them and been allowed into their daily lives. Others I want to thank for their help in making the writing of this book possible in various ways are: Mark Read, Janet White, Ian Patterson (poet and life-changer), and Chloe Diski (who believes that I have stolen her attitude to country walks for my own, though I think that the fact that we are related might have something to do with it).

Part of the final section appeared in another form in the *Observer*, and some of the chapters on New Zealand appeared in the *London Review of Books*. The story 'Star Stuff and Nail Parings' was broadcast on BBC Radio 4.

The Sámi tourist companies can be found on the following websites:

Britt-Marie Päiviö: Min Eallin
+ Per Nils   Box 115 98014 Övre Soppero
                        Sweden
                        Email: info@mineallin.com
                        Tel: +46 (0)98130058

Nils-Torbjörn Nutti: Nutti Sámi Siida
                        Marknadsvägen 11
                        981 91 Jukkasjärvi
                        Sweden
                        Tel: +46 (0) 98021329
                        Email: info@nutti.se

Håkan Enoksson: Giron Siida
                        Fågelvägen 19
                        S-981 Kiruna, Sweden
                        Email: info@gironsiida.se
                        Tel: +46 (0) 706491887

Pär Svonni: Sámi Experiences
                         Södra stallvägen 8
                         98134 Kiruna, Sweden
                         Email: per.svonni@samiland.se
                         Tel: +46 (0) 706687248

Hotel Ralleren Kiruna: Hermelinsg 10b
                         981 39 Kiruna, Sweden
                         Mobile: +46 (0) 703995864
                         Fax: +46 (0) 98061126

Anna Sarri: Nikkaluokta Sarri AB
                         Nikkaluokta 1104
                         981 29 Kiruna, Sweden
                         Email: nikka.sari@telia.com
                         Tel: +46 (0) 98055015

The owner of the cottage in the Quantocks can be contacted at:
cantoc@msn.com